To Jimmy and Rosalynn
Carter,

With love and admiration,

Glenn Wilkerson
July 7, 2022

This book is a set of essays on the fact of our mortality and the issues that death raises for every person. Written by various professionals in the fields of medicine, healthcare and religion, the reflections offer highly contrasting yet interesting views on the meaning of the human person and the role of our mind and heart, of our intellect and emotion, in meeting our finitude. It allows us to glimpse real joy and meaning in life by consciously facing death. As a religious believer, I found the book helpful in setting out so many issues surrounding our death and dying.

His Eminence Daniel Cardinal DiNardo,
President of the U.S. Conference of Catholic Bishops

Confronting our mortality is hard but necessary if we are to take our lives seriously. Brooks and Wilkerson have performed a noble service by compiling this book in which people of very different backgrounds offer their perspectives, so that everyone should find much that is helpful in it.

Rabbi Harold Kushner, author of
When Bad Things Happen To Good People

You know a book represents a true publishing event when you find yourself marveling at its scope as well as absorbing its personal power, poignancy, practicality, and depth. This is what I experienced in being moved and taught by the chapters in *Reflections in Mortality: Insights into Meaningful Living.* As I moved through each subsequent chapter written by a pilot, psychologist, social worker, minister, hospice worker, funeral director or other person intimately connected with a sense of mortality and its impact on how we might live our lives more fully, I found myself asking, Why wasn't a book of this scope and impact available until now? Well, now *Reflections in Mortality* fills that gap and then some. It is a true gift to all of us—including professionals who seek not simply knowledge but true wisdom on the topic.

Robert J. Wicks, Psy.D., author of *Perspective:*
The Calm within the Storm; Bounce: Living the Resilient Life

This work is lovingly dedicated to my wife, Marilyn; my sons and daughters-in-law, Rich and Cybèle and Doug and Suzanne; and my four grandchildren, Maya, Teddy, Sophie, and Lyla—all of whom have enriched and provided meaning and purpose to my life.

—Bob Brooks

To my five beautiful children—Kevin, Kelly, Shane, Shay, and Shanyn. Each of you in your own way has taught me so much regarding the importance of living passionately and fully in the present. Your laughter, uncompromising devotion, and unconditional love fill my heart with joy.

—Glenn Wilkerson

I think the sooner we face that we're going to die, the easier it is to appreciate the moments in life. ... When we realize that our lives will end, we take less for granted. That is what I've learned from loss. The whole thing is a fantastic mystery—so all we can do is appreciate each moment.

—Diane Keaton, American stage and screen actress

By accepting your mortality, you walk right through its shadow into the light on the far side.

—Isaac Clausen in James Lee Burke's *Rain Gods*

Reflections on
Mortality

Insights into Meaningful Living

**Robert B. Brooks, PhD,
and B. Glenn Wilkerson, DMin**

REFLECTIONS ON MORTALITY
INSIGHTS INTO MEANINGFUL LIVING

iUniverse books may be ordered through booksellers or by contacting:

iUniverse
1663 Liberty Drive
Bloomington, IN 47403
www.iuniverse.com
1-800-Authors (1-800-288-4677)

Because of the dynamic nature of the Internet, any web addresses or links contained in this book may have changed since publication and may no longer be valid. The views expressed in this work are solely those of the author and do not necessarily reflect the views of the publisher, and the publisher hereby disclaims any responsibility for them.

Any people depicted in stock imagery provided by Thinkstock are models, and such images are being used for illustrative purposes only.
Certain stock imagery © Thinkstock.

ISBN: 978-1-5320-0766-8 (sc)
ISBN: 978-1-5320-0767-5 (e)

Library of Congress Control Number: 2016917754

Print information available on the last page.

iUniverse rev. date: 02/21/2017

CONTENTS

PART II
Personal Perspectives

PART III
Faith (and Nonfaith) Perspectives

PREFACE

Robert B. Brooks, PhD

In his thought-provoking book *Being Mortal,* Dr. Atul Gawande, a surgeon on the faculty of Harvard Medical School, offers a very personal perspective and critique of the physician's role in dealing with patients who are dying. His observations include experiencing the care and death of his own father, who was also a physician, to cancer. In the introduction to the book, Gawande writes,

> I learned a lot of things in medical school, but mortality wasn't one of them. Although I was given a dry, leathery corpse to dissect in my first term, that was solely a way to learn about human anatomy. Our textbooks had almost nothing on aging or frailty or dying. How the process unfolds, how people experience the end of their lives, and how it affects those around them seemed beyond the point. The way we saw it, and the way our professors saw it, the purpose of medical schooling was to teach how to save lives, not how to tend to their demise.[1]

Gawande's words resonated with me, touching upon an issue that was a major catalyst for Glenn and me creating this book. Thirty years ago, Dr. Duke Samson, a neurosurgeon and lifelong friend of Glenn's, wrote a paper titled "Mortality and the Neurosurgeon," in which he addressed the denial of mortality that often infuses medical practice. After dealing with mortality issues as a minister for the past forty years, Glenn reread Duke's paper and decided to share his thoughts about the subject of mortality from the perspective of a minister. Glenn also received a one-page poem from another childhood friend, Billy Moore, a former professor at Texas State University who was just beginning treatment for cancer. Sadly, Billy died within a year of the start of his treatment.

Glenn shared Duke's, Billy's, and his own writings with me to obtain feedback about their content and to inquire where they might be published. I was very moved by the personal stories and ideas these authors expressed about mortality. In my role as a clinical psychologist, I have worked with patients of all ages who were coping with issues of loss, death, mortality, and grieving. I have also provided workshops about these topics and have long held the belief that there is need for greater discussion of these themes among professionals as well as the lay public. I suggested that Glenn consider soliciting additional chapters and editing a book about mortality. Glenn immediately embraced that recommendation and invited me to coedit the book with him—an invitation I accepted.

Our next step was to decide whom we should ask to contribute a chapter, our choices guided by the vision that the book be informative and helpful to both professionals and the lay public. Creating the list of contributors was an ongoing process that transpired over many months. We composed a letter to prospective authors, emphasizing, "In asking you to contribute to the book, we are hoping for a sharing of personal thoughts, feelings, and stories about death and dying." In addition, we requested that if their profession dealt with mortality issues on a regular basis, they share how their professional activities impacted on the ways in which they led their personal lives, and in turn, how experiences in their personal lives influenced what they did as professionals.

We arrived at three major groups of contributors, although the groups had permeable boundaries; that is, several of the authors could be assigned to more than one group, given their personal and professional experiences and training. One group included professionals whose responsibilities involved issues of mortality, some as an essential ingredient in their work. This group included Duke, who provided an updated, revised version of his original article; myself, as a clinical psychologist; hospice directors Jeanette Coffield and John Foster; funeral home director Jeff Staab; and the director of pediatric oncology social work, Fran Greeson, at the renowned St. Jude Children's Research Hospital in Memphis, Tennessee.

A second group was composed of individuals who had faced life-threatening situations or had family members who had done so. We included Billy Moore's poignant poem written just as he was to undergo treatment for cancer. Terri DeMontrond wrote a very insightful, emotional account of dealing with her adult daughter's suicide, while Todd Herzog shared his story as a three-time cancer survivor and having a daughter diagnosed with breast cancer shortly after she was married. Finally, Wesley Hunt, a West Point graduate and helicopter pilot in Iraq, not only paid tribute to classmates who were killed in Iraq and Afghanistan but also conveyed how he coped with his own possible death each time he flew a mission.

For the third group, we invited clergy or representatives of various religions to share how their faith interpreted and dealt with the issue of mortality and the ways in which their religious beliefs guided their decisions and actions on a daily basis. The authors included Dr. Javed Aslam, a Muslim; Bracha Etengoff, an atheist and humanist; Dr. Paul Foxman, a Buddhist; Dr. David Mason, a Christian minister and philosopher; Dr. Ramesh Patel, a Hindu; Dr. James Stovall, a Christian minister; Dr. Rifat Sonsino, a rabbi; Fr. Leon Strieder, a Catholic priest; and Glenn, a Christian minister. The positions they express about mortality, rooted in their religious—or, in Bracha's case, nonreligious—beliefs, provide insight into the diverse opinions and behaviors about mortality that exist among different religious faiths.

We believe the authors who have contributed their insights to this book represent a comprehensive and wide spectrum of viewpoints about mortality. However, as inclusive as we attempted to be, we recognize that some readers might have suggested additional contributors from other groups. Our goal was to include authors who would elucidate different perspectives of mortality and the ways in which these perspectives are rooted in our values and our religious or nonreligious beliefs. We wanted the words of our contributors to motivate each of us to reflect upon how we perceive and respond to our own mortality and to consider how we might reply to a number of questions that often arise, including the following:

- Do I believe in an afterlife, whatever that might be?
- If so, do I believe that the behaviors I display during my life determine what my afterlife will be?
- If I do not believe in an afterlife, how does that impact on my behaviors in this life?
- How do I handle thoughts of mortality?

- What emotions arise as I consider my own mortality?
- How do I respond to these thoughts and emotions?
- Do I use denial and push thoughts about mortality to the background?
- Do I become anxious or depressed when considering my own mortality?
- Does consideration of my own mortality, whether I believe in an afterlife or not, prompt a more purposeful and meaningful life, or does it lead to a more pessimistic, less satisfying existence?
- If I died tomorrow, what regrets would I have about things I should or shouldn't have done?
- What steps might I take to address these regrets while I am still alive?
- If I became seriously ill, would I want extraordinary measures taken to extend my life, even if those measures included additional pain?

Consideration of the theme of mortality invites these and many other questions—questions that we believe deserve to be openly explored. Exploration should not be interpreted to imply that we become obsessed with our own mortality but rather that in considering and accepting our mortality, we actually become better able to lead more meaningful lives.

Gawande observed that even when confronted with death and dying on a regular basis as a physician, he was taught little about dealing with issues of mortality with his patients. "When I came to experience surgical training and practice, I encountered patients forced to confront the realities of decline and mortality, and it did not take long to realize how unready I was to help them."

Gawande added, "Our reluctance to honestly examine the experience of aging and dying has increased the harm we [physicians] inflict on people and denied them the basic comforts they most need."

It appears that Gawande's realization that he was unprepared to deal with the patients who were dying is slowly being addressed in the medical field. An article by Felice Freyer published on the website of the *Boston Globe* noted that new Medicare rules will require health care providers to openly discuss end-of-life care with patients. There is a Medicare proposal to begin to pay physicians, nurse practitioners, and physician assistants to initiate discussions with patients about their end-of-life wishes. Freyer's piece emphasized the importance of medical professionals obtaining training on how to enter into these difficult discussions with patients, noting that change is taking place with "at least 136 medical schools including end-of-life care in a required course and 94 in elective courses, according to the Association of American Medical Colleges."

Glenn and I are encouraged to learn that the issues of death and mortality are receiving increased dialogue and training in the field of medicine, especially in terms of end-of-life care. However, we wish to emphasize that our goal in editing *Reflections on Mortality* was not to focus on the final days of our lives, although certainly several of the chapters do. Rather, it was our desire that the various chapters be relevant to our readers regardless of their age and whether they or their loved ones are faced with life-threatening illness.

Psychoanalyst Erik Erikson asserted in his classic book *Childhood and Society*, "Healthy children will not fear life if their parents have integrity enough not to fear death."[2] We would extend his observation by emphasizing that as we come to terms with our own mortality, we will be better equipped emotionally and spiritually to engage life with energy, hope, and resilience.

---

1   Atul Gawande, *Being Mortal* (New York: Metropolitan Books, 2014), 1, 3, 9.

2   Erik H. Erikson, *Childhood and Society* (New York: Norton, 1950), 233.

PART I

*Perspectives of Health
Care Professionals*

TO FACE ONE'S OWN MORTALITY: WHAT WE CAN LEARN FROM CONNECTING THE DOTS BACKWARD

A Psychologist's Perspective on Mortality

Robert B. Brooks, PhD

I N 2005 THE late Steven Jobs, cofounder, chairman, and CEO of Apple Inc., gave the commencement speech at Stanford University. The insights he offered during his talk have influenced the writing of this chapter, including his perspective about "connecting the dots backwards."[1]

Jobs explained, "You can't connect the dots looking forward; you can only connect them looking backwards. So you have to trust that the dots will somehow connect in your future. You have to trust in something—your gut, destiny, life, karma, whatever."

Jobs recounted a personal example. He told of dropping out of Reed College. "After six months, I couldn't see the value in it. I had no idea what I wanted to do with my life and no idea how college was going to help me figure it out ... The minute I dropped out I could stop taking the required classes that didn't interest me, and begin dropping in on the ones that looked interesting ... Much of what I stumbled into by following my curiosity and intuition turned out to be priceless later on."

Jobs sat in on a calligraphy class at Reed College and found it intriguing, even if at the time he did not believe it would have "any practical application" in his life. "But ten years later, when we were designing the first Macintosh computer, it all came back to me. And we designed it all into the Mac. It was the first computer with beautiful typography. If I had never dropped in on that single course in college, the Mac would have never had multiple typefaces or proportionally spaced fonts." Indeed, that was one of the distinguishing features of the Mac when it was first introduced to the public.

I would like to expand, to some extent, on Jobs's notion of connecting the dots backward. I believe that during our lives, we will experience events that are destined to have a major impact on our journeys in life, our beliefs, our emotions, our behaviors, and our relationships. Yet, at the time of their occurrence, whether the events appear important or not, we have no idea what their profound significance might be in years to come.

Connecting the Dots Backward: Questions to Consider

Jobs's commencement speech and his description of "connecting the dots backwards" resonated with me. While it was not a phrase I had previously used, its meaning was embodied in different threads of my work. For instance, during my presentations I frequently described situations that had occurred early in my career as a clinical psychologist that had a far greater influence on my professional activities than I would have predicted. I recall that while attending colloquia and seminars in graduate school, I always wondered what factors prompted speakers to investigate the topics they were addressing. I was pleased when they provided information about these factors during their lectures.

This chapter, which includes more personal information than many of my other writings, invites a description of those dots that have influenced not only my views about mortality but, in addition, the approach I have adopted with patients when exploring their questions and issues about death. This approach directs the kinds of questions I ask in my clinical practice and in my presentations. The following represents a small sample of these questions. As you read them, consider how you would respond.

- "What have been two or three of the best experiences you have had as a parent [or teacher, administrator, businessperson, spouse, etc.]? What made them so positive?"

- "What have been two or three of the worst experiences you have had as a parent [or teacher, administrator, businessperson, spouse, etc.]? What made them so negative?"
- "What did you learn from both the positive and negative experiences?"

I have also asked these kinds of questions in a more general way without indicating a specific role, such as follows:

- "What have been two or three of the best experiences you have had in your life? What made them so positive?"
- "What have been two or three of the worst experiences you have had in your life? What made them so negative?"
- "What did you learn from both these positive and negative experiences?"

I should emphasize that prior to asking these and related questions to others, I first reflect on what my answers would be. I have found that such self-reflection has refined the questions I raise and has helped me to become more understanding and empathic.

How would I answer several of these questions? As I review my life, I feel that I have been blessed in many ways. I had two very loving, encouraging parents. I have a wonderful family, including my wife, two sons and daughters-in-law, and four adorable grandchildren. I have some very dear friends. I have received much satisfaction in all aspects of my career as a psychologist. I experienced few losses during the first sixteen years of my life, with the exception of a beloved grandmother who died when I was eleven years old. I felt her loss keenly, since she lived with us for the last couple of years of her life. At the time of her death, she was eighty-seven years old; and although she had been relatively healthy, her passing at that age, while painful, was not totally unexpected.

The Death of a Young Brother

In answering questions about one of the worst and most painful experiences in my life (as well as in the life of my entire family), I would immediately cite what occurred just as I was to begin my senior year of high school. It would prove to be an event that prompted thoughts of mortality and made me aware of the different ways in which people grieve and mourn.

I am the youngest of four sons, although the title of "youngest" was achieved by a close margin, as I was born seventy minutes after the birth of my twin brother Michael. (Actually, seventy minutes is a relatively long time between the birth of one twin and the next twin.) As the story is told, when my oldest brother, Henry, was twelve and my brother Irwin was nine, my mother convinced my father that they should try for a girl. My mother became pregnant, but instead of giving birth to a daughter, the number of sons in the household increased by 100 percent.

My parents were not aware that my mother was carrying twins until Michael was born. I can only imagine what it was like—especially for my mother—as they were awaiting my birth, hoping that the fourth child would be a girl. Alas, it was not to be. However, my mother once told us that the disappointment of not having a daughter disappeared rapidly, especially since a woman in the same hospital room as my mother lost her infant during childbirth.

Irwin joined the air force a year after he graduated from high school. He loved his experience in the air force. He sent us postcards from cities throughout the United States and the world with messages filled with excitement. Promotion followed promotion as Irwin met every challenge with enthusiasm and passion. Adding to his joy was his meeting his future wife, whom he married when Michael and I were in our junior year of high school.

Several months after the marriage, both Irwin and his wife were thrilled to learn that his next assignment would take them to Japan. The future held such promise, joy, and adventure for them. However, as I was to painfully learn, all of this promise and joy can end in a split second as one's life is taken. A few months prior to the move to Japan, Irwin and members of his crew were on a mission that took them from their base in California to Guam. It turned out to be Irwin's last flight.

I don't remember the phone ringing in our apartment in Brooklyn in the middle of the night on that Labor Day weekend. What I do recall at some point during that night was having what I thought was a dream in which my parents were crying. I awoke a little later to discover much to my horror that it was not a dream; my parents had received a phone call from an officer at Irwin's air force base to inform them that his plane had crashed in the ocean and there were no known survivors. We were to learn later that a bomb had been placed on the plane by a terrorist in response to political tensions in the region.

The fact that the plane exploded over the ocean and that Irwin's body was never recovered prompted me to entertain for months the possibility, the hope, that he and the other crewmembers had survived the crash and were now stranded on an uncharted island. Since the air force announced that everyone on the plane had perished, in accord with Jewish tradition we sat shiva (a weeklong period of mourning in which family members gather together in a relative's home), but it took me many months to finally accept that I would never again see my twenty-five-year-old brother.

Irwin's death was the first I experienced of someone so close and so young. As I absorbed the reality of his death, I thought of how fragile life is and how one could be so full of life one second but gone the next. As might be expected, an intense sadness pervaded our home. During the following months, Michael and I were consumed with many activities that helped distract us, if only temporarily, from thoughts of Irwin dying. As seniors in high school, we were busy with class requirements and completing college applications. We spent hours working on the high school yearbook, and we maintained jobs outside of school.

I think it wasn't until I became a father myself that I could truly appreciate the depth of Irwin's loss to my parents. It wasn't that I didn't feel the pain associated with losing a beloved brother at such a young age. However, when my sons were born, I experienced emotions toward them that were different from those I had felt in other relationships; in many ways they were more intense, and I felt more protective. In that context, I came to understand with increased clarity the profound grief and sadness accompanying the death of a child at any age. I have heard many times the comment that it is not in the order of things for a parent to bury a child. Sadly, it is a far more frequent occurrence than many people realize.

We all cope differently when confronted with our own mortality or the mortality of a loved one. For several years following Irwin's death, my parents had difficulty talking about him or even using his name. They put away some photos of him, including one in his air force uniform. Without being told, I learned that we were not to discuss Irwin's death unless my parents initiated the discussion, which during the first couple of years rarely occurred. The pain was too raw.

I believe the intensity of my parents' emotions was heightened by our never having an actual funeral for Irwin. It's true we sat shiva in our apartment, and family and friends visited to offer condolences; but without a body and a burial site, no formal services were held. I'm not certain why a memorial service was not conducted at our local synagogue so that memories of Irwin could have been shared. I now wish I had asked my parents that question.

Although it is difficult to know for certain, I believe that if Irwin's body had been recovered, if there had been a memorial service, and if he had a grave site, it would have proven therapeutic for all of us. While we would have experienced profound emotions of sadness while visiting his grave, I hold the opinion that the presence of a grave site would have provided a location for healing and a place for us to speak with Irwin and say our good-byes over time.

Interestingly, for the literary section of our high school yearbook I wrote a piece about a boy coming to grips with a death in his family. When I read the essay years later, it seemed obvious that in addressing this theme I had found a vehicle through which to articulate issues related to Irwin's death. Yet, although it seems obvious now, at the time of the writing I was not consciously aware of the connection to Irwin. I do recall experiencing a feeling of relief after I finished the essay and a sense of satisfaction when the faculty adviser of the yearbook complimented my writing and told me she found it very moving.

With hindsight, bolstered by insights I have gained as a psychologist, I now appreciate that the process of authoring the article allowed me not only to express feelings of grief but also to find a means to respond more actively to an event—a bomb being placed on a plane that killed my brother—over which I had no control. I will return to this notion of what I call personal control later in this chapter. The concept of personal control is a basic foundation for being resilient.

Questions and Issues about Mortality

Many of the therapy sessions I have conducted with children, adults, couples, and families have included discussions of the loss of a loved one and ways of coping with the loss. As I attempted to assist my patients with this issue, it was not unusual for me to think about what I learned from Irwin's death. Nowadays it is common for therapists and other professionals who deal with loss to recommend to the bereaved that they visit the grave site of the person who died, that they have conversations with that person, and that they say things that had been unsaid. Such actions, unless taken to an extreme degree so that all other parts of one's life are neglected, are no longer viewed as pathological but rather as healthy ways of coping and coming to terms with the loss.

My patients, especially children, have raised numerous questions about death. Of course, one need not be a therapist to hear such questions. As any parent or grandparent can attest, children in our own families repeatedly pose questions about death in their quest to understand this phenomenon. I assume that most parents and other caregivers have heard some of the following questions:

- What happens to people when they die?
- What is heaven?
- Can you see heaven?
- What do people do in heaven?
- Why did my daddy [or mommy] have to die?
- Do I have to die?
- I thought only old people died. Why did my sister die?

Children who have lost a parent frequently experience increased anxiety about the surviving parent dying, and they often ask that parent, "Will you die soon?" or "If you die, who will take care of me?" Worries about being cared for when a parent dies are not unusual and are to be expected.

Studies have shown that the finality of death is not an easy concept to grasp for young children (and perhaps for older ones as well). The following is a comment uttered by a four-year-old: "My grandma died, but she's coming to my birthday party."

Parents at my workshops and in my clinical practice have frequently asked how to best explain death to children. Some shy away from using the words "death" or "dying," instead finding it more comfortable to use euphemisms such as "passed away." I once gave a workshop for parents titled "Talking about Difficult Topics with Your Children," which included such themes as how to discuss how babies are conceived, sexuality, drugs, and death. A mother of teenagers remarked, "I found it easier to discuss how babies are born than to try to explain death and heaven."

Many parents wonder whether or not to allow a young child to attend a funeral service or the service that takes place at the grave site. In addition, they ask about a child viewing an open casket. Not surprisingly, there is no simple answer to these questions, given the many variables that are involved, including the age and cognitive and emotional level of the child, how easily the child can be prepared for what he or she will experience during the funeral, and the support to be provided by the adults closest to the child.

For instance, Samantha is an eight-year-old girl I saw in therapy several months after her mother died suddenly of a brain aneurysm. Samantha requested to attend the church service and then be at the grave site at the time of burial. However, given the chaos and grief that followed her mother's sudden death, no one had prepared Samantha for the intensity of the sadness and crying that would be present at the church. Samantha became overwhelmed and began to scream, refusing to go to the grave site. Anxiety attacks followed, including fears that her father would also die and she would be left all alone in the world.

Even if Samantha had been better prepared to witness the emotions expressed by her parents, grandparents, and other family and friends at the church, she still might have become overwhelmed. However, such preparation might have eased some of the extreme anxiety that was triggered. Samantha was very insightful when she revealed in therapy how scared she was at the church and that she thought everyone "would even be sadder when my mommy was put in the ground in the cemetery. I didn't want to be there and see that."

In one of our sessions, Samantha voiced regret that she had never visited her mother's grave site. In the past, when her father suggested they go to the grave, Samantha said she didn't want to do so. However, she now felt that she had not really said good-bye to her mother. In a meeting with her father, we discussed his taking her to the cemetery, but unlike the situation in church that caused her to feel overwhelmed, the two of them prepared for the visit to the grave.

What Samantha found very helpful was writing a note to her mother in which she said how much she loved and missed her. She read the note at the grave. Her father reported that he and Samantha shed many tears and then hugged tightly. Samantha told me that she was very sad while reading the note but later felt better having done so. She made other visits to her mother's grave site, and there was a noticeable decrease in her anxiety. Although the actions are seemingly different, Samantha writing a good-bye letter to her mother and me writing an essay for the high school yearbook about death in a family may have served similar purposes.

A Shift in a Therapeutic Approach

In the 1970s, I shifted my perspective as a psychologist. Years later that shift was to find expression in my thoughts about mortality and death and the approach I adopted in helping my patients deal with these themes. I was trained in the late 1960s and early 1970s, when what has been referred to as the "medical model" dominated the field of mental health. Psychiatric diagnoses were given, and interventions were predicated on identifying and fixing problems. An emphasis on a patient's strengths—which is a prominent feature of psychology's current landscape, especially with the emergence of the field of positive psychology—was absent. The focus of the day was on pathology.

In 1973 I accepted a position at McLean Hospital, a private psychiatric facility in the Boston area; this was to prove a turning point in my career. The position I assumed at McLean was perhaps the most challenging of my career. I became principal of the school in a locked-door unit of the child and adolescent program. Within several months, I began to feel disillusioned, frustrated, angry, and burned-out. Contributing to these emotions was that the youngsters in my care seemed to become increasingly angry and provocative rather than more cooperative.

After many frustrating months during which I thought the solution to increasing patient cooperation was to impose more and more rules on them, a student angrily said to me, "You don't get it, do you, Dr. Brooks?"

"Get what?" I asked.

"We're going to outlast you!"

Little did I realize the impact that the words "we're going to outlast you" were to have on my career. Years later, in counting the dots backward, I came to appreciate that this child's angry warning became one of the significant catalysts for the strength-based approach I was to adopt in my clinical work—an approach that was also to influence my perspective about mortality and death.

What were the changes in my mind-set and behaviors that emerged from this patient's words? One insight, which seems evident now, was that if we continued to apply the same ineffective treatment strategies day after day, why should we expect our patients to change their behavior? Instead we had to take responsibility for changing our behaviors if our patients were to change theirs.

A second insight closely related to the first was that both children and adults are more motivated to make changes in their lives when they feel they have a voice in these changes. When people feel that rules and dictates for change are arbitrary and imposed, they are more likely to resist these rules than accept them.

The third insight was that while we should never ignore the problems and vulnerabilities that burden people, we must also focus on identifying and building upon their strengths, or what I began to call thirty-five years ago their "islands of competence."[2] Appreciating the strength of people proved to be far more beneficial in helping them to cope with life's challenges than did labeling them with diagnostic categories.

If I were to summarize these three points, I would do so by stating that we are the authors of our own lives and that if difficult situations arise, we must take responsibility for what we can do to confront the adversity; and when we take responsibility, we must honor our strengths and the strengths of others. These points capture the concept I mentioned earlier of personal control, or focusing on what you can influence in your own life. Parents and caregivers must attend to strengthening personal control in themselves as well as in their children.

The Question of Heaven

I have been asked if I believe there is such a place called heaven. I struggle with an answer to this question. I believe (perhaps "hope" would be a more accurate word) that our spirits continue to exist in some form after death. But when I entertain this hope, I have difficulty defining what I mean by "spirit."

I was moved when I read Dr. Eben Alexander's remarkable book *Proof of Heaven: A Neurosurgeon's Journey into the Afterlife*. Alexander details the near-death experience he had when the area of his brain that controls thought and emotion was attacked by a rare disease. He was in a coma for seven days, and his recovery was considered a miracle. Although an essential part of his brain was shut down, showing no activity, Alexander describes a visit he took during this time to what could be best described as heaven.

Alexander acknowledges that there will be people "who will seek to invalidate my experience anyhow, and many who will discount it out of court, because of a refusal to believe that what I underwent could possibly be 'scientific'—could possibly be anything more than a crazy, feverish dream. But I know better … I see it as my duty—both as a scientist and hence a seeker of truth, and as a doctor devoted to helping people—to make it known to as many people as I can what I underwent is true, and real, and of stunning importance. Not just to me, but to all of us."[3]

For me, the mysteries of an afterlife, of a heaven, remain exactly that—mysteries. I hope that Alexander's incredible experience and his belief in the reality of heaven prove to be true. However, what I take issue with is the belief espoused subtly, or not-so-subtly, by some individuals that the main reason for leading a kind, charitable, compassionate life on earth is for the reward that follows—namely, being accepted into heaven. I believe we should lead such a life not as a guarantee of entry into a heavenly afterlife but rather because leading such a life is what contributes meaning and purpose to our existence, whether an afterlife exists or not.

My wife and I did not teach or model for our sons those behaviors we considered commendable because we thought such actions would help open doors to heaven for them. Our goal was that they would learn and practice values that would enrich their lives and the lives of others in today's world.

The thought that heaven exists is reassuring. However, as I learned years earlier while working at a psychiatric hospital—an experience that has often prompted me to connect the dots backward—I feel most comfortable when focusing my time and energy on what I have control over in my current life. If that leads to future rewards in an afterlife, that is fine; but my intention is to have a positive impact on the world I live in now.

Mortality and Purpose in the Face of Adversity

I believe that people can more comfortably accept their mortality when they feel that their legacy is defined by the good they have accomplished and that they have few regrets when they die about actions either taken or not taken during their lives. I would argue that if we face death burdened with many what-ifs and with many unresolved problems—especially those housed in our relationships with others—it is more difficult for us to accept our finite existence. An ambivalent life is one that is dominated by a preoccupation with what could or should have been rather than one in which individuals focus on what they accomplished not only for themselves but also on behalf of others.

This view is endorsed not only in two of my favorite books—*When Bad Things Happen to Good People*, by Rabbi Harold Kushner, and *Man's Search for Meaning*, by Holocaust survivor and psychiatrist Dr. Viktor Frankl— but also in the words of my twin brother, Michael. The perspectives of Kushner, Frankl, and Michael provide examples of courage and resilience in the face of great adversity. To embrace their outlook invites us to appreciate life so that we are less frightened by our own mortality.

Kushner's bestselling book was first published in 1981. He wrote it not only to honor the memory of his son Aaron, who died at the age of fourteen in 1977, but also to share his understanding of why a benevolent God would allow people to experience intense anguish and pain. Kushner poignantly describes that authoring the book reflects his struggle "as someone who believes in God and in the goodness of the world … to rethink everything he had been taught about God and God's ways."[4] I will quote extensively from his book, since I am concerned that in paraphrasing his words I may lose the eloquence of his thoughts.

When Aaron was three years old, his sister Ariel was born. Kushner and his wife, Suzette, had been concerned about Aaron's development since he stopped gaining weight when he was eight months old and his hair began to fall out after he reached his first birthday. On the day of Ariel's birth, the Kushners were devastated to receive a diagnosis of Aaron's condition from his pediatrician. They were told that Aaron had a rare disease called progeria (rapid aging) and that he "would never grow much beyond three feet in height, would have no hair on his head or body, would look like a little old man while he was a child, and would die in his early teens."[5]

In an article written by Sandra Balzer Tobin and published in *MetroWest Magazine* in the Boston suburbs, Kushner observed,

> As Aaron grew older he became aware that there was no hope and that he would not survive. When he realized he was going to die, he became anxious about dying young without having left any kind of legacy. So I promised him I would tell his story … The book posits that all tragedy is not God's will and even God cannot solve all suffering. It encourages readers to learn from their losses and turn them into something good.[6]

In a very personal manner, Kushner shared with his readers the struggles he encountered, especially as a member of the clergy, in believing in a benign and kind God. He reviewed possible explanations for Aaron's death that he could not accept or find comforting—although they might be to other people dealing with loss. He rejected the notion that God gives people "what they deserve and need" or that God gives you only what you can handle. He also has difficulty accepting that Aaron and other deceased children are in a better place, citing his disagreement with the following views expressed by another clergyman while giving the eulogy for a five-year-old boy, Michael, who was hit by a car and died. "This is not a time for sadness and tears. This is a time for rejoicing, because Michael has been taken out of this world of sin and pain with his innocent soul unstained by sin. He is in a happier land now where there is no pain and no grief; let us thank God for that."

Upon hearing this eulogy, Kushner wrote, "I heard that, and I felt so bad for Michael's parents. Not only had they lost a child without warning, they were being told that they should rejoice in the fact that he died so young and so innocent, and I couldn't believe that they felt like rejoicing at that moment."[7]

Kushner countered the notion that we can explain the death of a young child by promising an idyllic afterlife: "Since we cannot know for sure, we would be well advised to take this world as seriously as we can, in case it turns out to be the only one we will ever have, and to look for meaning and justice here."[8]

Kushner expanded on this thought by noting,

> I don't know why people are mortal and fated to die, and I don't know why people die at the time and in the way they do. Perhaps we can try to understand it by picturing what the world would be like if people lived forever ... Either the world would become impossibly overcrowded or people would avoid having children to avoid that crowding.
>
> Humanity would be deprived of that sense of a fresh start, that potential for something new under the sun, which the birth of a baby represents ... We have to acknowledge that mortality in general is good for people in general. It is something else again to try to tell someone who has lost a parent, a wife, or a child, that death is good ... It would be cruel and thoughtless. All we can say to someone at a time like that is that vulnerability to death is one of the given conditions of life. We can't explain it any more than we can explain life itself. We can't control it, or sometimes even postpone it. All we can do is try to rise beyond the question of "why did it happen?" and begin to ask the question "what do I do now that it has happened?"

This last question dovetails with my work in the area of resilience. I emphasize in my writings and presentations that when difficult situations arise, resilient people do not blame the situation or others, and they do not blame themselves, but rather they ask, as Kushner suggested, "What is it I can do to deal with this situation?" Theirs is a proactive approach, ensuring that they do not succumb to the role of a victim.

What conclusion does Kushner finally arrive at in attempting to determine not only why bad things happen to good people but also what one is to do once bad things have occurred? Once more his insights are thought-provoking and, I hope, serve to help us to understand and accept our mortality. Kushner's words represent a transformative lesson for all of us.

> Is there an answer to the question of why bad things happen to good people? That depends on what we mean by "answer." If we mean "is there an explanation which will make sense of it all?"—Why is there cancer in the world? Why did my father get cancer? Why did the plane crash? Why did my child die?—then there probably is no satisfying answer … But the word "answer" can mean "response" as well as "explanation," and in that sense there may well be a satisfying answer to the tragedies in our lives … In the final analysis, the question of why bad things happen to good people translates itself into some very different questions, no longer asking why something happened, but asking how we will respond, what we intend to do now that it has happened.[9]

Kushner's questions deserve considerable reflection as we consider how to give meaning to life so that we do not fear death. He asked,

> Are you capable of forgiving and accepting in love a world which has disappointed you by not being perfect, a world in which there is so much unfairness and cruelty, disease, crime, earthquake, and accident? Can you forgive its imperfections and love it because it is capable

of containing great beauty and goodness, and because it is the only world we have?[10]

Kushner ends his book with a poignant remembrance of Aaron—a remembrance that holds significance for all of us as we confront life's adversities. "I think of Aaron and all that life taught me, and I realize how much I have lost and how much I have gained. Yesterday seems less painful, and I am not afraid of tomorrow."[11]

The insights offered by Frankl in *Man's Search for Meaning*, first published in 1946, parallel the reflections of Kushner. The first half of the book details Frankl's experience in the Nazi death camps, while the second describes a form of therapy he developed called "logo" or "meaning" therapy. As noted above, Kushner came to the realization that while bad things can happen in our lives over which we have little, if any, control, what we do have control over is our attitude and response to such situations; years earlier, Frankl arrived at a similar observation. He wrote:

> We who lived in concentration camps can remember the men who walked through the huts comforting others, giving away their last piece of bread. They may have been few in number, but they offer sufficient proof that everything can be taken from a man but the last of the human freedoms—to choose one's attitude in any given set of circumstances, to choose one's own way.[12]

Frankl articulated another key point that relates to our sense of mortality and our thoughts and emotions about death—namely, the need to identify a goal—a future activity that can offer meaning to our lives even in the direst of circumstances. He offered as an illustration the despair felt by inmates in the concentration camp. "The events and the people outside, all the normal life there, had a ghostly aspect for the prisoner. The outside life, that is, as much as he could see of it, appeared to him almost as it might have to a dead man who looked at it from another world."[13]

What did Frankl do to deal with this sense of hopelessness? He imagined a future goal that would bring purpose to his existence. "I forced my thoughts to another subject. Suddenly, I saw myself standing on the platform of a well-lit, warm, and pleasant lecture room. In front of me sat an attentive audience on comfortable, upholstered seats. I was giving a lecture on the psychology of the concentration camp!"[14]

In fact, this was a goal that Frankl was to realize after the war!

In describing his struggle to counteract hopelessness, Frankl quoted Nietzsche's words: "'He who has a *why* to live for can bear with almost any *how*.'"[15]

The words of Kushner and Frankl were to take on an even more personal meaning with the death of my twin brother Michael. In 2006 Michael was diagnosed with a rare disease called amyloidosis. I had never heard of the disease prior to Michael's diagnosis, and after he and his wife Shirley described it to me, I went online to learn more. I was dismayed by what I read. It was incurable and associated with a limited life expectancy.

Only a few sites in the United States offered a treatment protocol for this disease. Michael chose the Mayo Clinic in Rochester, Minnesota, not only because of its reputation for excellent care but also because there was a Mayo Clinic near his home in Scottsdale, Arizona, that could provide the extensive follow-up treatment that he would require.

Michael spent almost two months undergoing treatment at the Mayo Clinic in Rochester, and it went very well. However, not surprisingly, he faced many challenges to his health once he returned home. He used many medications as part of his treatment program. Progress and setbacks appeared with regularity. Michael never wavered in displaying a determination to live as normal, fulfilling, and healthy a life as possible. Normal was markedly different for Michael than most people, involving constant appointments with medical specialists and a daily regimen of medications. As one year led to the next, Michael surpassed the life expectancy of many individuals afflicted with amyloidosis. He experienced the birth of new grandchildren and spent much time with family and friends.

Shirley observed that whenever my wife Marilyn and I visited, for whatever reason, we seemed to catch Michael at his healthiest. Such was the case during our last trip to Scottsdale in January 2012. He appeared to be doing well, and we had a very relaxing, enjoyable time that included going out for dinner and a movie. One evening, all of Michael and Shirley's children and grandchildren came over. They all live close by. On our flight back to Boston, I commented to Marilyn how well Michael seemed to be doing and how upbeat he was. Little did I know that visit was to be the last time I would see my twin brother alive.

A few weeks later, while visiting my brother Henry in Florida, we received word that Michael had been admitted to the hospital because of problems with his heart. His defibrillator and pacemaker were adjusted, and he was released. However, a couple of days later the problem reoccurred, and he was admitted to the ICU. We called every day, and except on one occasion when Michael was very tired, we spoke directly with him.

When we returned to Boston from Florida, we immediately called Michael at the hospital. He answered the phone. His voice sounded weak, but he was happy to have been moved out of the ICU and into a regular hospital room. I told him I would call again the following day.

Given his recovery from past hospitalizations, I was not expecting the call I received early the next morning from Shirley. She was crying and said, "We are losing Michael." I was stunned. Apparently, shortly after I spoke with him the day before, his weakened heart started to fail. He died later that afternoon with his family by his side. I was overcome with sadness at the loss of a wonderful, loving twin brother.

I was asked to give one of the eulogies at his funeral. I described memories of our childhood together, of our love of sports, and of meeting our respective wives at almost the same time. After recalling childhood events, I shifted to Michael's struggle with amyloidosis, noting, "Some of you know that I have been very fortunate to write books about resilience. While I may have written the books, my brother lived what I wrote."

I shared thoughts about resilience, noting that one of the main features of resilient people is that when challenging situations arise, they don't blame the situation or other people, and they don't blame themselves. Instead they recognize that while they may not have had any control over the emergence of a particular situation—such as Michael developing amyloidosis—what they do have control over is their attitude and response to the situation.

I told those who attended his funeral that in the almost seven years that Michael battled amyloidosis, I never once heard him utter, "Why me?" He never accepted the role of a victim; nor did he feel sorry for himself. While he did not want to die at a relatively young age, he did not seem to fear death. His attitude was remarkably upbeat as he endured constant doctor appointments and an extensive medication regime. Even during our last phone conversation the day before he died, he told me, "I just take life a day at a time."

At the end of the eulogy, I encouraged everyone to honor Michael's memory by adopting his positive outlook, by not living a life filled with regrets, and by keeping in focus the importance of our connections to family and friends. Remarkably, a day or two later I was to learn of something Michael had written months before his death that contained almost the same words I used in my eulogy. It was as if Michael had been present as I was planning and delivering the eulogy, ensuring that I would be precise in explaining his outlook toward life and death while I honored his memory.

Michael and I have two very dear cousins from Toronto—Todd and Carol Herzog. Todd is a three-time survivor of cancer; he beat it once as a teenager and twice as an adult. Todd has authored a chapter in this book to describe his experiences battling cancer. His wife, Carol, is one of the loveliest, most caring people I know. About six months prior to Michael's death, their daughter Steph Gilman was diagnosed with breast cancer. After receiving treatment, she is now in remission. She detailed her experience in a blog, passmeanothercupcake.com, to capture the many emotions associated with her battle with cancer.

Todd and Carol were not aware of what I had said at Michael's funeral; nor did I know that Michael had written them a letter. Shortly after Michael died, Carol sent an e-mail to us and others in which she wrote, "I was looking through some old e-mails and came across this one that Michael sent to us. Our daughter is currently fighting breast cancer, and Michael, in the middle of his ordeal, took the time to offer us words of encouragement and love. This is who the man was … selfless and loving. We all miss him very much. Here is his e-mail to us."

Dear Carol and Todd,

We have followed the plight of Stephanie and your family and would like to take this opportunity to let you know that our thoughts and prayers are with all of you. Todd's own experience will serve as an inspiration to all of you in meeting the challenges ahead. The most important aspect in the day-to-day living is the positive attitude. Many people ask "Why me?" I always asked, "Why not me?" Having fought a rare incurable disease (8 in 1,000,000 get amyloidosis) for the past 6½ years, I have come to appreciate life from a far different perspective than most people, as I am sure Todd has as well. From Stephanie's blog, I can see that she too has adopted a great attitude and maintained an incredible sense of humor. I have always said that there are no real problems, only opportunities and challenges and I am sure that you will get through these difficult times. When you do, you will all be stronger and grateful for the support of your wonderful, loving family. You and your family are very dear to us. You always exuded such genuinely positive vibes. We will always keep you in our thoughts. If there is anything else that we can do to ease your burden, please let us know.

In reading Michael's remarkable letter to Carol and Todd, I was reminded of the idea expressed by a number of renowned people—namely that while death is inevitable, our fear of dying is lessened if we live life to the fullest. For example, Mark Twain observed, "The fear of death follows from the fear of life. A man who lives fully is prepared to die at any time."[16] In a similar vein, Leonardo da Vinci noted, "While I thought that I was learning how to live, I have been learning how to die."[17] Benjamin Franklin said, "Many people die at twenty-five and aren't buried until they are seventy-five."[18] Developmental psychologist and psychoanalyst Erik Erikson asserted, "Healthy children will not fear life if their elders have integrity enough not to fear death."[19]

Life without Regrets

I began this chapter with a quote from Steven Jobs about "connecting the dots backwards." In drawing to a close, I would like to share another insight from Jobs. "For the past 33 years, I have looked in the mirror every morning and asked myself, 'If today were the last day of my life, would I want to do what I am about to do today?' And whenever the answer has been 'No' for too many days in a row, I know I need to change something."[20]

Jobs's words might be viewed from another perspective—namely, if a person knew he or she were to die tomorrow, what regrets would the person have? Susie Steiner in an article "Top Five Regrets of the Dying" published in *The Guardian* in February 2012, addressed that question. The article is based on the recordings of Bonnie Ware, an Australian nurse who devoted several years working in palliative care with patients in the last twelve weeks of their lives. Ware wrote a blog titled *Inspiration and Chai,* describing the reflections of these patients, which she then compiled in a book titled *The Top Five Regrets of the Dying.* Steiner reported, "Ware writes of the phenomenal clarity of vision that people gain at the end of their lives, and how we might learn from their wisdom."[21]

The following are the five regrets highlighted by Ware:

- I wish I'd had the courage to live a life true to myself, not the life others expected of me.
- I wish I hadn't worked so hard.
- I wish I'd had the courage to express my feelings.
- I wish I had stayed in touch with friends.
- I wish that I had let myself be happier.[22]

While we may possess regrets similar to or different from those voiced by dying patients, the key issue for me is taking time to identify existing regrets in our lives and then taking actions to address them. Imagine if you were one of Ware's patients with just a short time to live and she asked what, if any, regrets you have about the life you have led. How would you respond?

Since I assume that most people reading this chapter have more than a few weeks to live, your answer can serve as a catalyst and guidepost for the behaviors you adopt in the future. Regrets are part of the human experience, but if we are burdened by too many of them, there is a lessening of joy and satisfaction, and, I would argue, there is a greater fear of dying, given all of our unfinished business.

Let's listen one more time to the perspective expressed by Jobs in his commencement speech, which certainly ties to the issue of regrets:

> No one wants to die. And yet death is the destination we all share … Your time is limited, so don't waste it living someone else's life. Don't be trapped by dogma—which is living with the results of other people's thinking. Don't let the noise of others' opinions drown out your inner voice. And most important, have the courage to follow your heart and intuition. They somehow already know what you truly want to become. Everything else is secondary.

A Final Thought

In reflecting upon my own mortality, I find it helpful to connect the dots backward and consider significant events in my life, including those detailed in this chapter: the deaths of my brothers Irwin and Michael, my early experiences and perspective as a psychologist, and my adoption of a strength-based approach. These and other events have helped me to clarify and strive for those goals that provide meaning for my life—namely, nurturing caring and loving relationships with others, living life in concert with my values, and lessening regrets. I have found that by focusing my time and energy on achieving these goals, I leave myself little time to worry about my own mortality. It is my hope that what I do now will live on in the legacy I create for my children, grandchildren, and the many others I have been fortunate to meet during my life.

---

1   Steven Jobs, commencement speech at Stanford University, 2005.

2   Robert Brooks and Sam Goldstein, *Raising Resilient Children* (New York: McGraw-Hill, 2001); Robert Brooks and Sam Goldstein, *The Power of Resilience: Achieving Balance, Confidence, and Personal Strength in Your Life* (New York: McGraw-Hill, 2004).

3   Eben Alexander, *Proof of Heaven: A Neurosurgeon's Journey into the Afterlife* (New York: Simon & Schuster, 2012).

4   Harold S. Kushner, *When Bad Things Happen to Good People* (New York: Schocke Books, 1981).

5   Ibid.

6   Sandra Balzer Tobin, *Metrowest Magazine*, October 2007.

7   Harold S. Kushner, *When Bad Things Happen to Good People* (New York: Schocke Books, 1981).

8   Ibid.

9   Ibid.

10   Ibid.

11   Ibid.

12   Viktor E. Frankl, *Man's Search for Meaning* (New York: Pocket Books, 1959).

13   Ibid.

14   Ibid.

15   Ibid.

16   Goodreads, Mark Twain > Quotes, accessed October 15, 2015. http://www.goodreads.com/quotes/5785-the-fear-of-death-follows-from-the-fear-of-life.

17   BrainyQuote, Leonardo da Vinci > Quotes, accessed September 23, 2015. http://www.brainyquote.com/quotes/quotes/l/leonardoda104789.html.

18   Goodreads, Benjamin Franklin > Quotes, accessed October 15, 2015. http://www.goodreads.com/quotes/85334-many-people-die-at-twenty-five-and-aren-t-buried-until-they are seventy-five.

19   Erik H. Erikson, *Childhood and Society* (New York: Norton, 1950), 233.

20   Steven Jobs, commencement speech at Stanford University, 2005.

21   Susie Steiner, "Top Five Regrets of the Dying," *The Guardian*, February 2012.

22   Bonnie Ware, *The Top Five Regrets of the Dying* (Carlsbad, CA: Hay House Publishing, 2012).

Robert B. Brooks, PhD

Robert Brooks grew up in Brooklyn, New York, the youngest of four sons (seventy minutes younger than his twin brother). Both of his parents were immigrants from Europe and cherished the opportunities their sons were afforded in the United States. Bob received his undergraduate degree from the City College of New York and his master's and doctorate in clinical psychology from Clark University in Worcester, Massachusetts. He then did his postdoctoral training at the University of Colorado Medical School in Denver.

After completing his formal training, he returned to the Boston area. He initially worked at the Boston University Medical Center and then at McLean Hospital, a private psychiatric hospital, which is also a teaching hospital for Harvard Medical School. He eventually was appointed director of the Department of Psychology at McLean, and after twenty-three years of full-time status at the hospital, he left to have more time for writing and lecturing.

During his career, Bob shifted from what is often referred to as a "deficit" model to a strength-based approach. Rather than focusing on what is wrong with people and how to "fix" their problems, he believed it was more important to identify and reinforce their strengths, or what he called their "islands of competence." This perspective, which is now an integral part of the positive psychology movement, led to Bob's interest in the concept of resilience across the lifespan. Many of the sixteen books he has authored or coauthored pertain to the themes of resilience, motivation, family relationships, and creating positive home and work environments.

Bob met his wife, Marilyn, at City College, and she has been a constant source of strength and support in both his personal and professional life. They are the proud parents of two sons, Rich and Doug, and have two wonderful daughters-in-law, Cybèle and Suzanne, and four adorable grandchildren (an unbiased view): Maya, Teddy, Sophie, and Lyla.

Contact Information:
e-mail: contact@drrobertbrooks.com
website: www.drrobertbrooks.com
Twitter: @drrobertbrooks

"WE'RE NOT TREATING THE MEASLES HERE"

A Neurosurgeon's Perspective on Mortality

Duke S. Samson, MD

Introduction

THE PROFESSION OF neurological surgery is no stranger to dying patients and grieving families. A large percentage of Americans will ultimately die of diseases or afflictions of the brain and central nervous system (e.g., traumatic brain injury, stroke, cancer, dementia, and infections)—diseases that strike at the core of individual humanness, and all have important neurosurgical implications. Unfortunately, the rapidity of onset of many of these diseases will often rob a stricken patient, very early in the disease's time course, of the unique personal identity that is synonymous with real life. Thus, a patient's "dying trajectory" may often be far advanced before a neurosurgeon actually sees the patient in consultation.

Neurosurgeons recognize that this emotional separation frequently shields us from some of the often unsettling experiences of caring for the dying. This relative lack of in-depth experience, coupled with the typical can-do personalities attracted to neurosurgery, results in a somewhat paradoxical situation; despite being routine custodians of the final common pathway for many terminally ill patients, the "high-speed low-drag" brain surgeon may well fail to develop any special skills useful in the management of patients and families during their confrontation with death.

Any personal progress I've made in that development over a long clinical career is the direct product of my wife's influence. Patricia Bergen is a trauma/critical care surgeon; her professional life focuses on the most

27

seriously ill and critically injured patients in the most famous acute-care hospital in America. Over the past thirty years, her personal example and our in-depth discussions, which began on our second date, have taught me almost everything I know today about medicine "in the valley of the shadow." For this, as for so many things, I'm truly grateful.

History

I went to medical school in the late 1960s, a time of great social upheaval in American society. As has often been true historically, organized medicine came embarrassingly late to the revolution. In testimony, my freshman class of eighty-two was composed of seventy-seven white guys, five women, no African Americans, and no Latinos.

Part of our gross anatomy class involved the lengthy viewing of x-ray motion pictures (fluoroscopy) of Nazi concentration camp prisoners forced to exercise their limbs in slow motion for the edification of German medical students. Each of the subjects was later calculated to have received twice the lethal dose of radiation. Considering about a third of our class was Jewish, it's a little hard to believe this was part of our study program.

During the ensuing four years, we learned a staggering amount about all sorts of presentations, diseases, diagnoses, and treatments but disturbingly little about managing the consequences of "treatment failure," a.k.a. human death. In the final three months of my senior year, we attended a one-hour-per-week colloquium entitled "The Dying Patient." Led, not taught, by a hardworking, no-nonsense oncologist, it offered no cookbook answers—just some very hard questions. It was the only class in the entire four years that was voluntarily attended by every student.

After medical school, I spent six solid years in training, initially in general surgery and then as a neurological surgeon. I tacked on an additional year of fellowship in vascular neurosurgery, followed by two years in the Army Medical Corps, before beginning a career practicing and teaching neurosurgery at a large medical center. My entire formal exposure to issues related to death and dying occurred in that single brief encounter in medical school. After that, it was all on-the-job training.

The intervening forty-some-odd years have witnessed enormous progress in formal education in this area. Modern medical school curricula feature mandatory courses for young physicians at every level of training. Similarly, new emphasis has been placed on education in end-of-life issues for nurses and other health care professionals, while both lay and professional publications have increasingly featured extensive discussions of all aspects of terminal medical care.

Nonetheless, while care of the dying may now be easier to read about on the Internet and subsequently discuss over cocktails, up close and personal this stuff is still tough to teach and even harder to really learn. Lectures by "experts" dot medical school schedules, but frequently these experts aren't the folks actually doing the hard work in the trenches. There, at the sharp end of the stick, many if not most active practitioners remain reluctant to publicize their own important experiences with dying patients and their families. This blanket reticence makes the learning environment somewhat reminiscent of the old saying about combat: "Those who know don't talk, and those who talk don't know."

On-the-Job Training (OJT)

As I hope I'm about to prove, it may actually be possible to know at least a little about the medical aspects of death and dying and then to talk semicogently about that limited knowledge. As a caveat, I offer readers two cautions that will be important in an interpretation of what follows:

1. This is just one neurosurgeon's experience, not a summary of broadly held opinions or even a theoretical outline of "the way things ought to be." I can only tell you what I've personally seen and felt. In the cauldron of clinical practice, it's frequently difficult to stay in touch with even your own feelings about death, much less to claim any insight into those of other physicians.

2. The reader will find all third-person singular references in this brief manuscript to be masculine; there is no "his/her" nod here to gender correctness. This perhaps antiquated stylistic approach is not reflective of any personal or professional prejudice—as my wife, students, and colleagues would testify—but rather an idiosyncratic narrative preference. Mea culpa.

"We're Not Treating the Measles Here."

One of the first things any young neurosurgery resident will hear as he comes on service is a pithy statement about the unique nature of his chosen profession. This seemingly mindless old saying actually embodies several different messages. One is a cautionary admonition: "Get your head out of your butt; you're in the big leagues now." Another is almost congratulatory: "Thank God you're growing up to be a brain surgeon and not a dermatologist." But beneath the banter is a darker warning about what the fledgling neurosurgeon is about to see and do. Stripped bare of the romance, neurosurgery is mostly about bad diseases and worse outcomes.

For the young neurosurgical resident, death generally comes calling all at once and right away. On my first call day (July 4, 1970) I stood helplessly by with almost nothing to offer to two young men dying from penetrating head injuries or to an eighty-eight-year-old lady dying from the delayed effects of a massive stroke.

Bullets, motorcycle crashes, falls, brain tumors, infections, hemorrhages, even malfunctioning shunts in hydrocephalic children—it's a grim and lethal list here on medicine's front line. For the young clinician in a safety-net hospital, there is no normal; there's just *Wham!* and then a bloody, messy race against the clock that the good guys are pretty sure to lose, either immediately or with agonizing slowness over the next days and weeks.

This is the anonymity of acute neurological illness; to the enormous distress of family and friends, these diseases rapidly and ruthlessly depersonalize patients almost completely. Ironically, as mentioned earlier, this sudden cataclysmic loss provides the young surgeon an emotional shield behind which he learns to do his job. That job is to manage the basics, the scut work, of surgical care.

"Hey, suck right there."

"Pull this drain."

"Order that test."

"Stop that bleeding."

"Fill in that box."

"Get that x-ray."

And he must always listen. The novice keeps his mouth shut, his head down, and his ears open, and he listens to the decision makers. That's how surgeons have learned their craft forever.

"Oh, and one more thing, rookie ..." Usually that one extra thing is a reminder that he's the one elected to talk to the family—"Hanging the crepe," as it's brutally termed. Bad news rides a fast horse and is usually delivered by a young neurosurgery resident. The sicker the patient, the more likely the job will fall to the new guy.

This is where most neurosurgeons begin to learn about the dying patient, and realistically, it's not a bad place. Families in general realize the young resident isn't really responsible for their loved one's care; so, absent any major screwup, he doesn't bear that burden of inquisition. On the other hand, they do recognize him as part of the medical team—someone who may often have more time to spend with them than the big guys do. So right here, even on his first day, the trainee can learn a little about how patients die and families grieve. As an added benefit, he provides the team with insight into how a particular family is bearing the heavy emotional burden—information that may be helpful for the team if push comes to shove down the road.

In every surgery training program, there's a natural progression of medical responsibility as the resident moves from rotation to rotation and year to year. With that progression comes a definite change in the resident's role. Soon decisions and their consequences begin to revolve around him. His focus now becomes the patient, not the family, and inevitably his emotions become increasingly linked to the patient's clinical condition.

How do these maturing residents react? In the optimal situation, senior residents become avatars of their teachers, the attending surgeons—the guys who are really in charge. These are the "been there, done that" surgeons who, much more often than not, really exist to care for the whole patient—not just the sick organs. They're "real doctors" in the best sense of the term.

This is where the fortunate resident learns about truly being a physician. As a friend of mine often says, "You can teach a monkey to operate; it takes a human being to learn to care." It's a tribute to medicine that so often both teacher and student are focused on caring; in those circumstances, the resident's interactions with the dying patient quickly come to mimic those of his seasoned teachers. Then—in a year or a rotation, or in a startling moment of insight—the torch is successfully passed. As a rule, these are defining moments for the young surgeon's career; the events of the next decades will shape and refine, but not basically alter, his responses to dying patients.

Dealing with Death

For me, as for most neurosurgeons, a patient's death brings a wave of complex emotions. The exact mix is different for each of us. For me, first and usually foremost comes a sense of personal defeat. Regardless of the disease or the injury, my job description—the way I define my professional self—is to banish the badness and to make the patient whole. Having actually been to medical school, I realize everyone on the planet is going to die inevitably, but they're damn sure not going to do it on my watch. Death means I failed. I didn't work this hard, travel this far, and care this much just to fail.

I understand that perhaps that blanket condemnation sounds irrational or egotistical. Trust me here: if your neurosurgeon lacks that degree of passionate commitment, you're in the wrong office or operating room. For most neurosurgeons, and certainly this one, that unlimited commitment is a sacred duty. We are bonded to it by an unspoken oath so strong it embodies our own definition of self. So when my patient is dying, regardless of my insight or wisdom or experience, I am in violation of that commitment. When that result becomes inescapable, my next visceral response is anger.

Forget the "kinder and gentler" babble of the talk show psychologists; anger serves multiple purposes, many of them beneficial. For this neurosurgeon, anger in the OR makes me colder, harder and more determined. It helps me find solutions to problems that aren't even in the book, gives me the strength to hold my hands and body in impossible positions for hours, and fires my determination not to be defeated by whatever malignant process threatens my patient. It's a good thing.

Operative neurosurgery isn't about elegant theoretical science; it's one of the few places you can watch good battle tangible evil every day. Real neurosurgery is all about winning and losing. In that arena, anger gives me an edge; it makes me smarter, tougher, and more resourceful. I'm a better surgeon and you're a safer patient because of anger.

But that same anger, as a response to a patient's impending death, is a needless diversion from the real issue. Anger is either about me or about the disease; it's not about the patient. If I've taken good care of this dying patient, my anger isn't brought on by personal guilt, which means I can usually recognize it for what it is, choke it off into a corner for later, and prevent it from driving me away from the patient and, of almost equal importance, from the patient's family. While I've never been able to abolish this initial angry reaction, with time and painful repetition I have learned to control its manifestations and its effect on my ability to communicate. That is, unless it's fueled by guilt.

Two Kinds of Guilt

Many physicians experience a pervasive sense of self-recrimination when patients die in the natural progression of their diseases. This malaise, I believe, has more to do with sorrow at the global inequity of death and the inability of medicine to provide ultimate intervention than with a sense of personal culpability. In part it may reflect the guilty relief of having been personally spared by death temporarily, or even a vague sense of having failed to succor the patient. In that context, it is probably more closely related to the initial anger response I've described above than the soul-searing self-hatred that comes with fatal mistakes.

This unspecified form of guilt is generally transient, although it can and frequently does distance the physician from the patient and family. In some situations, this remorse—especially if cumulative—may even imperil the physician's ability or willingness to continue in active clinical practice. Young physicians sometime factor their own susceptibility to this type response into their own final career choices. I know personally a famous ophthalmologist who "selected eyes over brains" because he wanted a "happy specialty." Because this form of guilt is not a personally familiar emotion, I won't discuss it further, in favor of describing a different feeling with which I'm all too familiar.

Every neurosurgeon who lives his professional life on the edge of the serious-disease envelope has made at least one fatal mistake. Each of us has inadvertently caused exactly what we live our lives to prevent—our patient's death. This outcome isn't common, but it's not exactly rare either. The tolerances inside the skull are very tight, the brain and its vessels are incredibly fragile, and the consequences of even miniscule error are often irreversible. Those aren't excuses; they're just facts.

A fatal error is the most horrible complication in a neurosurgeon's life; if possible, it's even more horrible the second or third time around. No matter how many patients believe they're alive because of a certain neurosurgeon's skill or experience or luck, it's those he's lost in trying to save them that stay with him forever. The passage of time dulls this razor of agony only a small amount. If the guilty surgeon can avoid killing himself or changing careers in the first twenty-four hours, he's probably got a chance to make a comeback, but the pain will never go away. There is nowhere to hide, no pill to take, no confessor to tell.

This type of ferocious, consuming guilt is a professional secret that only the members of the club know; it's rarely admitted and almost never discussed, even among colleagues. It has ruined many a promising young neurosurgeon (dermatology, anyone?) and, worse, gutted other talented surgeons of their willingness to risk in order to cure. It leaves no life it touches unchanged.

As well I can determine, there is no way to prepare for, or even to imagine in advance, the intensity of this emotion, much less to predict one's reaction when it occurs. The very best surgeons accept, endure, and somehow find the courage to risk again, but they never forget. This awareness of personal guilt is the most intense emotion I've encountered in the practice of medicine, and naturally, it's just another little thing they forgot to mention in medical school.

Running Away

These intense emotional responses to a patient's impending or actual death are stressful in the extreme; therefore, a natural, almost instinctual response is for the physician to separate himself from the afflicted patient and family. In other formal contexts, this has been termed "distancing behavior"; in the surgeon's lounge, sometimes it's referred to as "looking for running room."

In my experience, surgeons who are searching for this emotional distance usually adopt one of three widely divergent approaches. Having personally tried all three, I can testify that none actually work. I can also verify that, if unchecked, each of these behaviors can destroy a doctor's relationship with patients, families, and even colleagues. These aberrant responses to stress probably exist in other highly emotional contexts; superficially, each seems so spontaneous I think it's important to recognize and identify each by name to avoid falling prey to their traps. The first response I'll call "vanishing."

Despite what a nonmedical person might think, there are multiple ways for a physician to isolate himself from intimate contact with any inpatient or family. Making rounds at odd hours, signing out to a colleague, visiting the patient/family with a large retinue of nurses or medical students in tow, or even taking unscheduled weekends or quick "spur-of-the-moment" vacations all will buy the physician an amazing amount of space and time. Space and time for what? Avoiding controversy, confrontation, and "proximity to failure" while waiting for the world to turn and disease to run its natural course. It's kind of like hiding out near the OK Corral until the smoke clears. To "vanish" and then to return to work with a clean slate is a very understandable impulse; every physician recognizes the allure. It's just wrong to surrender to it.

A slightly more subtle approach is what I term "spreading the blame." This tactic consists of enlisting as many other professionals in the patient's care as is humanely possible. This is not heavy work; the list of available consultants for a terminally ill patient is limited only by the attending surgeon's imagination and the potential consultant's naïveté or avarice.

This approach is especially easy for "uber" specialists like neurosurgeons to adopt, since we basically don't know anything about any part of medicine distinct from the nervous system. In addition, the sick neurosurgical patient always has multiple problematic issues involving other peripheral organ systems ripe for investigation.

Not too surprisingly, spreading the blame works well in private hospital settings where each consulting physician is destined to receive his own slice of the remuneration pie. It often fares less well in public and teaching hospitals, where generally there's less money to be shared and often more work to be done. In these latter environments, a surgeon with a reputation for spreading the blame is likely to be told directly to take care of his own problems, as in the phrase "There's plenty of misery to go around, Jack." Unfortunately that response may just cause the physician to redirect his consultation requests.

A third approach is more popular than either vanishing or spreading the blame, and it represents a major ethical and fiscal dilemma for American health care. Not infrequently, when faced with a well-defined medically hopeless situation, a physician will wrap himself in the dirty shirt known as "doing everything that can be done." In so doing, the doctor diffuses responsibility for the patient's inevitable outcome, and simultaneously protects himself against any suggestion that he might have overlooked a potential treatment or even—God forbid—withdrawn support ("given up") too early.

This approach abrogates the physician's responsibility to the patient, to the patient's family, to the broader society, and to medicine itself. It squanders precious medical resources, raises unrealistic hope where none exists, and needlessly prolongs the agony of death. In polite company, this concept of aggressive therapeutic intervention (not pain management) in situations of terminal illness or disease is known as "futile care."

Currently in medicine at large, and specifically in the subspecialty areas of critical care and medical ethics, futile care is a hot topic. An in-depth discussion of this practice is beyond the limited scope of this paper or the expertise of its author; however, in many cases of advanced brain injury or demonstrable irreversible neurological deterioration, some clinicians resort to pulling out all the stops—not to benefit the patient, but rather to ameliorate or mitigate their own feelings of anger, guilt, and inadequacy.

The futile care approach is superficially very family friendly, since naturally families feel better when they're told, "We're doing everything known to medicine," as opposed to the frank "There is nothing we can do except make her comfortable." With futile care, everyone lives a lie—at least for a while—and we all pay for it. This is spineless medicine at its finest.

Reasons

So why do we (meaning neurosurgeons) go through all these emotional contortions? You've already read most of the excuses that I've been able to identify:

1. I didn't become a brain surgeon to have my patients die.
2. I know life isn't fair, and death isn't either.
3. I didn't make it happen.
4. If I did, I'm really sorry.
5. This failure has been a real team effort.
6. I've done everything known to man to help.

After a long career dealing with critically–ill patients, distressed families, and concerned physicians, it strikes me that basically all of these behaviors, from anger to avoidance, stem from a pervasive misunderstanding of medicine's role in human life. Our expectations as professionals are outrageously unrealistic and often incredibly self-centered. In fact, we know we can't cure everybody all of the time or, in fact, anybody some of the time. The physician's real job, at every level of medical care, is to provide comfort—to cure whenever possible, but always to provide comfort. The real question is why putting this mandate of comfort as our top priority represents such a stumbling block for many of us, especially neurosurgeons.

When I don't practice neurosurgery in the face of death the way I know it should be done, it's because even this secondhand involvement with death and dying is a dreadful business—dreadful because we ourselves are so afraid of dying. I believe that, in large measure, our inability to recognize and conquer that specific fear underlies most of our (physicians') inadequate responses to the dying patient.

The Bad News

Death is not an abstract concept; rather, it's an unavoidable and, consequently, critical component of human life. For that exact reason, it scares the hell out of each of us. The questions death asks are universal; the potential answers are frankly a dime a dozen and have been multiplying since before recorded time. Perhaps the real answers are unique to each of us, but there is no certainty that our own answers are correct, and that uncertainty lies at the source of much, but not all, of the fear we share. Unfortunately, most of us neurosurgeons haven't yet come close to reconciliation with this uncertainty surrounding our own deaths, and we know it. That makes it difficult in the extreme to deal effectively and compassionately with the deaths of patients charged to our care.

As a physician, I can offer the best treatment possible to a dying patient only if I'm willing to grapple with the nature and magnitude of our common fear about this ominous unknown that looms over every life. It's not a one-off event but rather a recurring struggle to understand as clearly as possible the fear and its component parts, and then to do everything possible to mitigate its causes.

The Good News

When you practice and teach serious medicine for a living, almost every day harbors some startling revelation, assuming you're just willing to be an intern again and listen.

If he thinks you care, the dying patient will tell you that, beyond death's enigma, he fears pain, suffering, and, perhaps most of all, the loss of his personal dignity. Death itself is frequently a riddle we neurosurgeons can't solve for this particular patient, but here, with these last issues, we can really make a difference if we're just willing to draw close enough to listen.

Historically many physicians, especially those with limited clinical experience, have been reluctant to prescribe large amount of analgesic medications, even in obviously terminally ill patients. The reasons underlying this reluctance are complex, and there is an increasing awareness in the medical community that what is important is how well the drug works, not how much is administered. However, there remains a pernicious insufficient use of sophisticated opioid analgesics in end-of-life situations, and almost more importantly, an insufficient awareness on behalf of patients and families of our growing willingness to employ them early and often. Upfront reassurance and prompt, consistent intervention by the involved medical team can almost always successfully manage this portion of the equation. Pain is bad; relief of pain is a blessing. Full stop.

Patients define "suffering" with a variety of terms; certainly there is considerable overlap among pain, uncertainty, and apprehension, but a very common component of end-of-life suffering is simple dyspnea—"air hunger," or shortness of breath. Just as there is no single cause of air hunger, there is no universal panacea, but it is truly amazing how frequently the alert, engaged intensivist can minimize this oppressive syndrome with a varying combination of medications and surprisingly minimally invasive ventilation maneuvers. The dying patient whose pain is under control and whose respirations are unlabored rarely expresses the uncontrolled panic that is the hallmark of overwhelming fear.

Finally, there is a growing awareness in the lay public that some of the extreme measures medicine has developed to deal with imminent death are brutal in nature, potentially harmful, and infrequently successful. Despite inspiring anecdotal stories of "great saves" secondary to cardiopulmonary resuscitation, the percentage of adult patients who survive such efforts, even in hospital settings, is quite small; in patients undergoing unwitnessed cardiac arrest outside the confines of a medical facility, the percentage of survivors is minuscule. The most eloquent testimony to this little-known fact is the overwhelming percentage of physicians whose advanced medical directives specifically preclude so-called full codes. In fact, the most common physician-to-physician comment regarding CPR is "Don't ever do that to me."

The aggressive use of indiscriminant resuscitation procedures is one glaring aspect of the futile care scenario discussed earlier. Most family members who have demanded that "everything be done" and then have been present during such attempts are understandably appalled at the violence of the interventions and the hopelessness of their outcomes.

Each one of us deserves a good death—a death defined as "good" by the one doing the dying, not by onlookers in the audience. What none of us deserve at the end of our road is to be abandoned by our caretakers, smothered by useless medical intrusions, or treated as experiments to determine how long the human heart can endure. We deserve physicians who can recognize death and not flee, who can honestly share their knowledge without flinching, and who will use their special skills to treat our pain, sate our air hunger, and fiercely preserve the dignity of our persons.

Closing

It turns out they were right about neurosurgery; we're damn sure not treating the measles here. Neurosurgery is a microcosm of life and death on steroids. Examples of breathtaking courage, of awe-inspiring kindness, and of incredible human caring beyond description have been commonplace in every ER, ICU, and OR where I've had the privilege to work. The practitioners themselves have been patients, families, coworkers, and students, all struggling to help others—and themselves—deal with the latest life-threatening catastrophe and ultimately with this death sentence we all share.

These supercharged environments tend to generate surgeons who thrive on living on the edge, taking charge, and being in control. On occasion folks like that have serious issues trying to remember exactly who they are and whom they came here to serve. However, beyond the posturing and self-important behavior, these neurosurgeons mostly think of themselves as caregivers, family members, and patients-to-be—regular people with a little extra ability to help when the crisis comes. And that's what really makes this medical specialty a great career.

Neurosurgeons are short on illusions; despite our interval successes, we're well aware that no one's leaving this episode alive. That realization brings with it an understanding that the most important thing in our power is to help those in our care reach the end of their allotted shift with a minimum of pain and suffering and a maximum of human dignity.

As a neurosurgeon, I don't need to intellectualize very much to judge whether I'm doing my job in end-of-life situations. All that's necessary is to examine the issues in the first person singular: "When I am dying, will this suffice?"

That's the gold standard for us all.

Duke S. Samson, MD

Duke S. Samson was born in Odessa, Texas, in January 1943. Following graduation from Odessa High School in 1961, he attended Stanford University, where he majored in psychology and played intercollegiate football and rugby.

He graduated from Washington University Medical School in 1969 and completed a surgical internship at Duke University Medical Center. His neurosurgical residency at the University of Texas Southwestern Medical School was highlighted by fellowships with Professor Gerard Guiot in Paris and Professor M. G. Yasargil in Zurich.

Dr. Samson entered the United States Army Medical Corps in 1975, serving both at Clark Air Force Base in the Republic of the Philippines and Walter Reed Army Medical Center. In 1977 he joined the faculty at UT Southwestern, focusing his clinical and investigative interests on vascular diseases of the nervous system. Dr. Samson was promoted to professor of surgery in 1984 and assumed the chairmanship of the division of neurological surgery the following year. In 1987, neurosurgery at UT Southwestern achieved departmental status, and he accepted the W. Kemp Clark Chair, established in honor of the division's first chairman.

On September 1, 2012, he relinquished the departmental chairmanship and the Lois and Darwin Smith Distinguished Chair in Neurological Surgery to his friend and partner Dr. Hunt Batjer. He was appointed emeritus professor in 2014.

Duke's wife, Dr. Patricia Bergen, is a professor in the Department of Surgery at UT Southwestern. They are the proud parents of 1st Lt. Lorne Daniel Samson, USMC, and Gabriel Stanford Samson, a senior at the University of Montana.

Contact Information:
e-mail: Duke.samson@utsouthwestern.edu

ON DEALING WITH MORTALITY

A Hospice Director's Perspective on Mortality

Jeanette Coffield, BBA

W E IN THE hospice community deal with death in clinical, spiritual, and social terms when families very often cannot. During the twenty years that I have spent in this field, I have been at the bedside of many friends, neighbors, and strangers. Each experience remains with me. Death can be, and often is, a gift, especially for those who come to us when any chance for good quality of life is over.

Hospice helps patients and families with the many choices and challenges that have to be faced at the end of life. When someone elects to receive hospice services, there are few defenses left against the onslaught of disease. The disease has had its way with the body, and medical science cannot extend the body's ability to function properly. One bodily system fails, and others rapidly follow. The patients try to reason their way through the decline with a list of defenses, such as anger, avoidance, and bargaining. Fear of dying can even make matters worse. Hospice guides the patients and their families through this maze of emotion, decline, and pain.

To illustrate how hospice helps with the many choices that everyone must make at the end of life, I will relate some of the more unusual ways in which some of our patients chose to live their last days. Each person dealt with his or her mortality with fierce independence and individuality.

For example, family members called our office one day to say that our hospice patient had gone to bed and would not get up. Also, he did not want to talk and refused food. Our hospice nurse had been in the home for a routine visit just a day or two before and found nothing unusual, and there was no indication that the patient was declining significantly. In fact, he had been out in the field on his tractor that day and seemed to be enjoying fairly good quality of life for someone with his diagnosis. He was doing well with the interventions our care team had put into place. A sudden decline seemed unlikely.

Our hospice nurse went to the patient's bedside, examined him, and found nothing unusual or anything to indicate that his death was imminent. The nurse sat by his bed to observe the patient and to try to get him to talk. When he finally spoke, his comments were words of innocence and trust. His understanding was that when a person is admitted to a hospice program, he has six months to live. According to his calendar, those six months were up this week. He thought that he was going to die, so he went to bed to await the event. Our nurse carefully explained that no one could predict the time of anyone's death, that the six months to live was just a guideline, and that he was doing well. The next day, the patient returned to his usual activities. He died several months later while riding his tractor in his fields. He chose to die doing the things he loved.

Another remarkable individual barreled her way through end-of-life choices with a vengeance. She was thirty-some years old and had been successfully battling breast cancer for several years. She had small children and good family support. She was passionate about life and was strong in her fight to beat her disease. That had worked in the past, but now the disease had taken over her body. She refused to believe that she was going to die and have to leave her family. Hospice managed her pain and symptoms and helped her family cope with her decline. She fought relentlessly. She asked the nurses why this was happening to her and why we could not change the course of her fate. She was so determined to pull out of her decline. She became fearful, agitated, and combative at the end. One of her last comments as she was grasping our nurse's arm was, "If I have to die, you are going with me." Her death was an emotional tsunami for everyone around her. She chose to fight and resist death at every turn, but the ultimate choice was not hers.

Another young woman in her thirties had had a lifetime of unhealthy choices that left her with a broken body and an unstable lifestyle. She was suffering from alcohol-related, end-stage liver disease. She had been a rodeo barrel racer and had traveled extensively and been successful in competition. Her drawings of horses and rodeo gear were strewn about the walls in her room in her father's home. She was small and by now very frail.

She spent time alternately with her father and with her boyfriend. Both living spaces were dark, without much food, filthy, and completely unfit for a person who needed medical attention. The boyfriend supplied her with alcohol, and the father just gave her a place to sleep.

Because she had declined so much, she agreed to nursing home care. Keeping her in the facility even on her good days became a challenge for our staff and the facility staff. Her boyfriend would come by, pick her up, and take her out to drink beer. That pattern continued until she was no longer able to get up. Her choice was to continue the alcohol abuse at all costs. The hospice staff helped to make her comfortable and to bring as much dignity as possible to her death.

On a different note, some choices involve a brush with danger for our patients and the hospice staff. We were called to help a man who lived in a family compound deep in the woods of East Texas. The admission process went fairly well, but there were some unanswered questions to keep us on our toes. First, it was difficult to determine who the primary caregiver for the patient would be. Who would be making the decisions when the patient could not? Second, the family had asked that we visit the patient only during the daytime. We respected that unique request. However, one night the family called to tell us that the patient was having difficulty and needed attention by our staff.

The nurse arrived at the compound to see a beehive of activity. There were floodlights beaming and welding torches flashing, and the usually quiet compound was bustling with activity. The patient was cared for, and the nurse left without fanfare, but she was worried for the patient's safety. We learned later that the compound was a chop shop—a place where stolen cars are reworked for sale.

Our hospice staff tried to convince the patient to go into a facility where he would be safer, but he chose to remain in the environment where he had worked and where he felt comfortable in spite of potential dangers. He stayed there until his death. There is no further information about the chop shop.

Other daunting situations often occur when patients who are living in public housing ask for hospice care. People might not want to live in that situation, but their choices somewhere along the line have brought them there. They have lived in areas known for drug dealing, fighting, and general chaos. Our fear as health care providers is that the drug dealers will target us or our patients to get their hands on drugs to sell.

Hospice workers sometimes require police escorts to enter patient homes in public housing to deliver care. We design plans of care that include safety measures and health care services for the patient and the family. Some patients have to be moved to nursing facilities to ensure their safety and the safety of the caregivers. Many of these patients have no financial resources; so most of our care is not reimbursed. Some of the patients qualify for Medicaid and can be moved into nursing facilities for their last days.

Hospice workers choose to give their time and talent to serving others. This is not always easy for them either physically or mentally. The hours can be long and very often are spent in the middle of the night. Death and dying do not have schedules. We are very careful here at our hospice to be sensitive to one another and to watch for signs of stress. Caring for people you know are going to die on your watch takes its toll on the staff.

One nurse in particular became a worst-case scenario. He was a burly middle-aged guy who wore cowboy boots and seemed to be just a good old East Texas boy. Everyone loved him, and he had a great family, most of whom were in the nursing field also. He seemed to enjoy his work, and the patients adored him. He could swap hunting and fishing stories with the best of them.

We were stunned one day when we were told that this big, loveable guy sat on his front porch, pointed a shotgun at his chest, and killed himself. The truth was that as a youngster he had witnessed his father killing his mother, and he had never gotten over it. Even though he had tried to deal with his personal grief by caring for the dying, the agony of that horrific event rendered him unable to cope with his own life. He chose just to give it up.

On the other hand, some choices made at the end of life can make us stronger. I had no idea that hospice care was even available to her when my mother was dying of breast cancer. Our community had no hospice services, and most people had not even heard about hospice. But my mother's death and the choices we had to make throughout her decline gave me the inspiration to be part of starting a hospice program in our community. Her last days could have been much more peaceful for her and for me.

The many decisions that had to be made to help with her care were challenging. She died of breast cancer, but the nearest cancer care center was more than an hour away by car. Very often, because she was so weak, she would lie on an egg crate mattress in the back of my station wagon as we made the journey to her doctors. Upon arrival at the cancer center, I would have to go inside and request assistance to put her into a wheelchair to be brought into the lobby to sit for what seemed like hours. Many of these visits would result in the need for further diagnostics, which were performed somewhere down long hallways in adjoining buildings three elevators away. Mother would then be sent home with another handful of prescriptions. She was so exhausted.

When she returned home and I had retrieved the prescriptions from the pharmacies, then came the challenge of getting the correct doses and making sure that the new drugs would not interact adversely with the existing ones. I knew very little about the medications, but I tried to educate myself, because as Mother's condition worsened, she became unable to keep track of what she had taken and when. I turned to the local pharmacies and physicians who had treated her. The pharmacists were unaware of what the others were filling, and the doctors at that time were not sharing information very well with each other.

In the same course of events, I discovered that the lady who had been hired to care for Mother at night was taking some of Mother's pain medication for herself. Care was being compromised at every turn. There were many decisions and choices revolving around controlling my mother's pain and symptoms and trying to balance those decisions with making sure that she kept her dignity and independence as long as possible. Mother died in the local hospital where I served as a member of the board. She had stated frequently in her later life that she did not want to go to a nursing home no matter what her condition; and that wish, her choice, was granted. I think that my position as a hospital board member helped to keep her in the hospital and not a nursing home. Months later, when a hospice sixty miles away came to talk to one of our church groups about the services they offered, I was overwhelmed with what a difference they could have made in my mother's end-of-life experience. The choices were difficult, and hospice could have helped.

In the early '90s, most elderly people whose health was failing were put into nursing homes, sometimes far away from the communities where they chose to work and rear their families. They were moved closer to their now adult children, who supposedly could keep watch and help with care. Their sense of place was altered. These new and different surroundings added to their problems at the end of life. There were new faces and caregivers. Adult children had their own families to care for and found it difficult to visit.

Again, the place where a patient is located has special meaning at the end of life. Those of us who chose to live in southeast Texas love it here, but end-of-life decisions and choices are more complicated. Jasper is a small community where there are a limited number of physicians and almost no specialists. The nearest health care centers are seventy miles away in Beaumont or sixty miles away in Lufkin. Families and patients can spend days and weeks away from home while receiving specialized care. Family members sleep on couches in the hospital and bear the burden of expenses for travel, hotel rooms, and food. Also, the health care system is overburdened and difficult to access. Patients and family members have difficulty understanding complicated treatments and whether their insurance or Medicare or Medicaid will pay for their care. Hospice helps with all of these decisions and choices.

Another area where hospice can be especially helpful with choices is when the time comes for a terminally ill patient to leave the hospital in one of the larger medical facilities. If he or she is being referred to hospice care, the discharge is usually made at the end of the day. The patient must travel by personal vehicle or be transported by ambulance to his or her home, sometimes arriving in the middle of the night. Hospice arranges for our nurses to be there with all necessary equipment and medications to begin care. The patient and family are spared the burden of "What do I do now?" There is a sense of relief from being home and having a professional waiting to help.

We don't choose our family members, and they are very often the ones who make end-of-life decisions for us. Some make the process of dying even worse by denying that their loved one is dying. "Please do not tell Momma that she is dying or that you are with hospice. She just could not handle it." This is a common remark among relatives. The truth is that Momma probably knows she is dying and might like to talk seriously to someone about it. Honesty and open discussion often ease the pain and fear of dying, but families are upset by end-of-life issues and cannot or will not face the situation. Hospice encourages patients to talk openly about how they want to spend their last days.

Dealing with death and dying on a daily basis is daunting for hospice workers as well as patients and families. Our agency addresses the stress that staff members carry by encouraging them to take breaks often, to take days off, and to back away from stress before it takes control. Employees are encouraged to participate in their children's activities, to become active in their churches, and to become involved in civic projects in hopes of providing relief.

How do hospice workers deal with mortality? Those of us here at Lakes Area Hospice ask this question daily. Easing the process of dying is our job. To bring physical and mental peace and comfort to someone who is dying is the ultimate goal of hospice workers. Dying does not come with rules, but we deal with the process one step at a time. Hospice workers' lives are enriched by helping others cope with their end-of-life issues.

Helping to create a hospice program, learning the rules for care, directing staff, raising funds for a nonprofit, and educating the community about end-of-life care were some of my tasks as director of Lakes Area Hospice. Nothing in that toolkit prepared me for dealing with my husband's death. Most of the guidelines went out the window. When he died, my husband and I had been married for forty-seven years and had two wonderful sons. My husband was a brilliant lawyer, a musician, and an artist. I knew what to expect when someone is dying, when to make critical decisions, and how to work through the health care maze, but nothing worked the way it should have.

My husband had great expectations that heart surgery would fix his problems. Based on my prior experiences with hospice patients, I doubted that the procedure would work, but my suggestions to him were not enough. He was in the ICU following his valve replacement. I was watching the monitors and his responses and expressing my concerns to the ICU staff. The response from the nurses was that the surgery was "successful." One by one, his systems began to fail—first the kidneys, and then the liver. He suffered a stroke. The doctors ordered one intervention after another, and time dragged on. My expertise told me that this was not going well, but the medical experts continued to try interventions. Dialysis would correct the kidney failure. Exploratory surgery would address the liver failure. The stroke could be dealt with later.

The voice of reason finally reached me. It was time to stop. Once I made that clear to the medical community, my husband was sent home by ambulance. Our hospice coordinated the transfer from the hospital back to our hometown. Hospice staff members were there to care for my husband. He died the next day with our sons, hospice staff, and me surrounding him.

While I had packed my toolkit for dying with all the right stuff, I learned that when dying comes close to you and your loved ones, there are few rules and guidelines to pull you through. The important thing is that we help our loved ones finish life with dignity and grace.

Most of us who work in hospice have felt the anxiety and pain of others dying and have chosen to try to help ease their fear. I feel personal satisfaction for having been able to create a place where people can die without chaos, agony, and confusion—a place where families and friends can experience the patient's death much like they have witnessed the birth of a child.

I pray daily to become more sensitive to those around me who are troubled and to be able to offer help when help is wanted. I pray for good decision making and for the opportunity to reach those in need. I plead for honesty and fairness in the health care industry, particularly when dealing with those who are at the end of their lives. I ask for hospice workers to be very sensitive to each other as well as to patients and families. I want to leave a legacy of trust and truth.

Jeanette Coffield, BBA

Jeanette Havard Coffield was born in Jasper, Texas, a small rural town in the southeastern part of the state. Her parents worked and struggled through World War II to provide a home for her and her older brother.

Jeanette attended Jasper schools and graduated from Jasper High School. She went to Lamar University in Beaumont, Texas, and received a bachelor of business administration in marketing. Following graduation from Lamar, she married March Coffield; they moved to Austin, Texas, where he completed his studies at the University of Texas Law School. She worked in retail and mortgage banking there.

Jeanette took an opportunity to return to her hometown, where March practiced law, and they reared their two sons. She was fortunate enough to be a stay-at-home mom, a church and community volunteer, a golfer, and an advocate for any good cause that came along. She served on boards for the State Board of Pharmacy, the local hospital district, and the Women's Texas Golf Association; and she served as county chair and senate district committee member for a national political party.

After her sons had completed college and were making their way in the world, she became the caregiver for her mother, whose health was rapidly deteriorating. This made her acutely aware of the health care access problems that arise from living in a small rural town at least an hour away from any significant medical facility.

The year after her mother died, she was invited, as a member of the hospital district board in her town, to observe a hospice program in a larger nearby community. Hospice became her passion when she discovered the wonderful help that it could have provided for her mother and now does provide for families and patients who are experiencing life-limiting illnesses. She helped to found a not-for-profit hospice program in Jasper and was proud to serve as its executive director for twenty-one years. She was engaged as a consultant by a major corporation when her agency merged with that company.

Jeanette is currently retired, still volunteering, and looking for another worthwhile cause where she can focus her energy.

Contact Information:
e-mail: jeanettecoffield@gmail.com

A Lasting Legacy: An Approach to End-of-Life Care

A Second Hospice Director's Perspective on Mortality

John D. Foster, MS, CPM

AFTER A STINT in the Army Medical Corps, I was hired as an orthopedic technician with a four-part job description at a large Catholic medical center. I assisted with setting up traction beds and transferring equipment. As a male orderly, I administered enemas and performed male catheterizations. As a psychiatric technician, I restrained physically aggressive patients. And finally, and most daunting, I served as a morgue orderly as well.

I approached my first night of being on call as the morgue orderly with excitement, interest, and high anxiety. I had an orientation on the procedures and protocol, and I even had a short lesson from the sisters about the sanctity of life and the human body—so there was to be no messing around in the morgue. This lesson proved to be extremely important because, as the rookie, I was on the receiving end of many bizarre jokes and tricks delivered by my fellow morgue orderlies, who were also, for the most part, medical students. I learned not to flinch at three feet sticking out of the bottom of a blanket on a morgue tray.

A few hours into my first shift, I received my first page: "Go to room 431 North." I went to the morgue and picked up the magical morgue cart, an ingenuous device that appeared to be an empty gurney with a clean white vinyl top that held a folded sheet. It was actually a false top that covered a morgue body tray that could be loaded and then cranked down to just above the bottom axle, over the wheels. Because of this design, morgue orderlies could maneuver through the hospital halls and even ride crowded elevators without anyone knowing there was a dead body in the cart. When in the elevator alone with one of the older nuns, it was not unusual for her to stoop over, lift up the sheet near the bottom, and say, "Bless your heart, you dear soul." The morgue cart encapsulates my first lesson in my ever-evolving primer on how Americans deal with death.

When I arrived at the morgue, I found a tall, chain-smoking pathologist waiting for my precious cargo.

"Put him on the table, lad."

I did so and learned how to place the rubber head block, turn on the water canal, and place a sheet over the private parts of the deceased. He turned on a floor microphone and began to record his report while questioning me about my career and intentions. He never removed the cigarette from his mouth, and I worried about ashes dropping into the open cavity before us.

After a couple of minutes, I felt comfortable enough to ask a few questions. "What do we call them? Are they bodies? Cadavers? Specimens?"

"Damn, son, they are our patients. They always have been, and they always will be as long as they are in our charge."

Another note went into my primer. I began to sense that my path through the health care industry might be different than I had imagined.

In retrospect, I see now that I was starting on a path of diverse health care experiences that would eventually become the infrastructure of my personal and professional health care philosophy. The training and experiences that I received in the Army Medical Corp provided me with a great base to build on later in life. I received training as a battlefield corpsman, aid station specialist, medical specialist, ward master, and medical noncommissioned officer.

Each new role added dimension and depth to my understanding of the diverse needs and vulnerabilities of patients and their families. The terms "patients" and "families" are used jointly because it is vital to recognize and appreciate the impact and the complex role the family has on the patient and vice versa.

I quickly developed an interest in the motivation and therapeutic practices adopted by health care providers. I wanted to know how they replenished themselves and how they coped with the stresses and compassion fatigue inherent in the health care field. Why and how did folks come to be health care workers, and what caused them to continue in their careers or switch to other fields? These are particularly relevant questions in hospice care because most patients in that arena do not get better. The traditionally rewarding milestones for health care staff in helping a patient achieve wellness are not achievable for hospice workers.

Over the years, I have observed a phenomenon I call the replenishing loop. Most staff members come with a reservoir of compassion. That reservoir has been built from their previous experiences in health care and an as yet untested commitment to serve. Usually this reservoir lasts about two years. If a refilling source or fresh stream of compassion does not refill the reservoir, the practitioner is empty in fewer than two years. This helps explain the early and serious turnover in end-of-life personnel.

Senior staff, mentors, and coaches have to help the staff to recognize the need for replenishing practices because they are, in fact, actions, deeds, interventions, insights, and operational tasks that eliminate, dilute, buffer, or cloak the pain and exhaustion that come with the job. Replenishing the reservoirs of compassion of the staff can improve the quality of care significantly. Replenishing practices include the following:

- listening
- managing pain and symptoms
- interpreting medical jargon
- accepting—without judgment—decisions, cultural differences, and family traditions
- demonstrating patience
- exhibiting calm and minimizing anxiety alarms
- sharing one's own pain and sorrow
- maintaining a realistic life clock
- avoiding showy interventions and maintaining stealthy actions and quiet deeds

Some health care workers have observed that maintaining high levels of compassion also include the following:

- repairing and adjusting reading glasses (Patients with sore ears or cuts on the nose may just stop wearing their glasses without verbally complaining. They don't want to ask for help anymore, and they are just too tired to explain the problem. Remember: most patients are locked into a world of vision. Addressing every challenge to adequate vision will help maintain as good a quality of life as is possible. Sometimes it is important to note what the patient is not saying or complaining about relative to his or her own care.)

- building up dentures that rattle around in the patient's mouth (Patients with ill-fitting dentures may just stop wearing them without verbal complaint. Since no one has witnessed or talked about the problem, they believe there is no answer. Again they don't want to ask for help anymore, and they just reduce their eating as a result of the poorly fitting dentures.)

Following my tenure at the medical center, I spent seventeen years in night school earning four degrees. I also held down two long-term part-time jobs, working both for a major pharmaceutical company and as a night social worker and psych technician in a large public charity hospital. Working in the locked mental health and drug-abuse ward, I discovered the fragmented and ever-changing line between balanced mental health and poor or fractured mental health. Our overused joke was that you could tell we were sane because we carried the keys and the matches. Those years in mental health care were invaluable to my growth in my profession. Not only did I learn to appreciate the complexity of human behavior, but also I adopted a strong desire to maintain equilibrium in my own life.

During those years, I was promoted several times at the medical center and moved upstairs from the morgue basement to the eighth floor to become the director of organization development. I was charged with designing and implementing patient education programs as well as staff education and in-service activities. A few more pages were added to my primer.

One of my early tasks was supervising and redeveloping the prenatal and parenting education programs. I had the privilege of viewing several births while making training films for new moms and dads. Based on that experience and lots of research and participation in the prenatal classes, I wrote my graduate thesis on well-baby clinics. I used that document to convince the sisters to open a prenatal community education center in a small shopping center three miles south of the hospital. In that process, I acquired some insight into the lives of pregnant moms and expecting dads. I was witness to the absolute wonder and joy of childbirth and the stages prior to delivery.

Movement to End-of-Life Care

After a few more years and a few more promotions, eventually to chief operating officer, I realized that I was not going to make it up the long ladder of hospital administration and that I really didn't want the job. I resigned and took two months off to figure out what I was going to be when I became a mature health care professional. I made the transition to working in hospice care.

For the next twenty-five years, I gathered keystones that supported my developing philosophy of care—a foundation that has guided me through the complex issues of living and dying. Below are some of those keystones.

- From the very first connection, work to keep the patient in charge and the patient's interest as the primary concern.
- Families are made up of diverse individuals who have the ability to swing from human frailty to angelic performance in a short period of time.
- If the patient was the decision maker in the family, chaos may rule until a new decision maker is identified. Often the family will attempt to shift too many decisions to the professional provider; hard work and determination will be needed to attain acceptance of this responsibility by the family. Remember: birthing, living, and dying are family experiences. Family consensus develops unity.
- It can happen that there will be a need to defend care objectives on numerous fronts, including primary care physicians, family members, hospital staff, insurance carriers, clergy, and even one's colleagues. Debate usually leads to the best outcome for the patient.
- Family-direct caregivers generally fare better in the grief and bereavement phase than family-care questioners who were not bedside caregivers.

- The hospice provider staff will react to the death of a patient with different degrees of intensity. If the patient was a fifty-five-year-old mother with cancer and the staff member has just experienced a similar situation with his or her mother, the challenge of care and level of grief may be too intense. The death of a child is always difficult and draining for hospice workers; yet serving the terminal child and family often provides the greatest reward.

- Realize that although the pain meds and end-of-life clinical care techniques are valuable, there is potency in the power of the hospice caregivers and hospice volunteers. The astute administrator must stay in compliance and pay the bills, but the premier administrator recognizes and complies with the needs of his staff by providing access for listening, understanding, replenishing, mentoring, and seeking new opportunities for staff when the time has come for them to leave hospice care.

- When a staff member exhibits excessive involvement or commitment to a patient, it is time to ask, "Whose needs are you attempting to meet?" In the long run, neither party will be appropriately served and supported by an overzealous hospice provider.

As a patient and his or her family face a possible termination of life, there are serious minefields to negotiate and cumbersome hurdles to overcome. These minefields, represented by the following questions, can lead to a lack of family unity that lasts long after the patient's death:

- Do we have to make these decisions?
- Are there spiritual answers we have not utilized or discussed?
- Do we code or not code?
- Do we treat aggressively or not?
- Do we listen to the physicians, or do we listen to ourselves?
- Are we letting him die if we don't treat?
- What would he want?
- Who should make the decision?
- Who will pay for all this?
- Should he be at home or in a facility?

- How will his death affect me?
- Who gets what?
- Will this destroy our family?

After a patient meets the official hospice admittance criteria, the provider staff begins to digest the physicians' orders and assesses what the patient and family know and understand. The team must now determine, based on the desires of the patient, what the best care plan is and how to initiate it. A number of scenarios will emerge depending on the sources of the information and the level of understanding, requiring the provider team to determine the voice of truth as it echoes above the choir of disgruntled and self-declared experts singing their own refrains.

Today's patients and families often present a multitude of emotional, social, and economic conflicts and dysfunctional relationships. Therefore, it is necessary to staff for these challenges by adding social workers, counselors, chaplains, and business agents to more effectively meet the needs of the patients and their families.

As an administrator, it is important to remember that people do what you inspect—not what you expect. It is easy to confuse activity with productivity; the hustle and buzz around a patient, especially when an administrator is present, may not reflect the real level of care the patient is receiving.

In the world of end-of-life care, positive-outcome diplomats are more beneficial than care-plan warriors. Finesse almost always wins out over force. Patience diminishes, understanding becomes exhausted, tolerance wears thin, anger surfaces, and self-interest remains a powerful trait. It is important to reject the temptation to react forcefully or aggressively. Liberal use of the powerful pause, and the great silence, often allows the shady emotions to yield to the sunshine. Without becoming the commandant of the family's collective consciousness, the provider team must adjudicate their communications and plans for the patient with compassion, understanding, and forgiveness because of the fragile environment in which they are operating. Successful providers become sources of strength and support that help families evolve to a good place.

Finding the Appropriate Path

I contend that people lay down stepping stones before us as we make entry into their lives. They are spread before us as alternative routes, cultural hints, psychological maps, family values guides, generational protocols, and practices. Only the patient knows the formula; and as his or her condition or dying perspective evolves, the placement, size, and relevance of the stepping stones may change. It is not uncommon to start a case following the wishes of the patient and spouse only to make serious changes when the adult children arrive and usurp the leadership role.

If the adult children failed to engage their parents in exploring the entire situation and all options, then they may—inappropriately—remove the ownership of the care plan from the primary decision makers.

Here is a simple stepping stone example of building a care plan that is patient-appropriate. If you pull up in front of a house that sits behind a chain-link fence and you see rubber toys in the grass next to a bowl of water and a worn path to the front steps, you can conclude there is a dog in the family. Exhibiting your awareness of the existence of that dog early in the relationship might allow you to step into the world of the patient more quickly.

When you enter the home, you may notice numerous religious icons, artifacts, and literature in the home. This should raise a religious awareness flag in your mind that helps you frame your message in a spiritual fashion that is readily acceptable to the patient.

There are hundreds of nonverbal, physical, cultural, and traditional messages from the patient and family. The challenge is to listen and observe in order to assess, create, and modify intervention plans that reflect such awareness. Despite all the answers on all the health care forms, health care providers still lack the almost intangible information that helps determine who the patients and their families really are.

As a hospice professional, sooner or later it must be admitted that the knowledge of how to do hospice or how to be a pathfinder, guide, or coach to the dying is learned from the love that the family has for the patient. The love of a family member often serves as a guide to specific caring interventions.

My colleague and I once entered a room to find it dimly lit with a thin, colored nylon cloth over the lamp shade. A family member explained, "It seems the bright light hurts his eyes, so we decided to just throw my scarf over the lamp shade for a while." We learned from this and adapted it into our practice. When we entered bedrooms in the future in our hospice outfits with our name badges, we would suggest that the lights be dimmed by placing a piece of colored nylon fabric over the lamp shade, explaining, "You see, many patients who have had extensive radiation develop some sense of photophobia, and we need to buffer their light exposure." This example functions as a reminder that, in selecting colleagues, we must find those that yield to mentoring by the family. It often became our task to create a therapeutic language for those natural, loving acts—practiced as second-nature in caring families—that would be acceptable to our peers and the reimbursement sources.

As we mature, we develop coping skills. We use these when we are called to action to protect ourselves, our core values, our friends, and our families. These are often the roles we adopt when confronted with difficult situations. Some may mask their reactions, while others may be demanding, controlling, melodramatic, nasty, righteous, babyish, or overly analytical. People cope with dying by assuming the roles they have used in the past to cope with difficult situations they have faced throughout their lives.

I have witnessed several episodes that illustrate this phenomenon. I once sat with a noted cell biologist. As we sat on each side of his dying wife's bed, he gently held her hand while describing to me the process by which the cells in the body die and ultimately cause death. He was not a bad man; rather he used his exceptional scientific skills to cope with his wife's death by adopting a role he had played throughout his life. On another occasion, I sat and talked to a truck driver who kept his clean uniform and cap in a cleaning bag next to his bed. They were a badge of his achievement and success as a superior driver, because his company provided an attractive uniform to all of its senior drivers. The uniform truly was his badge of honor, denoting his professional role, and having it near helped him cope.

One of the most heartrending coping observations I have witnessed occurred as I worked with the children's cancer unit in a major cancer center. I had been working to spend more time in support of our bereavement activities and therefore spent hours on the units with parents and dying children. At one point, a mother could not come up with any more positive phrases, statements, or prayers, and she just broke down sobbing. After a few moments, the child climbed into the mother's lap, held her face, and said, "It is going to be okay, Mom. I am going to be all right. I won't hurt anymore, and I will wait for all of you until you come and join me in heaven." In this instance, the child adopted the role of the parent.

Maintaining Quality of Life

In contemporary health care, we pride ourselves on our focus on the patient. Because of the advancement of technology and our push to quantify every aspect of health and wellness, we push, design, and work to achieve the right numbers. We even use it as we talk to each other and our patients, saying such things as "Well, your numbers are in good shape," or "Your cardiac numbers are in a good range," or "Your blood sugar numbers are too high, and we must work to lower those numbers." While monitoring numbers is important, the end-of-life patient may not be as concerned with numbers as with more mundane aspects of life. He may adjust and define quality of life daily or even many times a day. This morning he may have been able to stand and urinate while only hanging on to one grab bar. That feat then becomes the goal for the rest of the day. The numbers might not have been good, but he gained self-reliance and a small level of privacy. While the next day it may take two hands on the grab bar, if he is unassisted, it will still be a victory. These very small victories can build up and create or destroy his interpretation of quality of life.

To update the old axiom of walking in another mans' shoes, as a society we need to gain the ability to see and experience the world through patients' eyes, ears, and behaviors. Below are a few questions providers might ask themselves when trying to improve the quality of life for their patients:

- Where does the patient sit in the living room, and what direction does he or she face? Why?
- Does he or she lean to the left or right to see things, and what are they?

- Does he or she lean forward to hear someone—and who, and why?
- Does he or she hang his or her hand over the side of the chair, seeking to pet the dog or cat?
- Does he or she ask to have his or her glasses cleaned?
- Does he or she seem to look for the postal carrier, school bus, or farm equipment on the road?
- Does he or she want to wear a dress and not a gown?
- Does he or she want to be by the window and want it open?
- Does he or she ever request pain meds when the grandkids are there?

If observations are noted and shared, we can work jointly with the family caregivers to improve the patient's quality of life. It is important that any intervention be spontaneous. Many patients are reluctant to ask for small changes, because they don't want to make extra work or are unable to see the benefit a small change might make. Here are ways the above questions might be addressed to improve the quality of life for a patient.

- Face the chair, bed, or recliner toward an entry door or a window.
- Go outside and trim everything that might block the view from the window. On the inside, remove blinds and drapes and even furniture to create an unobstructed view.
- Open the windows whenever possible to bring the outside to the patient.
- Open the window, remove the screen, and work the soil right under the window as the patient watches and guides you as you plant new flowers under the window.
- If the patient lives in a country setting where farm animals are present, bring a few cows, goats, and lambs into view.
- Park the patient's car or truck nearby and let a grandchild wash it.
- Play music from an earlier time of the patient's life. A little Glenn Miller goes a long way.

- Use a baby spoon and a small bowl to serve food. Don't make the task of eating become a frustration, and don't serve unrealistic portions.
- When you have to move the patient from the recliner in the living room to the bedroom, don't forget to take the family photos off the mantel and move them to a good viewing spot in the bedroom.

I understand how trivial these lists appear when compared to the potent and proven techniques and clinical practices we institute with our patients, but I believe they enhance quality of life. If the patient were assertive and proactive, these would be simple things he or she would ask for.

When the patient determines that his or her overall quality of life has deteriorated below an acceptable level, he or she can initiate some withdrawing actions. Meals or liquids may be refused. He or she may refuse or change the schedule of his or her meds. The patient may restrict some visitors and increase visiting opportunities for others. He or she may not respond to questions or may become physically demonstrative. The patient may just state over and over again that he or she is tired and just wants peace. In that situation, we know—and the patient knows—it is acceptable to just sleep.

As caregivers and providers, we don't have to react immediately to these behaviors. We may initiate and seek some compromising interventions that, for a short time, bring balance back. We are supposed to be initiators of comfort, and we may have to sustain some discomfort in order to provide superior care and quality of life from the patient's unique perspective. It is important to be creative and observant while exploring what factors exist in the patient's world that, if changed slightly, would enhance the present quality of life, even if only for a few hours. Remember: it can take an extended period of time for some people to die. They may go through numerous and complex quality-of-life issues as they move toward death. Our challenge is to avoid using a scientific scale that may have been created months ago and stay in tune with the patient.

Similarities between Caring during Birth and Caring during Death

As the president and CEO of three hospices and president of the state hospice association, I was frequently called upon to speak about hospice. It was easy for me to talk about hospice, but I became increasingly uncomfortable and guilty regarding my routine speech presentations, and I experienced disappointment in myself for the shallow focus of these talks. I challenged myself to engage in an introspection of what I thought I knew and what I should be sharing with others. I decided to continue the presentations as they were for the general public and for occasions when development opportunities arose, but I felt compelled to present a more substantial premise to the providers, medical students, and other end-of-life practitioners.

I started by reading more about contemporary discoveries and issues relative to dying. I sought out the newest and most studied aspects of hospice care (such as the website of the National Palliative Care and Hospice Association, the National Association of Home Health & Hospice, End-of-Life Planning Guides, and the Annual Medicare Benefit Guide).

I knew I would find an answer. But repeated failure led me to question my own abilities and what I thought I knew and had achieved. In an attempt to protect and preserve that which I thought I knew, I engaged in a serious life review. That review led me back to episodes in my professional life that broke down barriers and set new norms of care. I began to journal my experiences from the prenatal care phase of my education. I knew it would be impossible to duplicate the joy and thrill of childbirth in the final phases of life and dying, but I hoped to reduce the potency and sting of pain and ease the final exit with demonstrations of love in caregiving. I also hoped for new levels of family dialogue and unity in grief support and legacy building.

I came to a startling conclusion. The answer rested not in the future but in the past. Premier providers and practitioners of the past had created and made significant contributions to childbirth education and preparation. But all the recent contributions to end-of-life care, though admirable, failed to match the positive experiences of the new moms and dads. My conclusion was that if the best place for a healthy baby to enter the world is a warm, safe, family-centered, loving environment that is controlled by the patient's and family's wishes and supported by health and social service professionals, then maybe this was a good model to help people exit the world. As I contemplated this fresh and fragile thought, a phrase began to repeat in the corner of my mind: "A little child will lead them." Or, as the prophet said, "The wolf will live with the lamb, the leopard will lie down with the goat, the calf and the lion and the yearling together: and a child will lead them" (Isaiah 11:6).

Possible Parallels between Birthing and Dying

I started to list phases and performance traits that I had witnessed in the new moms and dads more than twenty-five years earlier. When that list reached eleven statements, I went back to the beginning to see if there were parallels in the worlds of birthing and of dying. I was seeking and hoping for parallels, so my desire for balance may have caused me to stretch too far, but I contend that there is fertile ground in observing, analyzing, and questioning the common experiences of a natural entry into life and a natural exit from life. The following is the result of examining the parallels that exist between entering life and exiting life:

Time

> *Birthing*
> When most expectant mothers learn they are pregnant, their world experiences and worldviews change. They begin to create pathways filled with unsophisticated goals, destinations, and joys for the child growing within. They develop a new relationship with time and wonder, "How pregnant am I, and how long before I have this baby?"

> *Dying*
> When patients are informed and accept the fact that they are dying, their world experiences and outlooks on the world's future change. They develop a new relationship with time, which takes on new meanings and causes the

thought "How long have I lived, and how much longer will I live?"

Relationships

Birthing

This exciting, life-changing phenomenon usually focuses on one distinct partner or a very small circle of key people.

Dying

This pending closure of life prompts the dying person to weigh and assess relationships in order to get to the key people in his or her life.

Attention

Birthing

Expectant mothers take on a motherly glow and seek out social engagements where the glow can be noticed and appreciated by others.

Dying

Patients acquire a fragile persona and, while accommodating limited social engagements, they are recipients of excessive courtesy, soft voices, gentle touches, and sad stares molded into artificial smiles. The spotlight, though not bright, is on the patient.

Body Image

Birthing

The expectant mother's body image starts to change, and while at first it is a badge of honor, eventually it may turn the woman into a shape that prompts her to reduce social contact.

Dying
The patient's physical image may change and deteriorate. It is noticeable and shocking, but others often will make ambiguous statements that attempt to falsify the image the patient sees in the mirror.

Emotions

Birthing
Expectant mothers ride emotional roller coasters. Feeling the baby's heartbeat may prompt the highs; the lows may come when the back pain exceeds the woman's ability to endure it.

Dying
Patients ride emotional roller coasters. The highs may be prompted by the ability to keep down three teaspoons of oatmeal; the lows may occur when a person sleeps through his or her granddaughter's visit.

Beliefs

Birthing
Expectant mothers are bombarded with positive religious and spiritual issues, family-oriented messages, and gifts. Regardless of where she was before, the expectant mother has a human being growing in her, and all her previous beliefs are revisited because of this new circumstance. The expectation of the baby has changed her.

Dying
Belief demands fall upon patients like an avalanche of unanswered questions. They are on their way to the end of life. What lies ahead? What is beyond? Some may wonder, "How and where will I exist?" Their evolving perspective is measured in minutes and seconds instead of lifetimes.

Traditional Bible and clergy quotes become the vernacular of the day, and yet they may not bring comfort.

Changing Relationships

Birthing

New relationships will come, and others will be enhanced or diminish, often without understanding or transition. Expectant mothers are in the anteroom of a new sphere of influence, and the transition will be quick and complex. They can only prepare so much for this dynamic event.

Dying

Contemporary relationships are drastically narrowed. Some will be discarded, while others will become more intense. Patients will seek out those who affirm them quietly and those who are already demonstrating the pain of losing them.

Isolation

Birthing

Expectant mothers may seek isolation and freedom from caring inquiries. They are split between wishing for time to accelerate and, at the same time, hoping for it all to slow down because they are not ready.

Dying

Isolation often relieves patients from playing the role of the terminal host. They engage in reminiscence about the past and interpretation of the possible hallucinations of the present in regard to their final journeys. For example, "Aunt Jane stood at the bottom of my bed last night."

Pain

Birthing

Discomfort, pain, and suffering are introduced with the childlike activity of ranking them from one to ten or via a series of smiley faces. This is an exercise some hate but learn to indulge in as their coping reservoirs drop below self-imposed levels.

Dying

Discomfort rapidly and aggressively moves to pain and further into intense pain. Patients seek nothingness and yet demand consciousness and awareness. They may say, "Without the pain, I would not know I was still alive!"

The Future

Birthing

Probes into the future occupy vast expenditures of time. Expectant mothers wish to create successful and positive futures for themselves and their children and wish to adopt a life map to get them there. Expectant mothers often make statements like "The baby and I are going to share incredible adventures together."

Dying

Probes into the future are narrowed into unanswerable eternal questions and filtered by the actual act of dying. Very quickly, explorations of the future are turned completely around and add power to the act of memory and recall.

The Finale

Birthing

Labor begins, and vested parties gather to coach, cheer, offer advice, and engage in prayers and positive aspirations for the hardworking mom and baby. After some time, an inner-circle person asks, "When is she going to deliver? She has been in labor for six hours. She is hot, tired, sweating, and extremely restless. Isn't it time for her to deliver the baby?" In response, a senior staff person may respond, "She will deliver when she is ready. The baby is in charge, and the baby is not ready."

Dying

The active phase of dying begins. Restlessness is accompanied by shallow and irregular breathing. Words escape from the air-starved mouth and stretch the ability of the listener to catch meaningful statements. At the bedside vigil, caregivers and loved ones become impatient and seek answers from the support staff. "When will he die? It has been hours since he last spoke. He grimaces in pain, and he flails his arms and speaks no understandable words. When will he die?" A senior staff member will respond, "He will die when his is ready. He is in charge, and he is not ready."

Do parallels exist between a new life being introduced to the world and an existing life exiting the world? While one may or may not accept the common factors and may see no relationship between the events, health care providers accept the basic premise that the best place for a healthy baby to be born in is a warm, safe, family-centered, loving environment controlled by the patient's and family's wishes and supported by health and social service professionals. End-of-life professionals accept the basic premise that the best place for a person to die is in a warm, safe, family-centered, loving environment controlled by the patient's and family's wishes and supported by health care and social service professionals. I propose this as means of achieving balance in the daily dynamics of life and death.

Legacy

Pericles wrote, "What you leave behind is not what is engraved in stone monuments, but what is woven into the lives of others."[1]

One of my favorite times as a young lad was when my father's navy buddies from World War II visited our home. Eventually they migrated to the kitchen, and Red Top Ale, Pabst Blue Ribbon, and Schlitz kept their throats lubricated and the laughter hearty. My brothers and I tried to get as close as possible, without breaching the brotherhood circle, to hear their stories. My favorite listening spot was the top of the washer, where I was high enough to see everything and close enough to hear the stories—rough language and all. As I grew into adolescence, I realized the stories were censored by each storyteller. They didn't speak of the horrors of battles in the Pacific. They did not emphasize killing and death. They avoided details of lost comrades and shipmates. They talked about the good times.

"Remember when we climbed over that fence and went to the submariners' beer party?"

"Remember how long we stood in line to see the USO show with Clark Gable and Carol Lombard?"

"I'll never forget when Tiny drove that ambulance off the dock and into the ocean."

They were creating a legacy of the war that they thought was worthy of passing on and, more importantly, that helped them accommodate their participation in the war.

After years of grief- and bereavement-support activities, I recognize the creation of the legacy by the survivors as an extremely helpful and potent coping tool. All are unique in their dying, and the survivors are equally unique in their mourning, but the following anecdote illustrates how critical legacy creation can be.

The son enters his father's room at 11:45 p.m., and as he stands by the bed, he says, "He is really a good man." He returns at 11:55 p.m. and finds his father dead, and he says, "He was really a good man." In this action he has initiated the first entry in his father's legacy. The legacy is the sum total of all the perceptions held by all the people who knew and had contact with the deceased. From the moment of death, the legacy grows and changes. At the funeral home, visitors tell stories, and episodes are shared with survivors that are new to them and help to broaden their perceptions of the deceased. Eventually the legacy takes on a positive aspect and becomes a comfortable accumulation of unique memories about the deceased. This legacy reduces the pain of grief, filling the void with warm memories.

After my father's death, I remember my brothers and I looked through his wallet—an action that, if taken several months earlier, would have been a serious infraction and would have ended in a violent exchange. As we emptied his side pockets, we came upon a Teamsters union card.

"I didn't know the old man was a Teamster."

Other papers and artifacts introduced us to facets of our father that were new to us and enlarged the place he had held in our world.

Sometimes legacy building takes some priming on the part of the primary grievers. Friends and acquaintances may be hesitant to share stories and anecdotes until someone demonstrates it is okay. The legacy we build contributes to and perpetuates the new spiritual gift of a lost loved one—the eternal presence of that person in our ongoing lives. As we work to accommodate losing the person from our lives, we weave the memories and recollections into a warm blanket of legacy that might help buffer the chill of the loss.

Traumatic Loss and Grief

I had the honor and privilege to volunteer with the army for five years in the area of casualty assistance and military grief and bereavement when my fellow hospice volunteers and I taught a course about grief. Our students were exceptional men and women. Many were seasoned combat veterans from current wars. They were headed toward new careers in casualty notification duties and casualty assistance duties. These are extremely tough assignments.

On one particular day, we were emphasizing that if one failed to work through grief, it was likely the grief would negatively impact one's life. A serious platoon sergeant raised his hand to share his story. He said that since he'd come home, he'd worked very hard to avoid carrying bad news and tragic events home every night. He would pull into his driveway, and before he entered the house to greet his wife and children, he would extend his arm and place his hand on a large tree by the driveway. His intent was to transfer all the bad news and events from that day into the tree so that when he entered his house, he would be more wholesome and balanced in all things. He stated that he knew it worked because the tree died eight months later.

Our volunteer group also developed a support group for Gold Star Wives—wives who've lost their husbands in combat. We created events that provided professionally created grief and bereavement activities for children and support groups for wives. As my co-facilitator and I worked with the group of wives, we were struck by the enormity and complexity of their journey. We listened without judging, realizing that alcohol and medications were often a part of the coping process. We accepted their anger over trite and routine procedures initiated by the army. They spoke honestly of their repulsion when they heard "Taps" played for the hundredth time. They often talked about their crying place; when they reached the breaking point, they would put a happy video in for the kids and then go into the shower stall with water running full-force and break down and cry to the point of exhaustion. They were the bravest and strongest people I have ever met in my life.

After several sessions, I wanted to be able to capture some of their unique pain and suffering so that other helpers might be better able to relate to their challenges. For that purpose, I wrote this poem about their experiences.

My World Collapses

Uniformed men at my door collapse my world.
My inner body no longer holds me up.
Air eludes my lungs.
Screams fill my throat.
Vision is lost to pain-emitting tears.
My ears try to close to unwelcome words.
Beats from my heart attempt to break out of my chest.
Arms flail, and legs drop as low as they can go.
I try to redirect the message to another home.
All that mattered moments ago no longer matters now.
Roles and expectations of me flounder in disorientation.

I can't find anything to hold on to, and the floor stops my fall to nothingness.

Sobs lead to numbness, and numbness leads to voids unexplored.

I reach for the unreachable, and I want to restore that which is gone forever.

Ask me not to breathe deep, because breath only brings the devastating reality back again and again.

When I can finally touch my face, it is flushed with the burning heat of shock.

My fingers tremble as they encompass my squinting eyes and dropping jaw.

Lowering my head and diverting my eyes only connects my throbbing head to my pounding heart.

Some words finally breach the metabolic chaos, and I know what I hear is my new empty reality.

Pleas and the endless begging of God to intervene and stop this flood of loss and suffering are not instantly answered.

Future faith accommodations are yet to come.

Those precious e-mails and phone calls, only a few hours old, are now treasured artifacts of a shattered life and lifestyle, and final gifts from the part of us that died.

In a time unique to me, I grasp that which still physically embodies the love I have left in this world.

My family, my children, my friends reach beyond themselves to piece together fragments of false understanding.

Military condolences, protocols, entitlements, escorts, and paperwork pull me through imitation progress and coping.

Wives of others and warrior families wrap me in a cloth of unsought security and ill-fitting comfort.

Drums, bugles, flags, and salutes bid farewell for some, but for me they usher in an era initiated by new moment-by-moment loss episodes.

When my surviving loved ones are gently cared for, I alone greet the new loneliness that will be my companion from this day forth.

I pull myself up and search for the me I knew in a nearby mirror in the hall.

I appear flat, without luster, and the mirror does not reflect the absent partner I want to see beside me.

As I move away, I steady myself for the rocky path of loss accommodation that begins with these new and unsure steps.

Anticipation becomes an unfriendly trait; I seek the error message and only receive confirmation.

I desire peace of mind, and I am supplied with peace-diverting procedures.

I regret past affiliations and yet yearn for the comfort of relationships past.

A new identity is forced upon me with paper, ID, and terms.

I am surrounded by a contagious isolation that reminds too many others of future situations they can't imagine.

The shower stall becomes the crying vault where tears, moans, and sighs are drowned out, not cleansed by water.

Our closet holds uniforms, and each treasured piece is touched and fingered for a link to a love ripped from my world.

In a quiet, unspoken way, he now tells me I must go on. But go on where?

Where do I belong?

The military world is withdrawing from around me, and the civilian world requires credentials new to me.

I separate from others and ask that all not separate from me.

Tell me when the markers are made.

Tell me when the stones are laid, and tell me when the units return home, for I am eternally linked to the warrior world regardless of where I roam.

It is true. You do not get over it. There is never enough time to heal all wounds.

Days will come and months will accumulate and years will mount. With love, work, memories, compassion, and sheer tenacity, I will eventually accommodate the love I lost, the partner I had, and the future that faded when uniformed men collapsed my world.

A fallen soldier creates a wounded family that deserves a supportive community.

Conclusion

People are gifts in our lives. Some are very evident and easily accessed, while others take energy, time, and unique circumstances to unwrap and gain access to. Those of us who are professional providers bring our professional gifts to challenging health care opportunities. Sometimes when doing so, we let those professional and clinical skills crowd out and suppress the natural and compassionate love and care we have for those we serve. So remember to be bold in your goodness and be the total gift you are to all you serve.

---

1   As quoted in *Flicker to Flame: Living with Purpose, Meaning, and Happiness* (2006), by Jeffrey Thompson Parker, 118.

John D. Foster, MS, CPM

From his preteens forward, John D. Foster wanted to follow what his dad and his older brothers had achieved. His father was a navy medic, and his two older brothers had become army medics. He followed that path, attending five schools in the US Army medical school system and achieving the position of ward master at Fitzsimmons Army Hospital in Denver, Colorado. It was a great experience, but John came to the realization of how unprepared he felt in regard to making an impact on his own life and the lives of others.

For the next seventeen years, he went to night school and held various jobs in the sector of health and social services. He obtained four degrees and counseling certifications. John received a BS degree in business administration and a BS degree in social science education at the University of Indianapolis. He also received both an MS degree in health care administration and a certified public manager/administrator (CPM) accreditation at Indiana University. He also earned a counseling certification at Christian Theological Seminary.

As a leader in various fields of health care, John served ten years as director of organizational development at St. Francis Medical Center and twenty years as executive director and president of hospices in Brazos, Brenham, and LaGrange, Texas. He is the founder of the Texas Non-Profit Hospice Alliance and also is the founder of Operation Render Comfort (a military grief support organization).

During the course of his career, it became apparent to John that successful leaders in health care must achieve a balance between obtaining skills in the traditional business environment and also holding a deeply based philosophy in compassionate service. One of his greatest challenges was to build efficient and effective health and social service agencies that could interpret reams of codes, laws, and unlimited guidelines that were really hurtles to delivering care and receiving care. John believes that, after earning the trust of the client family, trust can be utilized to support and guide them through the grieving and dying process.

John will always be grateful to his mentors, guides, family coaches, and peers for the lovely and gentle talents they have shared and nurtured within him.

Contact Information:
e-mail: j_cfoster@verizon.net

EVEN FUNERAL DIRECTORS DIE

A Funeral Director's Perspective on Mortality

Jeff Staab, CLCC

SOME REALIZATIONS HIT harder than others, and some can land so suddenly and with such force that we're left feeling dumbfounded. In one such instance, a funeral director friend was discussing the loss of a loved one with the loved one's family when the director came to the abrupt realization that he was terribly uncomfortable with the idea of his own mortality. He worried that the discomfort would be apparent to the families that came to him for comfort and guidance. He asked himself if they would be able to sense, at least on some level, that he hadn't come to terms with his own mortality. How would he be able to help them and provide advice for coming to terms with their loved one's demise? Surprisingly, many funeral directors appear not to have arranged their own affairs in case of death.

I was at a recent presentation in a room of a hundred or so funeral directors, and the presenter asked how many in the room had made their own prearrangements. Only a handful of hands went up. You would think that being reminded of death every day would inspire some insightful planning. Funeral directors deal with the subject of death for a living, but many of them are discomfited by talking about their own deaths.

I believe that constantly seeing death and being involved with the deaths of others gives some funeral directors a sense that death will not touch them. They think they know the signs and will somehow dodge it when it draws near—an invincible feeling of "You can't get me; I know all about your death tricks!" I take great pride in my skills as an embalmer. I have personally embalmed more than three thousand corpses, and I admit to feeling that there is no way anyone is ever going to do that to me!

Most often, people who are bothered by the thought of their mortality and haven't considered what happens after death aren't going to be comfortable talking about it. But the death of a loved one is easier, on some levels, if it has been discussed and a plan for a funeral or, at the very least, a living will is in place. When families come into a funeral home for guidance, it might be helpful to ask them what they believe happens after death. Many will feel comfort and relief at discussing it with the funeral director. This can also help the director to be more compassionate and sensitive while the loved one's funeral is planned. In the end, planning one's own funeral can help a director or counselor relate to the families he or she serves every day.

Unfortunately the topic of death is a taboo in modern society—particularly in the Western world. One may occasionally hear death discussed briefly during religious services, but other than that, it's something that we learn not to think or speak about openly. Regardless of this taboo, death is natural and inevitable; so it's good to consider the topic of one's own death in order to help oneself and others come to terms with it.

Unease with One's Own Mortality

There are many reasons for being ill at ease with the idea of dying. Maybe something traumatic and life altering, such as an accident, is the reason. Or maybe death was never spoken of in one's family. Perhaps, as is often the case, one's particular faith paints death in a negative and fear-ridden light. Regardless of the reason, before one's own mortality can be accepted, it's important to identify why one is uncomfortable with it in the first place.

People fear what they don't understand, and the topic of death is not immune to this fact. Most people fear dying because they feel uncertain about what happens afterward. Therefore, the most common reaction is to resign oneself to crossing that bridge when one gets to it. Although it may be uncomfortable or confusing, thinking about what happens after death can be an excellent brain exercise. Asking friends and loved ones what they think can be a good place to start. This topic is richly discussed in books and on the Internet, and these sources can offer some helpful ideas and insights. Similarly, one can discuss it with a pastor or other religious adviser.

When one has a set idea of what happens after death, one is better equipped to handle losses in one's own life as well as in the lives of others. In my experience, individuals who have beliefs about what comes after seem better able to cope with death than those who have no such beliefs. In many cases, the hardest part of dealing with the death of a friend or loved one is facing the unknown, so having some idea can make one feel less distraught.

Studies have shown that people who are unsure of how they view death may occasionally reject their current religious beliefs. In some cases, they'll adopt childhood beliefs, or look for another form of spiritual guidance or teaching. Some may turn bitter and angry, while others opt to live a life in service to others by volunteering and donating money, time, advice, or assistance. The thing that all of these people have in common is that they're seeking to make sense of death and find greater meaning in being alive.

After someone makes sense of a particular experience with death, either from a religious perspective or by assigning some other meaning to it, that person is usually able to move on. Many people who have personally dealt with such grief say that there are good things about it. They got through the experience, and after great contemplation on the fragility of life and what it means to them, they came out of it with a different way of looking at that life.

I've often heard it said that we fear dying more than we fear death. Death takes little time, but dying is unpredictable and unfamiliar and can take months or even years. I think we can quell our fear of dying, but not until we recognize why we fear dying.

Five Reasons We Fear Dying

1. We're unfamiliar with dying.
   With death removed from our common experience, it's unfamiliar and unknown.

2. We fear dying in an unfamiliar place.
   In actuality here in America, only 7 percent of dying and death occurs outside of homes and institutions. And while most of this 7 percent is produced by tragic car

accidents or unpredicted cardiac events, the likelihood is that most people do not die in an unfamiliar place. The institutionalization of medicine means that the likelihood of dying in an institutional setting is greater than dying outside such a setting. In fact, nearly three out of four deaths in the United States occur in a hospital, nursing home, or long-term care institution.[1]

3. We fear that we will die alone.

    Thanks to the expertise of nursing staff, family can often be called and be present for the death of a loved one. But sometimes the event of a death happens without warning and the moment is missed. If you have a loved one in a nursing home, I respect your decision. Yet, to be honest, one of the hardest parts of my job is simply walking through nursing homes and seeing the aging residents in crowded loneliness.

4. We don't know our caregivers.

    With the advent of institutions like nursing homes and hospitals has come professional caregivers who do an outstanding job. But these caregivers are not our loved ones. It may be worth considering that the true caregivers are and always have been loved ones and family members.

5. We fear being a burden to our families.

    This is perhaps the fundamental fear that lies at the heart of the problem. Those who are sick and perhaps dying think that by removing themselves from their families (via entrance into a nursing home or retirement community), they relieve the burden. But one's dying doesn't burden family; it's what creates family. It allows families to love and to be caretakers, and most importantly, it allows the dying to die in familiar places.

Moving Past Denial

As a funeral director, I advise that it is better to plan on dying than to live in denial of death. I urge those who are capable of it to make plans so that when they die (and they will), the people they love aren't left with a huge mess to deal with—on top of grieving for the loss of their loved one. I have seen survivors thrown into the secret lives of their loved ones and having to deal with the guilt or the anger that they feel over the way the deceased left things. It's not thoughtful or caring to leave several loose ends for loved ones to handle. It is vital to be conscientious in regard to the fact that life will continue to affect others after one dies. For me personally, I don't think I will ever be ready to die, but I will be prepared.

I have met religious people who believe in predestiny and that God has already planned out their lives and purposes and deaths. Working in the funeral business has erased any notions of predestiny for me. I believe in creating your own path and that not a single second has been predetermined.

Death is not always fair! Have you heard that only the good die young? I take the "anyone, anytime" route. It pays to be careful, but being careful doesn't always pay. I once handled a funeral of a man you might say was a health freak. He ate all the right things, exercised, and did everything "right." He won a marathon and two days later had a fatal heart attack in his sleep. Once again, death is not fair; live for the day.

As for me, having worked in the death business for thirty years, life is precious. Besides working as a funeral director, I have also been lucky enough to have cheated death on several occasions. It has been a real eye-opener for me. And it has increased my desire to get the most out of life. My list of things I want to do and places I want to see is a long one.

I feel that I appreciate life more than the average person, who might see death only on TV or read about it in the newspaper. Jimmy Cliff wrote a song about living for the day but being careful because choices made that day could affect one's life forever. This has kept me in check most of my life. Every day is a gift, and I do not like to waste time worrying about what was and what could be. Yet I will think long and hard about the choices I make. It's all about balance. Family and friends are important to me. I have seen too many lonely deaths filled with the regret of not trying harder to get along. You have only one family, so look for the good and set aside the feuds.

Fill your world with all the love you can take. That's what death has taught me; life is and will always be about the love that we share. Enjoy every day by spreading love; it will someday come back and lift you up.

---

1   Aubrey D. N. J. de Grey, "Life Span Extension Research and Public Debate: Societal Considerations," *Studies in Ethics, Law, and Technology* 1, no.1 (2007). doi:10.2202/1941-6008.1011.

Jeff Staab, CLCC

Jeff has been a funeral director and counselor to the bereaved for more than twenty years and is a certified life cycle celebrant. He has been a leader and innovator in creating meaningful celebrations of life and a designer and resource of urns for ashes and jewelry for ashes. He is the founder and president of Cremation Solutions, a company that assists funeral professionals and the families they serve with funeral planning information Cremation Solutions is the number-one resource for information on scattering ashes. He is also the owner and operator of Life Tree Farm.

Jeff is a pioneer in the process of establishing guidelines for those who are cremated and choose scattering as the final disposition. He has developed methods, ceremonies, and scattering urns for ash-scattering events. Cremation Solutions has the most complete line of scattering products as well as cremation memorials, cremation urns, and new products that add dignity and ease to the cremation scattering ceremony. Jeff is an expert in memorial goods, such as cremation urns for ashes, cremation jewelry for ashes, and cremation monuments that hold ashes. As an educator to the death care industry, he has written for industry publications. Jeff is a Certified Life Cycle Celebrant (CLCC).

With his wife Stacie and daughters Jena and Shaana, he lives in Arlington, Vermont. He enjoys adventure in the mountains and on the sea, cooking for friends, social responsibility, and green living.

Contact Information:
e-mail: Jeff@cremationsolutions.com
website: www.cremationsolutions.com

Finding Balance While Helping Others Cope with Grief and Loss

A Director of Pediatric Oncology Social Work's Perspective on Mortality

Frances L. Greeson, MSSW, LCSW

W E ALL MAKE decisions in our daily lives. However, there are some decisions we realize in hindsight were pivotal decisions. These pivotal decisions can ultimately change the courses of our lives and continue to shape our own personal growth and development as adults. Such was the decision that I made to enter graduate school to pursue a master's degree in social work. I had been out of school for more than eight years and really never had any intention to return to school.

With a BA in psychology, I had worked in retail banking and in a state agency to determine eligibility for financial assistance. While sitting at my desk one day, I found myself daydreaming about what it would be like to find a job working in a pediatric hospital with children coping with chronic illness. At that moment, I made two phone calls to local pediatric hospitals, only to hear that both required a master's in social work. I felt somewhat defeated. However, after discussing it with my family, I began to plot a course to return to school part-time while I continued working full-time. My ultimate goal was now clear. I was determined to become a medical social worker specializing in children coping with acute and chronic illness.

I must admit that, at that time, I really had no idea what such a job would entail. I just knew I had always loved working with children. With the support of my family, I applied for a graduate program in social work. I also began looking for a different job that would afford me the opportunity to gain more exposure to working with children. Fortunately I found a position in an adolescent psychiatric hospital, where I worked with the primary psychologist, assisting with discharge planning and coordinating family therapy. Participation in family therapy sessions provided me a wealth of experience that was incredibly beneficial and affirmed what I was learning in my graduate course work.

When the time arrived for my second internship during my final year of graduate school, I was determined to find an opportunity in a pediatric medical setting. I immediately contacted St. Jude Children's Research Hospital. St. Jude is a pediatric hospital that treats children with cancer and other catastrophic diseases. I was lucky to have grown up in Memphis, where St. Jude was founded by the late actor Danny Thomas in 1962. Thomas founded his dream on the premise that "no child should die in the dawn of life."

The mission of St. Jude Children's Research Hospital is to advance cures and means of prevention for pediatric catastrophic diseases through research and treatment. Consistent with Thomas's vision, no child is denied treatment based on race, religion, or the family's ability to pay at St. Jude. Additionally, families never receive a bill from St. Jude for their child's medical care. When Thomas opened St. Jude in 1962, the survival rate for acute lymphoblastic leukemia (ALL) was only 4 percent. By 2014, 94 percent of children with ALL could expect to survive this once deadly disease, thanks in no small part to St. Jude.

When I contacted my potential field instructor at St. Jude, she commented that she had just spoken with my adviser and that I certainly seemed eager about this internship. She was right; I really wanted this internship because I knew it would help me achieve my goal to work in the field of medicine as a social worker. I interviewed and fortunately was accepted for the internship! When that semester arrived, I was very excited. Little did I know how this experience would change my life and teach me many valuable life lessons.

The Intern

Most people probably aren't aware of what a medical social worker can offer a patient and his or her family unless they've had some exposure to this. Unfortunately, much of what the public does know about social work in general comes from the media. To this day, I still find it frustrating to watch a medical show on television and see that a social worker shows up briefly in the script to swoop in and take a child away from his or her home and family. As an intern, I quickly began to learn the complexities of a social worker's role. Master's-level social workers are trained in counseling. They are available to patients and families to help them learn to cope with the diagnosis of a catastrophic illness. The goal is to help the family adjust and stabilize emotionally as they begin treatment. Social workers also practice systems theory, wherein the social worker identifies and can intervene in all the systems, or environments, that impact the child, such as family, school, peer group, and hospital or medical center. Social workers are also experts in linking patients and their families with community resources to help with financial stability.

After a very thorough orientation, and with supervision from my field instructor, I was assigned to my first patient and her family as their primary social worker. The primary relationship meant that, like the attending physician, I would remain the child's and family's social worker throughout the course of the patient's treatment and follow-up visits. In some hospitals, the patient changes social workers as he or she moves throughout the various areas of the hospital. This is not the case at St. Jude, where the viewpoint is that having a primary relationship allows the social worker to build valuable long-term relationships with the child and family. At St. Jude, many of our patients are followed at the hospital for a number of years. When I began working with one of my first patients, whom I'll call Jenny, and her family, I had to confront my own feelings about witnessing human suffering.

Please note that as I share stories about the patients and families I have had the privilege of working with over the years, for the purpose of ensuring patient confidentiality and privacy, specific identifying information has been changed, or the story may be a composite of my experience. But all the examples I provide represent actual cases and situations from my clinical practice in pediatric oncology.

I met Jenny and her parents the first day she came to the hospital. Her parents were quiet people with limited means and education. She was thirteen, and like her parents, she was very quiet. I provided supportive counseling to help her and her parents adjust to the hospital and the illness.

I also helped them connect with the resources at the hospital and in the community that could provide additional financial support. Jenny was diagnosed with a type of leukemia called acute myelogenous leukemia (AML). At the time, this leukemia was more difficult to treat than the more common type of leukemia, acute lymphoblastic leukemia (ALL). However, Jenny initially did well and went into remission after months of difficult chemotherapy.

As an intern, I had more time and a smaller caseload than the full-time social workers, so I often checked in on Jenny and her parents to provide support and monitor for anything that they might need. One day while she was undergoing inpatient treatment, the doctor asked me to join him for a meeting with her parents. Sadly, during that meeting, her parents learned that her leukemia had returned. She needed to change chemotherapy treatments in hopes of getting her back into remission. I stayed with her parents after the doctor left. This was the first time I observed parents actively grieving over the possible loss of their child. Both parents understood what this meant. They sat quietly crying, and I was at a loss as to what to do for them. Not being able to tolerate my own feeling of inadequacy, all I knew to do was jump up and run out of the room to get extra Kleenexes for them. Later, as I told my field instructor about my discomfort, she wisely told me that there are times when sitting and not saying a word is the right thing to do. However, hearing this from your field instructor and actually learning to feel comfortable with silence are two different things. Whenever I observed a child or a family member crying, it remained difficult for me to accept the fact that I could not make everything all right or come up with just the right thing to say to these parents or patients. I had to work hard to remind myself that it was okay to sit, say nothing, and be present with the patient or family member as they cried.

Since my internship cases, I have become familiar with the work of Dr. Alan Wolfelt, an expert in the field of grief and loss. He uses the term "companioning" when he describes the professional's role in the grieving process with patients and families.[1] Over time I have come to understand that as a pediatric oncology social worker, I am the patient's and family's companion on the journey that begins once they learn of the cancer diagnosis. While it has always been difficult to witness human suffering and open expressions of grief, the concept of companioning has helped me develop a better sense of how one's quiet presence can be a source of comfort and support during moments of suffering. It is important to sit and be present, lending as much support as I can while bearing my own discomfort in silence.

Later in my career, whenever I was mentoring students, I fondly talked about the importance of companioning and shared the story of "the Kleenex intervention" with the students. As for Jenny, she did go back into remission during my internship. I was there the day her parents learned this good news, and we all celebrated together. That is one of the great things about being a pediatric oncology social worker. I am there for the happy moments as well as the sad ones, which helps me find balance.

As the months passed and I worked with approximately ten or twelve families, it seemed I was going to make it through my entire internship without suffering the loss of a patient. I marveled at my social work colleagues and wondered how they were able to cope with the death of one of their patients. I watched curiously when a social worker came back to our offices following the loss of a patient. I noticed that they used the support of teammates, including other social workers, chaplains, and medical staff, to cope with the loss. I remember thinking to myself, "I don't know how I would do given that situation."

Sadly, though, that situation did occur. But through my first loss of a patient, I began to learn a valuable lesson that would actually help sustain me throughout my career in pediatric oncology social work. I was assigned as the social work intern for a very sweet five-year-old named Nicholas. He was a handsome little boy who loved T-ball and gymnastics. He was diagnosed with the most curable type of leukemia, ALL. His prognosis was favorable. I met with the family a couple of times to complete my assessment and begin to plan for ongoing social work services. They had financial stability and good extended family and community support. While I was nearing the end of my internship, I was not sure if they would need to be transferred to a primary social worker after I left, because everything was going well for them.

However, one day while back in my office, I received a call from the nurse on the inpatient floor; Nicholas had died suddenly from unexpected complications. I was stunned. I sat in my office thinking, "What in the world will I do for or say to this family?" My field instructor offered some very quick guidance and sent me on my way to see Nicholas's parents on the inpatient floor. When I arrived on the floor, the nurse told me the family had quickly gathered their belongings and left. I actually remember feeling relieved that I would not have to see these parents, but I also felt guilty for feeling that way.

I turned around and went back to my office. As I rounded the corner to the office, all of a sudden, waves of emotion came over me and I began to sob. My field instructor quickly took me to her office for support and comfort. When I finally stopped crying, she asked me if I knew any healthy children I could play with. At first I found that a puzzling question. I did identify my godmother's granddaughter, who was visiting, as a possibility. My field instructor told me to leave for the day and go play with her. For the remainder of the afternoon, I enjoyed being in the company of a healthy child and learned a very valuable lesson about balance. If you are going to work in a field that involves helping families cope with grief and loss, you must find ways to have balance in your life. You cannot forget that there are healthy children in the world. It is imperative that you find time to spend with those healthy children.

When my internship ended, I was grateful for the patients and families I had come to know and the incredible lessons I had started to learn about life and loss. I truly hated to have to leave when the time came, because I had grown to feel very passionate about this work.

Returning to My Passion

In a little less than a year, I received the call I'd been waiting for. There was a full-time position open at St. Jude. I was thrilled and applied immediately. I was hired and returned to St. Jude in the role of a primary social worker. I quickly settled into my new career path and began the climb up a huge learning curve.

I was assigned to one of the medical teams and began working with children newly diagnosed with cancer. What I began to love about this work was that I truly never knew what my day might hold. One minute I was meeting a newly diagnosed child and his family. Next I was called to celebrate with a child who had completed therapy or had just been told that his or her cancer was in remission. Calls came for me to rush to the ICU because a patient has experienced complications and I needed to be present to provide support to the parents while their child was put on a ventilator. There were truly many miracles I got to witness and many stories of survival I got to tell.

There were also those patients who had difficulty fighting their diseases. The following stories are about the patients who fought hard but ultimately lost their battles with their illnesses. As hard as it is for a social worker to work with patients who die, I have found that these experiences also shed light on many blessings and hold valuable lessons for life.

As I began to build up a caseload, I had a mix of patients. Some were doing well. But some began to relapse and had more difficult fights against their diseases. Consequently, my own exposure to grief intensified over time. I had learned about the stages of grief as defined by Dr. Elisabeth Kübler-Ross (shock, denial, anger, bargaining, depression, and acceptance).[2] Now I was actually witnessing it. I watched parents, whose children were not doing well, going through these various stages of grief as they coped with the ups and downs of their child's diagnosis and treatment. I was also beginning to experience my own feelings of grief and loss.

Everyone who decides to work in this field brings along his or her own beliefs and life experiences. As I share my very personal views and beliefs with you, I preface this by adding that these are solely my views and do not represent the views of St. Jude. Up until I became a pediatric oncology social worker, I had very limited exposure to death and dying. I experienced the loss of three grandparents as a child and young adult, but losing a grandparent was to be expected. I was fortunate to have both of my parents. The only other loss I had experienced was at age twenty-seven. I lost a dear friend's husband, who died suddenly from a brain aneurism at the young age of twenty-eight. His death was traumatic for me. It also caused me to wonder why God would allow things like that to happen. He left behind a young widow and a two-year-old daughter.

As I began working with children with cancer, I found myself asking similar questions about God. In hindsight, I realize that I began to move through my own stages of grief as described by Kübler-Ross. I honestly think that I spent much of the first two years of my career in the early stage, which Kübler-Ross identifies as denial. In retrospect, I believe that denial plays a very important role early in one's career. It buffered me and allowed me to be able to continue my work as I learned more about my role as a pediatric oncology social worker as well as coping mechanisms to make it possible to continue in the career. At the same time, when I experienced some anger and began to question why children had to suffer, I also found myself confronting hard questions about my own religious and spiritual beliefs.

I grew up in a Christian home and attended church regularly. In high school, I had many friends who were Christians involved in Young Life, an outreach ministry whose mission is to introduce adolescents to Jesus Christ and help them grow in their faith. These close friends had a big impact on my faith during my adolescence. As an adult, I considered myself a Christian as opposed to identifying myself with a particular denomination. I remained active in church. I also believed in salvation and heaven.

Seeing intense grief and suffering in children and their parents really forced me to examine my spiritual beliefs in depth, and I began to do some serious soul-searching. I wanted to make sense of why things like this happened. I frequently wondered why a loving God would allow such suffering, grief, and pain. While I never felt it was wrong to ask difficult questions in the context of my religious faith, I often reminded myself that, on the cross, Jesus expressed feeling forsaken by God, his Father. In my daily work, I really couldn't believe that my young patients were going to die. However, over time I realized that this was a reality I could no longer deny after witnessing several losses.

Early in my return to St. Jude, I expressed a special interest in play therapy. Not too long afterward, I had the opportunity to provide puppet therapy for my younger patients. This was no ordinary puppet. His name was Will. He was the size of a six-year-old boy. Will had been "diagnosed" with a type of kidney tumor called Wilm's tumor. He had a wig to take off or put on based on what was happening with the individual child I was seeing for puppet therapy. He also had a catheter, called a Hickman line, in his chest to receive his chemotherapy.

Another colleague had a puppet named Hope. We each got to name our puppets. It was important to us that their names communicated a positive meaning. With Will at my side in puppet play sessions, I quickly learned what an effective therapeutic tool he proved to be with my younger patients. He truly provided a window into the complex mind of a child.

As I engaged a child in puppet therapy, often his or her own fears about the illness and possibility of dying would emerge. I was working with a wide range of cancer diagnoses, and it did not take me long to learn which diagnoses came with a poor prognosis. I remember emotionally bracing myself when I was assigned a new patient with a disease that carried a poor prognosis. And so it was when I met two precious little girls, both six years old and both diagnosed with inoperable brain tumors.

One little girl, Anna, had bright, twinkling brown eyes. She was vocal and outgoing. The other little girl, Janet, had a very quiet and sweet personality. They both loved to come and have their individual sessions with Will, telling him about their treatments and what had happened to them that day. Will also showed them how to hold still for their radiation treatments. Their mothers had met in the waiting room while the girls were getting their radiation therapy, and the two little girls quickly became fast friends. In my head, I knew that children with their type of brain tumor did not survive, but in my heart, I remained hopeful.

One day while I was in my office, both of these little girls showed up at my door, so I picked up Will just to say hello, without any intention to do any therapy. They both grinned at him when he asked how they were doing. Then Will innocently asked them if they had gone to the lab that day. He proceeded to ask if they had given their blood while they were in the lab. Quickly Anna piped up to say that she had not "given" her blood, adding, "They took it from me." Janet quickly nodded in agreement. Not planning to engage in any sort of deep discussion, Will replied, "Oh, so they took your blood."

Anna then got a very serious look on her face and said, "Yes, and you know that if they keep taking my blood, it will be all gone and I will die." I honestly have to say I was shocked to see Janet nodding right along in agreement as Anna made this statement. I had learned that children at various developmental stages have major misconceptions about illness and what happens to their bodies during treatments. But this was the first time I had ever seen this play out in such a frightening scenario. I reached up to a shelf in my office and pulled down a children's book about leukemia that explained how the bone marrow continues to make blood for our bodies.

As Will and I read this to the girls, they both listened intently, and a look of relief came over both of their little faces.

After they left my office, I remember thinking how incredibly brave these girls were. Who knew that every time they went to the lab for blood draws, they wondered if their last ounce of blood would be drawn that day and they would die? They silently and very courageously did this on at least a weekly basis. I knew deep down that eventually their tumors would result in their deaths; but, at least for one day, I had been successful in allaying some of the fears they quietly endured.

Maryanne Radmacher authored a book of meditations titled *Courage Doesn't Always Roar*, and I think of those two little girls whenever I see the title of that book.[3] Without uttering a word about their fears, these little girls walked bravely into our lab and cooperated with our nurses for their blood draws. My hope was, and is to this day, that I might be as brave as they were when confronted with illness and its challenges.

I also met another patient whose story illustrates what it means to be brave in confronting death. Her name was Sarah, and she was all of seventeen years old. Sarah was diagnosed with a tumor that had relapsed. I would often check on Sarah, and on one particular day, neither of her parents happened to be in the room when I stopped by. When I entered the room, I asked Sarah if she felt like a visit, and she said yes. Then she quickly added that she would like to talk about her funeral. I must not have been very good at keeping a poker face, and my look of anxiety must have shown, because Sarah commented that if this was too hard for me, we could talk about something else.

I swallowed hard and said, "No, if you want to talk about this, then that is what we will do." I honestly have to say that I do not remember the details of that conversation. I just remember feeling incredibly sad. Sarah knew that her remaining time was not long, and this made it difficult for me to deny this reality myself. There I sat with a very brave seventeen-year-old girl who should have been planning for her prom, not her funeral. I remember struggling not to cry as she talked to me about her death. I left her room asking myself, once again, why God would allow such a precious girl as Sarah to go through this suffering.

I have found that during times in my life when I am struggling, someone comes along and says something that seems so simple but is actually quite profound and is just what I need to hear at such a time from just the right person. This was the case when I got a call from the clinic with a new referral.

Emily was eight years old, and she and her parents had recently been told that she had a solid tumor that carried a poor prognosis. The clinic wanted me to see her for puppet therapy because they described her as angry. She was no stranger to hospitals. She had already endured several surgeries for a previous health condition. The clinic sent her straight back to my office.

When she came in, I put Will on my lap and was ready to talk to her in Will's high-pitched puppet voice. She took one look at me and said, "Can you just put that puppet down and talk to me?" Well, of course, that is exactly what I did. It has been my experience that many children confronting life-threatening illness are much wiser than their years, which was true of Emily. She began to tell me that she had really been struggling with why God would allow something like this to happen to children like her. She felt that she had already been through enough. But then she added that she thought she had figured out the answer to this question.

When I asked her what she had come up with, she gave me this explanation: God allows things like this to happen to children so adults can focus on what is really important in life. At the ripe old age of eight, here was this child, talking in such simple language about getting priorities straight. I will never forget the impact this discussion had on me at a time when I was also struggling with why God would allow such suffering in children.

From that day forward, I walked with Emily on her journey with cancer. She was an amazing child who made the most of her counseling sessions—much to her benefit. If she was teased at school about her hair loss from her chemotherapy, she would pick up the phone to call me to make an appointment. She came from a family with deep Christian faith. She and her parents were really quite inspirational to me. Emily was always very brave and outspoken. She never hesitated to tell me exactly what was on her mind. I loved that about her.

One of the most difficult parts of my job included coming in at the time of a patient's death, or prior to the actual death, to provide bereavement support to the patient's family. Often this was done in collaboration with one of our hospital chaplains. Over the course of my career, I never found that this ever became any easier. It is incredibly painful to watch a family as they come to accept their loss and say good-bye to their child, regardless of the child's age. Such moments continued to force me, as the social worker, to accept the fact that I would continue to lose patients I'd grown to love.

Often the chaplain and I would debrief and support each other after a death. While it was difficult, at the same time—and it may sound strange for me to say this—it was also an enriching experience. I remember telling one of the chaplains, after coming in during the night for the death of one of our patients, that I felt as if we had been walking on sacred ground with the family because we were there to witness one of the most private, intimate, and painful experiences a family can endure. While this was incredibly hard work, at the same time I always felt blessed to be a part of these experiences.

St. Jude treats patients from all walks of life. Cancer does not discriminate. In my role with families, I was exposed to a bounty of various cultures and religions. I have learned so much about other cultures and religions and how families cope as they approach death and dying.

I found myself continuing to try to make sense of the grief and pain I experienced. One of the ways I coped was to turn to books and read during my struggles. Reading helped me to grapple with the questions I continued to ask about suffering and death. At one particularly difficult time, I turned to a morning devotional book, *Streams in the Desert*, compiled by Mrs. Charles E. Cowman. I was truly feeling down and struggling with the recent relapse of a patient to whom I had grown very close. Her pain and suffering filled my mind. As I said earlier, I have found that when you need them the most, the right words come along at just the right time. The Bible verse for the day was "For I reckon that the sufferings of this present time are not worthy to be compared with the glory which shall be revealed in us" (Romans 8:18, KJV). What caused me to stop and take stock of where I was in my own pain, suffering, and spiritual struggle was the story—about a person who had the cocoon of an emperor moth—that accompanied this Bible verse.[4]

As the story went, the person kept this cocoon for over a year, and he was present to witness the moth's first efforts to escape from its long confinement in the cocoon. He watched the moth "patiently striving and struggling to get out." He noted that the moth never seemed to be able to get beyond a certain point. After watching this for quite some time, his patience was finally exhausted, so he resolved to give the moth a helping hand. With scissors, he snipped the end of the cocoon to help the moth escape. The deed backfired. The pressure that the body of the moth experiences as it struggles to go out the small end of the cocoon actually is what gives the moth life. Passing through such a narrow opening is nature's way of forcing the juices into the moth's wings, helping the moth develop and live outside of the cocoon. In his wisdom, the man thought he was helping the moth, but instead he led to the moth's undoing, causing its death. He added that he had been shortsighted to think that the moth's pain and suffering could be spared.

I related so much to this story. Who was I to think that I would ever begin to understand or have the answer to why children suffer and die? As much as I wanted to spare my patients and families and understand how such pain and suffering could happen, I began to realize and move toward accepting this as something outside my ability to answer. I began to conclude that there are some things we will never understand while on this earth.

At about the same time, I also read the legend of the dragonfly—a story about a community of water bugs in a pond. Once in a while, sadness would come over the community of water bugs because one of the water bugs would get an urge to climb up the stem of a lily pad. Once the bug climbed up, it was never to be seen again. The bug's friends were certain that the water bug was dead. One day, when one of the water bugs had the urge to climb up the stem of the lily pad, he made a promise that he would return to tell his friends what he found at the top of the pond. However, when he did reach the top, he fell asleep. When he awoke, his body was new. He had become a blue-tailed dragonfly. He soared off into the air with his new wings.

Remembering his promise, he tried to return to the pond, but his body would not go down into the water. He could not return to tell his friends the good news. The story ends with the dragonfly saying he knew that when the other bugs' time came to climb the stem, they would know what he now knew. "So he raised his wings and flew off into his joyous new life."[5] This reinforced, for me, that there are many questions about suffering, loss, and death that we cannot answer here on earth. I decided to try to stop asking why and place my faith in God.

Approaching the Five-Year Mark

As I approached the five-year mark in pediatric oncology social work, I continued to work with patients who had either relapsed or were approaching the ends of their lives. Thankfully I also continued working with other patients who were doing well. They were completing their treatments, surviving their cancer, and moving on with their lives. However, I seemed to spend a larger portion of my time with my patients who were not doing as well, and my work became more intense.

As I mentioned earlier, it is critical for a social worker to maintain a very balanced perspective—much easier said than done. Despite knowing this, at the five-year mark in my career, I wasn't doing a good job of finding balance, let alone maintaining it. I was feeling more stress. This was at the time when Emily, the eight-year-old who helped me put priorities in perspective, was approaching the end of her life. Additionally I had been working with another patient, named Aimee, for a couple of years, whom I had grown very close to; she also had struggles with cancer—and not just her own.

When I met Aimee, I couldn't help but love her immediately. She was four years old and had an infectious smile with a personality to match. Sometimes I had to remind myself that she was just four years old. From the day we met, I knew her cancer carried a very poor prognosis. Over the months, I saw her frequently for puppet therapy. At her age, she was a prime candidate for this type of play therapy. She loved talking to Will about her treatments.

Not too long after I began working with her, her mother was diagnosed with late-stage breast cancer. Following several months of rigorous treatments, Aimee's mother died of her disease. I supported Aimee throughout her mother's illness. One session still stands out in my mind. On that day, Aimee had come to the clinic with her uncle. Her chemo treatments were being stopped because she was having a good response to therapy and was technically in remission for the time being. As Will talked with Aimee about no longer needing her medicine, she began to cry. This was not a quiet cry. It involved racking sobs. I remember putting her on my lap and asking her why she was crying. She said that when her mother stopped her medicine, she died. Will and I were able to explain to her that there were other reasons that patients stopped taking medicine. We clarified for her that she was stopping her medicine because her medicine had done the job we wanted it to do, and her cancer had gone away. She seemed to be relieved, but I remember sitting and just rocking her to comfort her. She had been through so much more than any four-year-old should ever have to endure.

Unfortunately, later on, Aimee relapsed and was going to be sent home on hospice care. Shortly before she left to go home, she was brought to my office in a wheelchair. She had lost a lot of weight and was weak. She wanted to sing for me. It was a gospel song. In her childlike voice, she sang it so sweetly, yet very seriously. I sat quietly, listening to her. When she finished the song, being typical Aimee, she burst out singing a popular rock 'n' roll song that included the lyric "I love you from head to toe." Aimee always knew how to lighten up a moment.

Saying good-bye to her as she returned home on hospice care was incredibly difficult for me. I had also grown close to her extended family and knew I wouldn't see them again. Our good-bye was filled with lots of hugs. Words were inadequate, and this was again one of those times when silence and presence say everything that needs to be said. My journey with Aimee was coming to an end. I would stay in touch with her family, but I missed her terribly when she left; and when I received the phone call that she had died at home on hospice care with her family at her side, I felt the loss acutely.

I once heard someone compare the role of a pediatric oncology social worker to that of a Sherpa, an elite mountaineer who lives in the Himalayas. Sherpas are known for being experts in the mountainous Himalayan terrain. Because of this expertise, for years they have served as guides for climbing expeditions to Mount Everest. The Sherpas very skillfully guide groups of climbers through the passes and mountain peaks at extreme altitudes. Sometimes even the most experienced Sherpa loses a climber to the treacherous mountain. Then it becomes the Sherpa's responsibility to get the remaining group back down the mountain.

I do see some similarities between the Sherpa's role and the role of the pediatric oncology social worker. My journey with the family does not end with the patient's death. We continue to accompany the remaining family members on their journeys as we provide bereavement support and counseling. Just as Sherpas make multiple trips up and down the mountain, pediatric oncology social workers accompany multiple patients and families as they grieve and experience the losses of their children. Consequently, over time, the social worker experiences the cumulative effects of loss and grief. The impact of such effects can result in compassion fatigue if the social worker has not developed sound self-care strategies. Without self-care that works, it can become difficult to remain effective in this field.

Unfortunately for me, I was not doing a good job of self-care at the five-year mark. I knew my sadness over the cumulative losses I had sustained was taking a toll on me. I had moved into Kübler-Ross's stage of depression. I began to think about leaving this field, which I loved. I could not imagine continuing to sustain losing patients like Emily and Aimee. Remembering the advice of one of my professors in graduate school, I pursued my own counseling. Through these sessions and with much soul searching, I came to the conclusion that it was time for me to leave the field of pediatric oncology social work. Shortly thereafter I applied for a new position in adolescent psychiatry and changed the course of my career.

The Rest of the Story

It took only two years before I found myself missing the work with the children and families of St. Jude. I truly believed in Danny Thomas's mission and his philosophy that "no child should die in the dawn of life." I found myself once again longing to be a part of that mission. So I had a heart-to-heart talk with myself. I vowed that if I returned, I would do a much better job of self-care. I had to lay out a plan that included having balance in my life. I would need to stay in touch with healthy children if I was going to work with ill children. And I would need to rely on my faith to sustain me when times were difficult. After soul-searching, I made the decision to return to St. Jude. This time I was determined to find my balance physically, emotionally, and spiritually.

Not long after returning, I lost a teenage patient to leukemia. His mother and I had phone conversations following his death. She talked about a book that she found very helpful in her grief and suggested I read it as well. Written by hospice nurses, *Final Gifts* is a book about understanding the special awarenesses, needs, and communications of the dying.[6] Through case examples presented in the book, hospice nurses explain how those who are with the dying can be the recipients of final gifts from the dying. This could involve some sort of reconciliation that takes place between the dying and their family member(s). Other gifts may come in the way a person dies; for instance, if the dying person decides it may be too hard for his or her family member to be present at the time of death, the dying person may wait until the person leaves the room. Sometimes the dying wait to die until they know that their loved ones have the right kind of support present.

At this phase in my career, I found this book to be very beneficial. I began to pay closer attention to my own feelings and focus on what I could gain professionally as well as personally from my experience with dying patients and their families. I knew from my practice that some children who are aware they are dying need to hear from their parents that their parents will be able to go on without them before they are ready to die. From my experience, I have seen children hang on to life, waiting for additional family members to arrive, before they decide to depart this earth.

I saw this when my own mother died. My mom had struggled and fought chronic obstructive pulmonary disease (COPD) for years. Four months before she died, she fell and sustained a head injury that left her uncommunicative. On one of my visits, I felt as if she were ready to die, and I couldn't understand why she was waiting. I had a monologue with her, reassuring her that I would manage okay without her and thanking her for the many blessings she had given me throughout my life. I doubt I would have had a conversation like this one if I were not a pediatric oncology social worker.

However, she still continued to hang on to life. I knew she must have been unhappy without being able to communicate. That was especially difficult; I had always treasured our talks and the advice she so wisely imparted to me. I couldn't imagine how she could keep holding on while her body continued to fail. When she was going into multiorgan failure,

I truly didn't know how or why she continued to hang on to life. Later I came to realize what she was waiting for. My brother lived six hours away on the other side of the state. I remember telling her that my brother was on his way to visit her. My brother arrived at the hospital late that evening. When he arrived, I decided to return home to get some rest. Within twenty minutes after his visit with her, I received the call that she was gone. I have no doubt that she left us with two final gifts. She knew it would be too hard for me to be present when she died. And she also waited to have one last visit with her son.

In my practice, after I returned to St. Jude, I finally realized I had come to the stage of acceptance, as described by Kübler-Ross. I knew some of my patients would die. I also began to redefine hope, realizing that hope changes over time. Instead of hoping for a cure, I began to hope for good pain control and quality time for my patients with their families and friends. I worked very hard to strike a balance between my personal and professional lives. If I'd had a difficult session with a family that was losing a child, I'd take Will and do a play therapy session with a child who was doing well. I needed that balance throughout the day. As I worked with patients approaching the end of their lives, I began to look for the final gifts I might experience, as well as those gifts given to family members who may not know to look for them.

As I think of final gifts, I am reminded of one of my patients named Ellen. Ellen was nine years old and approaching the end of her life. I was engaging her in a therapeutic play session utilizing art. She was drawing and using rubber stamps to tell me a story. Her story began with a baby who had been abandoned by its mother. The baby was now in the care of another lady. The baby and this lady traveled until they came to a river. At the river, the lady told the baby that she would not be able to go with her, so the baby crossed the river alone. On the other side, the baby went to live with other children in the house of a clown.

The clown told all the children that if they had family to return to, and if they wanted to go back, they could return. The baby in Ellen's story decided to stay and live with the clown. I will never forget Ellen's words as she ended her story. Ellen looked up at me and said, "And the baby had peace in her heart." I later shared that story with Ellen's mother, who said this gave her some additional peace about losing Ellen.

I have been back at St. Jude for twenty-five years, for a grand total of thirty years. I moved into social work administration sixteen years ago. Now I pay close attention to staff as they approach the five-year mark. I remain well aware of the impact that cumulative losses may have on our social work team, and I try to apply the many lessons I've learned over the years in my work as a clinician and administrator. From a personal perspective, I have no doubt that I was better prepared to cope with my own family's losses because of the children and their family members I have had the privilege of knowing in my work. They have truly been my role models.

I have come to accept that death is a part of life. I do not believe that death is the end; rather, I believe it is yet another beginning. When I think about my own immortality and my death, I would not be honest if I did not admit to having some anxiety. My anxiety is not actually about death itself; it is about any suffering and pain I may endure. When I think about death, I imagine many children waiting for me in heaven. I believe that they will be some of the first souls I see, along with my own family members and friends who have preceded me.

Who knew, when I made the phone call to find out what I needed to do to become a pediatric medical social worker, how much I would change personally as well as professionally? I would not trade anything for the incredible lessons I have learned from my patients, their families, and my colleagues. I remain forever grateful to all of them.

---

1   Alan Wolfelt, *Companioning the Bereaved* (Ft. Collins, Colorado: Companion Press, 2006), 29.

2   Elisabeth Kübler-Ross, *On Death and Dying* (New York: Scribner, 2003), 265.

3   Maryanne Radmacher, *Courage Doesn't Always Roar* (San Francisco: Conari Press, 2009).

4   Mrs. Charles Cowman, *Streams in the Desert*, vol. 1 (Cowman Publication, 1981), 9–10.

5   "The Dragonfly," accessed September 29, 2014, http/www.steventrapp.com/dragonfly-story.htm.

6   Maggie Callanan and Patricia Kelley, *Final Gifts* (New York: Bantam, 1992).

Frances (Fran) L. Greeson, MSW, LCSW

A native of Memphis, Tennessee, Fran Greeson, LCSW, has worked in the field of pediatric oncology for more than thirty years. She began her career as a social work intern at St. Jude Children's Research Hospital and became director of the hospital's Social Work Department in 1998. A graduate of the University of Memphis (formerly Memphis State University), Fran earned a master of science in social work from the University of Tennessee. As a licensed clinical social worker, she has made presentations at numerous national meetings and conferences. Topics of these presentations include puppet therapy with pediatric oncology patients, ethics, educating pediatric patients to assume adult responsibilities, and leadership in mentoring and supervision. Additionally, Fran has served on the national board of the Association of Pediatric Oncology Social Workers (APOSW). In 2007, APOSW named Fran National Social Worker of the Year in honor of her commitment, expertise, innovation, and advocacy in the field of pediatric oncology social work. Her book, titled *Evangelization*, is published by Lectio Publishing.

When Fran is not working, she enjoys spending time with Bozeman and Kalispell, golden retrievers she fostered and adopted through a golden retriever rescue organization. She also enjoys traveling throughout the West to national parks and spending time in the mountains of Montana. However, her most treasured times are those spent with her family, including her nieces and their children.

Contact Information:
e-mail: flgreeson@bellsouth.net

PART II

Personal Perspectives

THE BIOLOGY EXHIBIT

A Dying College Professor's Perspective on Mortality

Billy Moore, BA

I only began to know,
After the deadly diagnosis
That spread, first slowly, then accelerating
Like a fire on a windy plain in damp, dead prairie grass,
Smoking and charring, then spreading in a low, persistent flame,
Sucking in all who knew even my name, a wide arc spreading.

I recalled the insects I had collected in my soft and seeking youth,
Sweeping across fields and flowered meadows, in the damp
Shadows of trees, near puddles and streams, swinging my net
And cupping my hands to snare them one by one,
Careful to take only one of any kind,
Moving them toward my deadly jar, where they succumbed.

I took them then one at a time, each and all, with exquisite care
Lest I spoil them for my display, almost tenderly arranging them
In rows and squares, by structure, name, color and size,
For science and for perfect view and understanding,
As all the freshmen did, time out of mind,
And taking righteous half-pleasure in the art of it.

I impaled each with precision on a glittering silver pin,
In the center of the thorax, to avoid disturbing in the least
The delicate arthropod legs, the elegant chitinous frame, or the wings,
Some spread for a glorious flight, some spread flat, some folded tight
To protect the treasure of the life now withdrawn into the dim light of
universe,

Assigning each an exact place in the order of things in a world of artifact.

I hid the nature of their truths in the curls of an ancient, magic artificial tongue
Lettered on a tab in the frame of a box, under icy-hard transparent glass
Which seemed to argue further otherness and distance
Even in their proximity, as if to deny the obvious reality of the silent scene.
So people could shuffle by, in tight focus or distracted by the coming lunch,
Or wavering between, mostly silent in their forward drift to God Knows Where.

And now, far from bejeweled meadows succumbed to fire and fog and smoke,
I perch, alone among the crowd, atop the silvery pin above the labels and
Beneath the glass that reveals at once all my myriad vulnerabilities and
Holds at bay the world still moving through space, through time now turned
Inside out, inverted and smeared into itself, and I see the faces I have known,
Moving on past, peering, with fearful, mostly close-kept, half-curious questions.
Questions indeed, the riddles of which I cannot know but the divers forms.
And so it is, has always been, and now forevermore shall be, in finite life.

Billy G. Moore, BA

Billy Glenn Moore died on September 14, 2013, at the age of seventy from cancer. He was the former mayor of San Marcos, Texas, and professor at Texas State University.

After moving around West Texas during his childhood, Billy settled in Odessa for his junior and senior years and graduated from Odessa High School in 1961 as president of his senior class. He earned an associates of art degree in 1962 from Odessa Junior College and then moved to San Marcos, Texas, in 1963, where he earned a bachelor of arts degree in English/counseling and guidance from Southwest Texas State University. Billy played basketball at Odessa High and Odessa Junior College, as well as for the SWT Bobcats. In 1968, he enrolled at Louisiana State University, where he pursued a doctorate in English literature. At LSU, he received a National Defense Education Teaching Fellowship for two years.

Billy began his thirty-five-year teaching career at Texas State University in 1965, retiring in 2003. He taught in the English Department for fifteen years. He served as director of public affairs from 1986 to 1999 and as director of regional and economic planning from 1999 to 2003.

Billy began his service to the city of San Marcos in 1980 as a member of the Planning and Zoning Commission, serving as chair for seven years. Elected to the city council three times, he served as mayor for two terms (1996–2000).

During the year preceding his death, Billy and his family had the opportunity to celebrate life together doing things that he loved: fishing at the lake, perusing his iPad for the latest news, contemplating religion and politics over long evenings at the San Marcos River, and gracing those around him with his customary intellect and humor.

BRUSHES WITH DEATH

A Three-Time Cancer Survivor's Perspective on Mortality

Todd A. Herzog, BA, BComm, CPA

MORTALITY WAS NOT much of a thought in my early years. I was blessed to have two living parents and three younger brothers and all four of my grandparents; the first grandparent to pass away did so four years after my first cancer diagnosis. While I had friends who did not have double pairs of grandparents, I generally was pretty naive when it came to death. And as far as I was concerned then, that was a good thing. Why bother with thoughts about death when we can go through life happy-go-lucky, right? I mean, we know it's coming, but what's the rush? Isn't that how it should be?

Or should it?

May 1971

Death came knocking, albeit fairly silently. It all started with a lump on my chest, and within weeks, it had grown. Within two weeks of seeing a doctor, I was under the knife. The word "cancer" was never used in the beginning—at least not that I can remember. It was called a tumor. The only surgery I'd had until that point was a tonsillectomy, and that wasn't a pleasant memory. So I tried to avoid surgery. I was told that radiation was possible but that it probably wouldn't get rid of the whole tumor. The recommended treatment was surgery, followed by radiation.

It was only when I was well into the radiation that I heard the word "malignant," and then I put two and two together to understand that I had *cancer*. It was Ewing's sarcoma, a fairly aggressive cancer. I'm not sure that any doctor ever mentioned the big C by its name. Like the word "death," "cancer" was whispered only in dark hallways; and kids—I was sixteen years old at the time—weren't supposed to be in dark hallways.

Now comes the hard part. Did I think about death at that point? I vividly remember, postsurgery, that the first question I asked my father after I woke up was who had won that night's Stanley Cup playoff game (it was game seven, winner take all). I didn't get an answer; my father didn't want to tell me that my favorite team, the Chicago Blackhawks, had lost the game and the cup to the Montreal Canadiens. After that, I spent a lot of pretty lousy days in recovery and then going through radiation. Because of my weakened immune system, I experienced some infections that took me close to the brink. All in all, I spent about eight weeks in the hospital that spring and summer. But I don't remember spending any of that time contemplating death.

What I did do was think about getting better, but I also thought that every little ache I had could mean a return of the tumor, and that any recurrence could mean it would be all over. So, in a way, I suppose I did think about death, but mostly as a vague, conditional concept that wouldn't be reality unless the tumor returned.

While being treated, I learned that the statistics suggested my chance of survival was less than 50 percent. Then I heard that, as rare as my cancer was, there was someone else in the hospital with it, and he didn't make it through the summer. I probably shuddered (I really don't remember), but then I figured, "Now the odds are on my side." In reality, as we all eventually learn, the odds don't mean a damn thing—for each one of us personally, they're either 0 percent or 100 percent. There is no in-between.

And it's not just the diagnosis of the big C that delivers the death threat. There are ongoing, often more imminent trials that come with the treatment. As one example, one of the tests I had was a bone marrow test to look for cancer cells. It was done by taking a biopsy from the collarbone. As it was explained to my parents (and only later to me), there was the possibility that the instrument used to take the sample could slip and puncture the jugular—and then it would be lights out. And then there were major infections, blood transfusions, and all the other fun stuff that comes with aggressive treatment. While there were some anxious moments, I wasn't thinking about dying; I had already survived major surgery. On the other hand, my parents suffered immensely. My whole family did, but I didn't have a sense of that at the time.

I asked my brothers how they thought my illness impacted the family. The youngest, David, was only seven at the time, but had this memory:

> Overall, it's been important for *me* to think about what your illness did to the balance of our family. Until you got sick, you were merely the oldest brother, and some/all that that implies in a family of four boys; whether it meant we were measured against you, or were measuring ourselves against you. And so when you got sick, as with any needy child in a family, most attention was diverted to you. In a way, your being sick, and all of us having to find ways to cope with that, sort of cemented the ways in which each of us has, it seems to me, as a common characteristic, the ability to be alone and entertain ourselves, be good company for ourselves (and of course are good company for each other). Suffice it to say, though, that it did have an impact on family dynamics.

David's comment really does say it all. A serious illness can have a major impact, but it's really its impact on living that matters—not its impact on thoughts about death. We might worry about dying and think more about it when faced with a life-threatening illness, but it's how the illness informs our life that matters, as well as how we respond to it, whether knowingly or unintentionally. And as David notes, the way it informs the lives around you also matters. That's an important message: an illness affects not just the individual but also those around the patient, and in many cases the illness has a lifelong impact.

For me, after the treatments were done and my cancer went into remission, life moved on. I found a girl, and we decided to get married. First, though, was the question of children—could I father a child after all that local and full-body radiation? It was not something that anyone mentioned at the time of the radiation, but it was naturally a question I had to consider. It turned out not to be a problem; I have three grown children (a son and two daughters). However, at the time of treatment, what the doctors *did* tell me was that there could be some long-term effects, such as a possible secondary cancer in about twenty years. My wife-to-be accepted the possibility (I guess she really was in love with me!), and we got married.

As the years passed, pains occurred, and many x-rays, CT scans, and so forth, were taken, and all were negative. On the other hand, I developed some lung problems associated with the surgery and radiation, but those have been mostly manageable. I've been lucky. As I developed various issues over the years (primarily heart issues resulting from the chest radiation), the scientific technology has mostly kept pace. So, for the most part, considering my medical history, life was good.

Then my father passed away at age fifty-five from a brain tumor. There was that ugly big C again. (It also took some of my grandparents, but they were "old.") Suddenly I was reminded that I was still waiting for a possible recurrence. It had been only sixteen years since my tumor, so recurrence was still a possibility. And now I had two children. Suddenly mortality seemed to become a thought to be reckoned with. Kids really do change everything.

My father's death made us think that life could be short. So what did we do with that lovely thought? Well, we decided it was time for a family trip to Disney World. Our kids at that time were just five and two years old, but we didn't care; life is too short. So off we went, and it was great. And with the advent of video, our kids still have a record of memories from that trip. So that's how I dealt with my first real taste of mortality.

And then we decided to have another child. Everyone said that with a son and a daughter, we had the million-dollar family (who knew?). But we just felt a larger family was better—maybe a hedge against living into old age—so we became a family of five and were very happy.

Vigilance for a recurrence of cancer was still on the radar. At the time of the birth of our third child, it had been eighteen years since my surgery—still within the twenty-year or so timeline to possibly have some form of recurrence—and a long life was looking like a real possibility. On the other hand, now having a family of my own, living wasn't just about me; it had become more about those around me.

Then my mother passed away from lung cancer at age sixty-three. She had been a lifelong smoker. In fact, she joked about how my grandfather taught her as a teenager to smoke the proper way. It didn't seem like a joke to me. And twenty-five years after my surgery, I wondered if I'd be the lucky one—the only one to get cancer in my family and survive. It all seemed so surreal and made me feel a bit guilty. Here I was, the one whom everyone worried would not live past age forty, and yet I was alive while my parents were taken far too soon by cancer.

Unsurprisingly, my kids were starting to get worried. Was there a faulty gene that they had inherited? While that question remained unanswered, in 2008, almost thirty-seven years since my surgery and cancer diagnosis, I thought I was home free. I had been getting checked for skin cancer on a regular basis for more than twenty years. I had frequent basal cell growths in the area that was irradiated back in 1971. None were a serious form of cancer, but they nevertheless demanded that I stay vigilant. At one checkup, I happened to notice a very small growth in the nipple area. The doctor and resident both had overlooked it. They weren't too concerned but did a biopsy just to be sure. The diagnosis? Breast cancer. The doctor actually didn't believe it and thought pathology made a mistake. But follow-up analysis proved it to be so. Who knew that men could get breast cancer? Well, apparently about one percent of all breast cancers are in men! I love learning new things, and I was about to get a whole new education.

When I found out that I was facing cancer again, it hit me like a ton of bricks, but not in the obvious ways. You see, while I was surprised, shocked, and bewildered, there was also a weird sense of relief. The secondary cancer had finally happened, and now I could see the enemy. And while breast cancer is no picnic, the odds of survival were better than my original diagnosis of Ewing's. So I just figured, "Let's deal with it and move on." Easier said than done.

Given my family history of cancer, doctors wondered if there was a genetic component that could be identified. After some blood work and detailed analysis, they determined that there were no known genetic links. The new cancer was likely a result of my earlier radiation—it just took longer than expected to rear its ugly head. But my kids didn't need to worry too much. That said, the doctors did note that there was much to be learned about genetic links; and they urged that my kids, particularly my daughters, start monitoring at an earlier age than normally recommended.

Before my own parents passed away, I hadn't really thought much about death and its impact on families, except for one time during my professional career as an accountant when a client came to us to help him manage his affairs because he was dying. His wife was distraught by such talk, but he was calm and organized, and he wanted it that way for his wife upon his passing. He wasn't young, but he wasn't old either. He knew he was dying, and what mattered to him was that his house be in order before he passed. (I later experienced the same scenario when my mother developed lung cancer; she was the strong one, wanting to get everything in order so we wouldn't be left with a mess. From these experiences, it would seem that acceptance comes much sooner for the dying than for the living.)

I still remember watching my father sit in a chair in our house with his two-year-old granddaughter on his lap. My mom commented how peaceful he looked. I wondered what he was thinking; he was scheduled for a brain biopsy the next day, and I thought maybe he was thinking about what the doctors would find. I knew that he was terrified of dying—or worse, living with a damaged brain. He'd witnessed firsthand how compromised brain function can impact quality of life when his father had a stroke many years before and never fully recovered. But he hid the fear. It was an unusually warm Sunday in March, and we spent some time looking at my newly planted trees in the backyard.

The next day was colder than average—a harbinger of things to come. I joined my mother at the hospital and found her waiting for him to return from the operating room. It took longer than expected, and no one came to explain. Ultimately we found out that he had hemorrhaged while they were doing the biopsy, and there was nothing that could be done; he was going to die.

It was the first time—and the last, I think—I really cried. When my father died, I didn't know what to think or feel. Here was a fifty-five-year-old man who had been doing normal things just a little more than twenty-four hours earlier. We knew the operation would be dangerous, but there really was no time to prepare. We had known for a only couple of weeks that something was wrong. And even in those last several hours, we kept hoping for a miracle. But then his heartbeat stopped, just like in the movies. It was awful, and I didn't care who saw me crying.

But who was I crying for? My departed father? Me? My kids? My mother? Probably everyone. It didn't matter. He was gone, and all the rest of us were left to pick up the pieces. Maybe I was crying for that—the uncertainty we faced in sorting his affairs. As the oldest son, and being an accountant, I was first in line to help mom with her financial affairs. And not long after that, I started to lose some of my hair. (Chemotherapy treatment for breast cancer took care of the rest of it.)

This was as close to death as I'd ever been—too close for comfort. But death is part of life, right? If you're born, you're going to die someday. So why is death so feared? Is it because we know it's coming but we just don't know when or how? Is it because we think of all the things we'll miss? Is it fear for those we'll leave behind—those who won't be able to come to us any longer for advice and wisdom? Or is it because we fear being forgotten? And does the reason even matter? These questions were all staring me right in the face. And frankly, I didn't have the answers then; nor do I now. All I knew then, which is all I know now, was that life goes on for the rest of us. We deal with it, and we carry on.

When I think about it, I've probably been living the last forty-odd years thinking that the grim reaper was always near and that my job was to stay at least one step ahead. When I was younger, I would not have been able to articulate that thought, but that's how it feels now that I have more than a few years under my belt. I can't say every day has been all bliss, but I generally have no right to complain about my life. In fact, I had a lot of reasons to want to stay at least one step ahead of the grim reaper. So that's been a key factor in shaping my life.

I've never been one to put up with nonsense for long. Anything that had a considerably negative impact on my life had to be changed because life is too short! I had no idea how long I had to live, but I've often felt I was living on borrowed time. I fought harder for changes at jobs I didn't like, and when that didn't work out, I made a move. For me, a bad job was worse than no job.

It's easy to think you're brave and strong when you survive three bouts of cancer, among other health-related issues. (I also had my thyroid removed a couple of years after the breast cancer. It was a malignancy that was caught very early and was almost a nonevent, at least in the scheme of my life.) Everybody tells you so. And maybe it is true for some. But I suspect that, at times, all people are frightened of having their lives cut short. Maybe it's not so blatant, but I've seen it manifest itself in other ways, such as moodiness, irritability, and depression. And really, there is no cure other than accepting that all we have is this moment. At least that's what I've learned over the years. I can tell myself that I'm brave, and everyone will likely believe me; but if I think too hard about the future, doubts and fears set in. And if I forget, there's always something or someone to remind me.

About two years ago, my oldest daughter was diagnosed with breast cancer. She had been married for just less than a year when she was diagnosed. In fact, she received the bad news just a day after we walked sixty kilometers (more than thirty-seven miles) to raise money for The Weekend to End Women's Cancers. I felt guilty that my genetics had a direct, very negative, impact on one of my kids (genetic testing showed there was no link, but I'm not so sure). At that moment, when my daughter shared the news with me, I realized that I wasn't just facing my own mortality, but I was also staring down the barrel of the mortality of my child. That's not supposed to happen! I have never forgotten watching my grandparents bury their only son, my mother's only sibling. He was barely forty years old. They never fully recovered from that loss. No one should have to go through that.

But living the possibility of that nightmare had a tremendous impact. You see, it had almost become a joke within our family; I'd get some illness, deal with it, and carry on. That's life. Death was never part of the equation, so why bother dwelling on the possibility? But now that it was *my child*, the equation was more complex, and the outcome was much more important. I didn't really have time to think about it. I wasn't just a parent; I was a parent who had faced similar challenges. Therefore, I was in a position to help my daughter navigate the journey. So I did what I had to without contemplating the future. There was no time, because I had work to do.

I did what any father would do. I took my daughter wig shopping in anticipation of the eventual loss of her hair. (As it turned out, she preferred scarves and hats as her chosen methods of covering up.) I also went along with her and her husband to some of the early appointments with her oncologist, who was also my oncologist. I was her sounding board, both as a parent and as a fellow survivor, which brought new meaning to our father–daughter outings.

What I didn't do was cry and yell. It's not my style. And besides, as a family, we'd been through this sort of thing so many times that I knew that there was no point in looking for reasons, blame, pity, or whatever. I knew that there was a job to be done—getting her cured—and my daughter needed all the help and support she could get.

By throwing myself into seeing my daughter get cured, I was blinded to a new twist. I was in the midst of a bout of depression, and it seemed that my daughter's diagnosis might have helped to deepen it. I'm not entirely convinced, but it's been in the back of my mind through her and my recovery.

Like many people, if not all, I ponder the meaning of life—more specifically, my life. Perhaps I do this a little more than average; I was a philosophy major at the university. No one really knows the meaning of life (although some think they do), but it has occurred to me that having children and raising them to carry on has to stand at the top of any list. If that stops happening, then the world as we know it will be gone within a hundred years or so. So the injustice of a person dying young isn't just about the unlived life of that person and those who may have followed; it's also a failure to the parent. Now, that might sound harsh, but it does explain, on some level, why people—my grandparents, for example—never get over the loss of a child (even if that child has already had children of his or her own, thereby sustaining the family line). Suffice it to say that losing a child is too upsetting to think about. So, for me, it feels better to just keep marching and not think about it.

Facing mortality is one thing, but facing one's child's mortality is quite another. It spreads a person thin and underscores the uncertainty of life. And that's what life with cancer is like. Life might be a roller coaster for most, but for those dealing with cancer, it's a really wild ride, never knowing when you just might run out of track. You see, most people think that once cancer treatment is over, and especially after you're five years cancer-free, you're back to normal. Maybe, but it's a different normal; you're always looking over your shoulder, always seeing more doctors than normal people, and always dealing with long-term effects from the treatment. It's great to be alive, but life is never really normal again. And death is part of that equation, in varying degrees, as time passes.

My accounting background has forced me to deal with mortality from the financial perspective with a number of clients, from those hoping there's enough cash flow for life, to those wondering if their kids will have enough. I've dealt with death planning and with the aftermath. I'd like to think I've been more empathetic than many, given my experiences. But thinking about your own death or the death of your child is different.

All I know is that I keep defying the odds, so my family thinks I'm going to live forever. (Try telling that to the insurance companies.) But I know the odds are stacked against me. If cancer doesn't do me in, then the ailments that have resulted from the treatments might. But odds are just that—odds. So, in many respects, I'm no different from anyone else. You just never know when the proverbial bus is going to hit you. So back again to living in the moment; it's all you have.

A few more thoughts:

I wonder, at times, why I survived while others, including another teenager with the same diagnosis in that summer of 1971, didn't? I don't know that I believe in any divine plan, but I've gone through much of my life somewhat justifying my reason for living. From raising a family that will go on to do great things of their own to helping my mother with her affairs when my father passed, I've often searched for reasons why I not only survived but also continue to survive. Are those the reasons that helped me survive three bouts with cancer, or does naming those reasons simply make me feel less guilty? Or is it just my way of dealing with the fact that with life comes death and there's ultimately no way to change that?

It would seem that everyone has a different way of dealing with the threat of potentially imminent death. We are all individuals, and no two are alike. However, some seem to deal with it successfully and others, not so (though even the definition of success likely varies). Is there a magic formula? Perhaps, but I'm not sure there's any way yet to know what it is without trial and error. We are all inching toward death; some just more aware of that fact than others. How you deal with that fact is what gets you through life. For me, it's been about taking care of myself physically and mentally, and doing the same for my family. That's meant some sacrifices along the way—working fewer hours, taking early retirement—but, for me, those sacrifices are worth it.

As time passes, I think a lot more about my dad's age when he died and how my brothers and I are measuring our time as we approach his age at death or as we pass that age. And soon, I imagine, we'll measure our time against the death of my mother.

One last thought: As you can probably tell by now, I have chosen to not let my cancers define me; and at every step, I have chosen to fight, very much wanting to remain among the living. There are still children to see married, grandchildren I have yet to meet, and many more years needed to travel and pursue new hobbies. And even after almost forty years, I still can't wait to spend a whole lot more time with my wife. Having had diseases that could have ended my life prematurely, my mortality is something of which I am keenly aware. However, I've beaten the odds a number of times and prefer to look forward to the future rather than reflect on death. As I mentioned earlier, life is too short. So I intend to live it to the fullest!

Todd A. Herzog, BA, BComm, CPA

Todd Herzog is no stranger to adversity, having been diagnosed with cancer three times and enduring all the various aftereffects that continue to come along years later. It's a lifelong journey, on which he's joined by his wife of forty years, Carol, and his three amazing children, Josh, Stephanie, and Lindsay. Born and raised in St. Catharines, Ontario, Canada (just a short bike ride from Niagara Falls), Todd obtained his BA in philosophy at the University of Western Ontario, followed by a BComm at the University of Windsor.

Todd started his working life as a professional accountant, becoming a partner and eventually striking out on his own. He followed that with a brief stint running his own retail store, and he then fulfilled another lifelong dream by becoming an investment adviser. This was followed by a long career in financial planning with a major Canadian financial institution.

Although now retired; he enjoys taking art lessons, practicing yoga and meditation, and just generally appreciating life. Todd lives just north of Toronto with his wife. His kids have left the house but still find their way back when their fridges are in need of a restock.

Contact Information:
e-mail: therzog@rogers.com

REMEMBERING FRIENDS AND SERVING OUR COUNTRY

An Army Helicopter Pilot's Perspective on Mortality

Wesley Hunt, MBA, MPA, MILR

Hortman, John David	May 6, 1981–August 8, 2011
Holbrook, Jason Ellis	January 28, 1982–July 29, 2010
Whitten, Daniel Preston	December 19, 1981–February 2, 2010
Pena, Paul Wenceslaus	July 8, 1982–January 19, 2010
Synder, Adam Paulson	November 18, 1981–December 5, 2007
Fraser, David Michael	October 23, 1981–November 26, 2006
Dennison, John Ryan	September 2, 1982–November 12, 2006
Bock, Amos Camden Riley	January 30, 1982–October 23, 2006
Seidel III, Robert Augustine	October 27, 1982–May 18, 2006
Avery, Garrison Charles	May 2, 1982–February 1, 2006
Britt, Benjamin Thomas	April 20, 1981–December 22, 2005
Zilinski II, Dennis William	December 23, 1981–November 19, 2005

(Eulogy pages can be found at http://defender.west-point.org/service/taps.mhtml.)

You may not know these individuals personally, but these are the members of my West Point class of 2004 who gave their lives in the defense of this great nation. Upon graduation, military academy graduates embark upon a five-year service requirement, but that commitment is not solidified until academic instruction begins in the fall of the cow (junior) year. Before that day, a cadet may opt to leave the academy without incurring a military obligation.

September 11, 2001, is a date, like the attack on Pearl Harbor on December 7, 1941, "which will live in infamy."[1] On that day, I was among the members of the class of 2004 who were yearlings (sophomores) at West Point, braving the daily rigors of cadet life. On September 11, we realized that we would likely enter our active duty military service during a time of war. Although we still had the option to depart West Point at the end of our yearling year, we vowed to stay.

For the ensuing years, we followed the war efforts closely because we knew that as each day crept closer to graduation, we were all moving closer to the opportunity to lead soldiers into combat. While at West Point, we never openly discussed the potential of not returning to American soil alive, but death is certainly an inherent reality when it comes to war.

The study of military art is a component of the curriculum at West Point. We studied numerous campaigns, spanning the time period from the American Revolution to the United States' involvement in Mogadishu. We studied the tactics of great military minds and West Point alumni, which included, but was not limited to, General Grant, General Lee, General Pershing, General Patton, General MacArthur, General Eisenhower, and General Schwarzkopf. We understood that these great leaders waged our country's wars knowing that human life would be sacrificed on both enemy and friendly sides. We read about the devastating death tolls of the Civil War, World War II, and the Vietnam War. When a West Point graduate is killed in action (KIA), his or her name is announced during breakfast in the mess hall, which is mandatory for all cadets, and a moment of silence is held in the graduate's honor. During the Vietnam War, on some days of especially high morbidity, the list of KIAs was so long that cadets would leave the mess hall while the names were being announced because of overwhelming feelings of loss and despair.

We cadets knew and fully understood the risks involved in war fighting, but no amount of education or storytelling could ever prepare us for the loss of one of our own, from our own class. As women and men in our early twenties, we believed we were invincible, given our pedigrees and our natural propensities to defy the odds. I recall a classmate and fellow aviator saying, "Hell, we got through West Point … Iraq is nothing!"

Graduating from West Point is truly empowering, and we left with a conqueror's mentality that permeated every aspect of our lives. Then our class left school, and members migrated to the war zone; and we were all forced to rethink this mentality when we lost our classmate Dennis.

Dennis Zilinski was killed in action by an IED (improvised explosive device) on November 19, 2005. He was the first of our classmates to pay the ultimate price. I'd had a few classes with Dennis at West Point, and he was known for his contagious smile and easygoing demeanor. Fifteen years later, I can still recall sitting across from him, dressed in "as for class" (class uniform for cadets), smiling about how great it was to be a firstie (senior). That year, Dennis was the captain of the swim team and one of the most highly respected cadets at West Point.

When a classmate is lost, the Association of Graduates notifies the class via e-mail. At the time of Dennis's death, I was in flight school at Fort Rucker in Alabama with roughly one hundred of my West Point classmates; and we were crushed upon hearing the devastating news. Dennis made this war real to me, and until that moment, I hadn't realized the true dangers of my profession. Dennis was born just one month after me in 1981; we were twenty-three years old at the time of his death.

There is nothing more difficult than trying to comprehend the loss of a friend, classmate, and fellow soldier with such a bright future ahead of him. I could not help but think about his mother, father, and other family members that lost a beloved son, brother, nephew, and cousin. Then I thought about my family and friends and how devastated they would be if I did not return home from combat. But these thoughts did not deter me from honoring the oath I made to this county to defend her against all enemies, both foreign and domestic, and I believe this to be true for most all of my classmates. Dennis's death brought a heightened sense of reality to this conflict; it grounded us, but it also galvanized our resolve to continue to honor him by honoring our country. To remember and honor my classmates, I occasionally peruse their eulogy pages as a reminder about the precious nature of life.

The class of 2004 is certainly not the only class that has suffered losses in the defense of the greatest county in the world. While I wish I had more than this essay to honor all who've paid the ultimate price, in reality, no quantity of words can adequately express the loss families and this country have suffered from their passing. It is incumbent upon us all to *never* forget their sacrifice and to honor them by living each day mindful of their legacies. We must live for them because they are no longer with us to live for themselves.

A soldier once said, "There are no atheists in foxholes." When faced with the threat of immediate mortality, I found that to be accurate. I was the pilot of an AH-64D Apache helicopter in Iraq in 2006; my crew and I put our lives at risk every time we left the base for a combat air patrol. I met my unit here in the States in 2006, and prior to my arrival, we'd lost four crewmembers and two aircraft. One aircraft was lost in a midair collision, and the other was shot down by a man-portable air defense system (MANPADS or MPADS). Army aviation is inherently dangerous, even during peacetime when performing routine training missions. I have lost two close friends to training incidents, and these accidents serve as constant reminders of the dangers associated with this profession. Adding a combat setting to these dangers heightens one's sensitivity to the sanctity of life.

Before every combat mission, I said the Lord's Prayer at the conclusion of the routine preflight aircraft checks. I believed that I had to make my peace with God before every mission in case I did not make it back alive. Before one mission, a pilot I frequently flew with saw me praying and asked what I was doing. I replied, "You know this flight might be our last one, and I just want to make things right with the man upstairs."

"Well, please send one up for me," replied the officer, a superb pilot whose skills and capabilities were matched by few. However he was not a religious man, and I never heard him speak of anything remotely spiritual during the deployment—until that particular request.

I believe it is human nature to contemplate mortality in combat. In contrast, while we all have the understanding that tomorrow is promised to no one, the average day in the comfort of the United States does not include insurgents engaging you with the intent to kill.

Oddly enough, I was not overly concerned with my personal well-being during the missions. The aircrews were laser-focused on accomplishing the missions; consuming one's mind with anything else infringed on a pilot's ability to fight. As I look back on my time in Iraq, I see that impending doom always lingered in the recesses of my thoughts, but I never actively contemplated the what-if scenarios. Most of us wrote final good-bye letters for our friends and families that we left among our personal belongings or with trusted friends so that our loved ones would know that we were thinking of them in our last moments. Although I did not actively contemplate becoming a soldier KIA, the thoughts were certainly a part of my subconscious; and over time, bit by bit, those subconscious thoughts deposited sediments of stress and tension in my mind that were unrealized until I returned to the safety of the United States.

About a month and a half after my deployment ended, I attended church with my family. Until then my emotions had been intact, and I was elated to be home, in the safety of my country, surrounded by the people I had missed the most during my time away. For some reason, which I cannot fully grasp or explain to this day, I was overcome with a wave of emotions ranging from happiness and relief to guilt and grief. I felt happiness because I was able to hug my mother again after so many moments when that possibility was in question. I felt relief because, at least for the time being, I did not have to fly a combat mission through the heart of Baghdad. I felt guilty because I had made it back home and some of my classmates had not. I felt grief for the parents and loved ones that would never see their children, siblings, relatives, or friends again in this natural life. These were only a few of the emotions I could pinpoint, but once that moment was over, I felt liberated, as if the weight of the world had been lifted from my shoulders.

I cannot say I have ever felt that way since then, and my combat experience has given me a humble appreciation for the sanctity of life. I am no longer in the military, but if my country ever needed me again, I would answer the call without question. Combat taught me to embrace my mortality and to live each day to the fullest. Waking up every morning is a luxury that many soldiers will not experience. Never forget.

---

1   Franklin Delano Roosevelt, "War Address," December 8, 1941, National Archives, https://www.archives.gov/education/lessons/day-of-infamy/.

Wesley Hunt, MBA, MPA, MILR

Wesley Hunt attended Cornell University, where he earned master's in business, master's of public affairs, and master's in industrial and labor relations degrees while studying at the Johnson School of Management and the Cornell Institute of Public Affairs.

After graduating from high school in Houston, Texas, Wesley accepted an appointment to the United States Military Academy at West Point, where he excelled in all facets of academy life and also played on the varsity football team. He graduated in 2004 and earned a BS in leadership and management with a field of study in mechanical engineering. Upon graduation and subsequent commissioning, he spent eight years in the US Army as an aviation branch officer and AH-64D Apache Longbow helicopter pilot. In addition to qualifying as an aviator, Wesley also completed the US Army Airborne and Air Assault Schools.

Wesley's service included one combat deployment to Iraq, where he served as a platoon leader, and two deployments to Saudi Arabia, where he served as a diplomatic liaison officer. As a platoon leader and air mission commander, he planned and led fifty-five combat air missions that supported Operation Iraqi Freedom. Wesley was awarded the Combat Action Badge for his successful combat engagements. In Saudi Arabia, he served as a liaison officer who represented the US government in missions involving the Royal Saudi Land Forces Aviation Corps.

While in the military, Wesley found time to contribute to society by volunteering his time to Big Brothers/Big Sisters and by serving as a high school camp counselor for his local church. He currently mentors and advises young men at the MacCormick juvenile detention center in upstate New York.

His hobbies and interests include fitness, skiing, current events, politics, and spending time with friends and family.

Contact Information:
e-mail: wesleyphunt@gmail.com

No Good-Byes: Losing a Daughter and Learning How to Live Again

A Bereaved Mother's Perspective on Mortality

Terri DeMontrond, LLC

THIS IS THE story of my daughter, Misty, and me, and how I didn't get to say good-bye before she died. Today I try to live my life as if there may be no time for good-byes.

"Bye, honey, I love you!"

"Bye, Momma, I love you more!"

For many years, this was our parting routine after a visit or after we signed off from a phone call, a text, or a Facebook message—sometimes multiple times a day. It was Misty's favorite way to end our conversations; and I adored that, even at thirty-five years old, she still called me Momma with a loving, slightly southern lilt.

My beloved daughter, Misty, remains one of the most amazing human beings I've ever known. Her smile lit up a room. She loved to laugh, and it was so contagious you couldn't help but laugh along with her. She was a beautiful, petite, blonde-haired, hazel-eyed creature. She was precocious, fiercely curious, and intelligent. Most of all, she was compassionate, always championing the underdog.

In the sixth grade, I glimpsed her growing social consciousness when she was assigned to read *Roll of Thunder, Hear My Cry*. She had come into my bedroom, book in hand, and read a passage to me. The book is written from the perspective of a young black girl shortly after the Civil War; it depicts the horrors of racism, and I could tell Misty was very upset. Tearfully, she asked me how people could treat each other so cruelly. I had no answer.

From that point on, I watched her world vastly expand. She became fascinated by other cultures and made friends of all races and backgrounds.

She was fiercely loyal to her friends and would instinctively soothe anyone she felt was misunderstood or mistreated. Misty frequently led me, oftentimes reluctantly, into situations involving unusual or alternative lifestyles I would not have otherwise experienced. As she matured, she became drawn to children with special needs and eventually studied to be a pediatric medical assistant.

That was one side of the picture. The other side was that from the start, despite our great love for each other, Misty and I battled. She warred with her emotions, and I with mine. It was a sort of war of wills neither one of us had officially declared. In the beginning, I chalked it up to the expected and usual teenage rebellion—the growth of her independence. But while her peers seemed to be outgrowing this phase, Misty's behavior rapidly turned impulsive and dangerous.

At fourteen, after multiple episodes of running away from home and school, she was placed in a recommended residential treatment center for overall evaluation, and as a consequence of declaring suicidal and homicidal ideations. She underwent long-term inpatient care about a dozen times throughout her short lifetime, excluding hospital stays. She received many psychiatric diagnoses over the years: oppositional defiant disorder, bipolar disorder, depression, sex/relationship addiction, alcohol and substance abuse addiction, and borderline personality disorder. With each relapse, psych medications were dispensed, which she frequently abused by taking too much, not taking enough, or adding her own drug or alcohol of choice to the mix. I can remember a particular conversation we had during one of the later relapse episodes when I asked her why she couldn't or wouldn't abide by the prescribed regimen. In despair, her response was that she wasn't trying to get high; she was simply trying to feel normal. My heart ached.

Throughout the years, we searched for solutions. We utilized all our resources, large sums of money, and much time and effort. There is nothing a parent won't do for his or her suffering child, and I was no exception. Each time a crisis occurred, we fought, and I like to think we learned something each time.

During the last two years of her life, Misty had three pregnancies, two of which were ectopic and required lifesaving measures—terrifying surgeries, horribly painful for her both emotionally and physically. That surely played a role in her deep depression. After her last failed suicide attempt in November 2011, she herself insisted on an inpatient treatment program.

The treatment center we chose was in North Carolina. They touted better statistics that any other center in the country. Misty was doing very well. As most addiction recovery programs do, this center held a mid-program family week. During family week, the family of a loved one in treatment comes to the treatment center and participates in a structured therapeutic process to help prepare the inpatient for the real world.

At that point in time, I had already attended seven family weeks, spanning the past fifteen years. I was a bit reluctant, and I felt financially overwhelmed. Despite my misgivings, I decided to go forward. I was exhausted and afraid, but I still wanted to do everything possible to participate and support her recovery. And the chance to spend time with her trumped everything. She seemed genuinely committed to her recovery. It was glorious to be with her and see her feeling empowered and proud of her accomplishments.

After she successfully completed the ninety-day inpatient program in late February 2012, it was time for her to select and move into a sober living environment for six months. Misty wanted sunshine and beaches and found a sober living community in central Florida. It would offer her shared/roommate-style independent living and an intensive outpatient program (IOP), which is basically a half-day of structured process groups and individual therapy. They had a special life skills component that sounded good. At night they had group activities, including twelve-step meetings. Arrangements were made, all expenses were paid 100 percent in advance, and off she went.

Trouble started on day three. She did not feel safe. She complained of bad roommates and a poorly run program, and most disturbingly, she said people were abusing drugs. When I spoke to staff there, they denied everything. Within two weeks, Misty called her boyfriend, Larry, who sent her an airline ticket, and she left the program. It was devastating for everyone, because the agreement we'd made was that if she didn't complete the program, she'd receive no further financial support. The experts insisted I had to strictly adhere to the guidelines of tough love; otherwise, Misty would never have a chance to become an accountable, healthy, self-sustaining adult. She needed to "experience reaching her own rock bottom," they instructed me, so she could begin her recovery built on her own foundation.

I was so scared for her, but she was happy and adamant that she was ready to use what she'd learned and move on with her life. She and her boyfriend lived with his parents in Louisiana for a couple of months and went back to the business of working on building a life together. In April 2012, they returned to Houston, and we began to spend time together. One day they brought me their résumés so we could update them and print them. It was a good visit, but I was guarded, waiting for her to ask for money. She didn't.

She left my home that afternoon brimming with enthusiasm for what was to come. I had an extended retreat planned and was preparing to leave for a couple of months to Arizona. I had no idea that would be the last time I would see and hug my darling, sweet girl.

You never know when you may have had your last conversation with someone you love so deeply you can't imagine life without him or her. It's as if you just can't imagine a day without that person in it.

I didn't know it at the time, but Misty's emotions were slowly unraveling. Shortly after she died, her boyfriend, Larry, told me that she had desperately wanted to become pregnant. I found her pocket calendar and noted that she'd clearly written "Baby!" during a time each month when she would be ovulating. She must have felt it would give her stability—something to be sober for. Maybe it would seem a fresh start; I can't be sure.

Larry also shared that when her monthly cycle came, she begged him, in disappointment, to get high with her. And he did. As she spiraled emotionally, she turned more to the drugs to numb her pain and disappointment.

She became more isolated and volatile with Larry. One Saturday in early July 2012, Misty called the police and stated Larry was being violent toward her. They cooled off, and she took back her complaint by the time the police arrived. However, the police found Larry had an outstanding traffic warrant, and so he was taken to jail. Now Misty was totally alone. I encouraged her to come and stay with me, but she declined.

I felt her slipping further and further away. In the last two weeks of her life, things deteriorated at lightning speed, but I was torn about exactly how much to swoop in and rescue, remembering the contract we had agreed to and the stern instructions from her treatment team.

She rarely left her apartment. She told me she felt as though the walls were closing in on her, but she couldn't bring herself to go out. She despaired and asked me what to do. We talked about her getting a part-time job nearby or volunteering at a local school—anything to jump-start her life once again. I asked to come see her or for her to come see me, but she always had excuses. Finally she told me she didn't want me to see her because she had been cutting herself and was ashamed and couldn't bring herself to let me see her. I suspected she was also using; I could always tell. I was worried sick she was taking too many pharmaceutical psychiatric medications unsupervised by a doctor.

Then, as if life weren't challenging enough for her, an old friend of hers died; she hanged herself, leaving a three-year-old child behind. Misty was devastated. She posted her feelings about her friend's suicide on Facebook. A day later, she also posted how much she missed her friends and family, how sad she was, and how she just wanted to go to sleep and never wake up. I called her. We talked. I asked her if she was feeling suicidal. She said she felt so lonely, but then she said, "Momma, I wouldn't take my life. It isn't mine to take, because you gave it to me." I was so relieved. She sounded sincere and in touch with her heart and the love I had for her. Then she finally opened up to me and admitted she'd relapsed.

I encouraged her to go to a detox center for three days, stabilize, and then come and stay with me. We got it all arranged quickly. After the many times I'd been through the relapse-and-rehab process, I had come to clearly understand that the period just before entering a program can be very dangerous for someone abusing substances. The desire to get high—that one last binge on the drug of choice—becomes very great, and I was terrified.

I called and texted her constantly. She would answer to say that she was showering, getting something to eat, taking a nap, or packing her things and would be on her way to the hospital shortly. I asked to come and drive her. "Mom, I can do this. I'll call you when I get there and get settled." She even gave me the name and phone number of the intake person at the hospital, and I called and spoke to her. It seemed she was all set to go.

And she was—I found her bags packed and sitting by the door when I cleared her apartment after she died. So close.

The night before going into detox, she called me to say that her longtime friend Sarah was in town from the Middle East, and they were planning a dinner and games at a local eatery. After that she would go to the hospital. I knew Sarah; she worked for a private contractor overseas and underwent random drug testing; she didn't do drugs. Misty sounded good and upbeat about seeing Sarah, so I was glad she would have some time out of her tiny apartment with a safe friend.

I later learned Misty had asked Sarah for twenty dollars for gas, and Sarah—who loved Misty dearly—gave her four hundred dollars to help her with bills and other necessities. This must have been too tempting to resist. A decline into a drug-induced oblivion ensued. She avoided my calls, refused to let me into her apartment, and insisted she'd be going into the hospital as soon as she'd had a nap.

We had a short telephone conversation the night before she died. Annoyed with my constant calling, her last words to me were to please let her be, to let her rest. She said that everything would be okay and told me to "please stop worrying or whatever it is you're doing!"

There is a well-known saying in many twelve-step programs that we adopted as our mantra: "Don't give up before the miracle." But we didn't get our miracle. Misty died. And a part of me died with her.

On August 1, 2012, my bighearted, beloved thirty-five-year-old daughter ended her life.

On that day—and for days, weeks, and months after—I didn't know if I would survive without her. Some moments I still wonder. At first I felt a numbing shock—a despair, a trauma—wash over me. Later came awful guilt and regret. What more could I have done? What should I have done? Most of all, I missed her. I still miss her—every day.

I failed her. No matter how much I did, it wasn't enough. Parents are supposed to protect their children, no matter their ages or circumstances. I replayed the events over and over in my mind. I knew how fragile she was—her most recent suicide attempt had been only nine months prior—and I had been in a constant state of hypervigilance, calling and texting her. How could I have let her slip away? Tough love may have been a viable strategy if Misty had been in a safe place, but with one of the possible outcomes being death, the costs of tough love were far too dear.

I imagine she must have felt that she was incapable of pulling herself up from the bottom she'd hit, and it left her hopeless, vulnerable, scared and full of despair. For sensitive people, the world can be too harsh, too loud, too much. So she got high and, as she had done during her suicide attempt in November, took every pill in her possession. Blood pressure medication, antidepressants, antianxiety meds, and cocaine were all cited on the autopsy report declaring the cause of death as suicide. However, this time no one was there to stop or save her. And she died all alone.

For years her counselors and doctors told me, "She might not make it this time." With each relapse, the odds kept being stacked against us, and the damage from crisis after crisis mounted. And the miracle we'd never once doubted would eventually come never came.

One particularly sorrowful night shortly after her death, I lay awake, and these words came to mind. They took shape as a poem to and about her.

She

She didn't want it anymore—her precious life we fought so hard for.
No amount of love and care would be enough to save her.

Weary of the battles in both her internal and external worlds, she decided the time had come to surrender and end the wars.

No good-byes were said—just the threat, finally, fully earned.
Determined to find relief, she went into the sleep of no return.

She leaves behind despairing loved ones
longing to hear, once again, her wholehearted laughter.

Striving to breathe through the tears—now facing a different struggle—
to carry on and somehow go on living a life without her.

I find myself asking what my role is now. What do I do? I continue to grieve for my hopes and dreams for my little girl; for Misty's innocence, lost when she was raped and left with an STD at the age of fifteen; for how she put herself in harm's way in dangerous situations with dangerous people; for how she was overtaken by addiction time and time again; for her loss of inner peace as her anxiety and depression set in and grew to paralyzing proportions.

Grief is my own personal spiritual war raging inside my soul. Grief numbs me into accepting that the loss is absolute. Grief crushes my heart and implodes my spirit. Grief closes my eyes and bows my head. Grief collapses my limbs and dulls my senses. Nothing looks, sounds, tastes, or smells the same. Grief pauses, paralyzes, and sedates me. Mothers are supposed to protect their children at all costs—no task too difficult, no hesitation, no exceptions. I felt the deepest of shame for not taking better care of her.

In a strange and surreal way, the unexpected and traumatic loss of my child by suicide disintegrated my core sense of who I thought I was. The hope I held was ripped away forever. Quietly and insidiously, trauma exploded my mind and greatly intensified my emotions. It brought hurried, fractured, frantic thoughts.

"No!"

"How?"

"Why?"

"She can't give up!"

"I just want one more chance!"

"Wait, what happened to our miracle?"

The days following her death are both as clear as crystal and as abstract as a fantasy sci-fi movie. Writing her obituary is one clear memory for me. I remember writing and crying and suddenly thinking, "How can this be happening?" But the words came. It was a mercy at the time, for it allowed me to make tangible the wonderful parts about the life she'd led.

I know she'd be disappointed that she didn't get to donate any of her organs. I didn't find her soon enough, and that pains me. At least I knew her end-of-life desire was to be cremated. I think back to when she teased me about how, after I was gone, she would keep my ashes with her always. I asked her to put my ashes in a nice spot and leave me there. I didn't want to burden her with carrying me from place to place. Ironically, I now carry her ashes with me with the deepest love and a commitment to never again leave her behind.

I still have her cell phone active so that we can call her number and hear her say, "You've missed me, so leave a message ..." And I often leave a message saying that I do miss her. I've kept her Facebook page active so that I can keep her memory present and so her friends can post loving comments.

A very empty and dark space is left behind. There are so many nooks and crannies filled with the details of each and every moment I shared with her. There are many trap doors that sweep me right down into the memories of all the times I now second-guess, wondering what I might have done differently. What if I'd chosen a different doctor, a different medication, or a different way of dealing with a crisis? It's endless—the wondering, the regretting, the awful longing. And yet there are respites—moments of peaceful, loving thoughts, and my heart aches in a good way.

It's been written that when a parent dies, the past is lost; when a partner dies, the present is lost; and when a child dies, the future is lost. For me it has been more. Misty was my past, present, and future all in one.

She was my past because all my life, my dream was to be a wife and mother. The family I built was my brass ring. Because I'd come from an unstable, abusive family of origin, I was very determined to create a safe and serene home for my family and myself. I was a young mother, and Misty was a difficult baby to bring into the world. Eight hospitalizations and two surgeries due to many complications during pregnancy culminated in a beautifully perfect five-pound bundle of pure joy. I had developed preeclampsia at the time of her birth, but I never lost consciousness and nursed her as soon as they allowed. Her birth was such a blessed victory, and I fell deeply in love with her at first sight.

She was my present because Misty and her daughter, Brianna—who was seventeen years old at the time of Misty's death—were and are such a big part of my life. Brianna has lived most of her life with me and had a somewhat sibling-like relationship with her mother, although Misty did her best to be a parent to Brianna when she was able. There was an almost constant need for hypervigilance to keep everyone safe for many years. Fear was always present, but hopeful optimism always trumped the fear.

By necessity, I became a crisis manager—calm on the outside, terrorized on the inside, always mindful that the present is where the magic happens; that is where wholeness returns and battles are won.

I planned my days around Misty's and Brianna's needs. I was caretaker to two precious girls, and I was determined to support them into wellness. Truthfully, I had many moments of resentment when my efforts fell short or were ignored and what seemed like needless suffering recurred. If only we could access and use the skills we had been taught for months and years. But when emotions become irregular, the more practical and sound part of the brain falters. However, the efforts continued.

I took many classes on mental health issues, nutrition, and holistic alternatives. I earned various certifications, trained to facilitate groups for families who had similar issues, researched, read, studied, practiced, taught … and prayed. I didn't allow defeat to enter my thoughts—at least not when anyone was looking. Terror gripped my heart when the phone rang late at night—and that happened often—but I knew that whatever it was would be okay. Because that's what mothers do; we are the holders of hope, the forever optimistic.

And finally, she was my future because that's where the payoff was to be. Misty was going to overcome her addictions and earn a good chance to stabilize her emotional issues, which would allow her to properly parent her daughter and live a life free of trauma and full of calm and contentedness. It would be her moment to model courage and determination to her child and her peers—an opportunity to use the many skills she'd honed to bring hard-earned experience to others who might feel lost. She was *my* future—to be a doting mother and grandmother, to plan weddings and grow old and properly prepare and enjoy grandchildren, and, most of all, to see her whole and content.

Fewer than eighteen months after Misty's death, I have to figure out a way to continue living without her. I'm no longer the mother I once was. Nor am I the altruistic socialite or the banking executive. I continue to be a champion and crusader for my child, for her child, and for other families dealing with similar issues. We are a tribe—a devastated yet hopeful group of embattled warriors determined to do whatever it takes to prevail.

I've joined groups and attended meetings for people who've suffered losses like mine. I've become a mentor for others who've lost a child by suicide. I know, from experience, their unique sense of regret, confusion, inadequacy, guilt, and even some shame. I understand and have begun the necessary and ongoing work of acceptance, encouraging them to let go of regrets and to embrace the self-forgiveness that is required over and over again.

During an intense therapeutic session, an incredibly wise woman asked me what I thought the worst-case scenario would be—which specific thoughts brought the most fear into my being and paralyzed me in my grief. She suggested "total annihilation of the self," and I agreed. However different my world had become, I was still breathing and moving about. I was alive with a broken heart.

I see now, as grief evolves and some time to process has passed, that Misty's death *was* a total annihilation of the self. Over the years, I had acquired a yoga therapist certification and trained as a Martha Beck life coach and an NEA-BPD Family Connections facilitator, and it all seemed so very ridiculous. I felt like a complete fake.

The moment I was aware of her death, I was completely deconstructed; my entire being was splintered into the tiniest shards of glass—a pile of dust on the floor. It seemed impossible that people still walked around casually in the grocery store or that people laughed, went to movies, and made plans for the weekend. All the hope, the huge expectations of a happy outcome for Misty, was forever and completely gone, as was my faith. All my tools, skills, resources, expectations, hopes, and dreams dissolved into the ether—useless by all measures.

Then, without conscious effort, I became aware that I was placing one foot in front of the other. In spite of it all, the clock still moved and the world still turned. Knowing this, accepting this, was the new starting place. Integrating what had happened and reorganizing a new reality were the invisible building blocks for carrying on. I would simply breathe, and a moment, an hour, would pass; an entire day would come to an end— and I survived. Preparing a cup of tea and a bite to eat, contemplating an occasional plan for an afternoon—these very simple things got me through difficult days. They still do.

Somewhere I read, "Forgiveness is letting go of the hope that the past could have been any different." I've read that healing is going from "what if" to "what now."

So … what now?

I am learning a lot about forgiveness. Unlike my feelings regarding the actions of others, the feelings and very deliberate act of self-forgiveness is an ongoing process for me. As memories come up and my self-doubt takes over about a choice I made, I notice and stop. I make an intentional effort to explore those thoughts and remind myself that while I can't admit I always did my best—sometimes I am lazy, imperfect, neglectful, angry, hurting, and selfish—I try to do my best as much as I can. With Misty, I tried really hard. And with the same compassion I extend to the other grieving mother I mentor, I offer love to myself in honor of my unquestionable love for Misty.

My close community has become very small. I talk to trusted loved ones. I learned quickly to be cautious of whom I trusted my grief with. The most well-meaning, loving people will say deeply hurtful things, ignorant of how painful their words of wisdom and solutions can be. The pain of my grief made them so uncomfortable, and they just wanted to relieve me of that pain; they wanted the old me back, and that person was forever gone. I've made peace with that, and I ask my loved ones to try to do the same. My child died; I am forever changed, and I am sorry it makes them uncomfortable. I ask that they accept me and my tears, allowing me to be true to my own feelings as I adjust to a different way of being in my life.

As this shift took place, I noticed that I was also making some peace with aspects of my grieving. One afternoon I was watching a TV special on grizzly bears and was fascinated at how their behavior in the wild of nature resembled my inner grieving beast at its most savage. In their natural habitat, they are the most feared, brutish, gluttonous creatures among both man and animal. From the insatiable appetite to the habit of hibernation, there seemed to be connections.

I reread *The Tao of Pooh*, a lovely book about the simple ways of Winnie the Pooh learning and living the practices described in the *Tao Te Ching*. Basic Taoism holds that there is a gentle way of appreciating, learning from, and working with whatever happens in everyday life and that allowing and accepting the natural way of things brings calm, order, and peace. "From caring comes courage. Those who have no compassion have no wisdom. Knowledge, yes; cleverness, maybe; wisdom, no."[1]

All of this came together one weekend, and I was inspired to compose a metaphor about how those two bears depicted how my grieving was changing. It's called "Bearing Grief," and it is about unwittingly surviving something that is so painful it tears the very fiber of one's soul. And yet, in surrender and acceptance, we survive. The human spirit is truly amazingly resilient. I'd like to share that metaphor here.

Bearing Grief
My Metaphor for Loss

Grizzly Grief comes lumbering in, growling fiercely and baring his teeth. His big paws swipe aggressively, greedily, tearing at my heart and mind. His hulking frame towers over me as he rips at my flesh and into the core of my being. No words—just a vast and intense entitlement to devour all there is of me. I don't resist or struggle; experience has taught me there is no escape. Grizzly leaves me bleeding, my soul flayed open to all the earthly elements.

I collapse. I cry. I scream and wail. I'm exhausted, totally spent, mortally wounded, and hopelessly defeated.

Sometime later, Winnie the Pooh arrives. Gently he snuggles up next to me and quietly whispers that I will not die in this moment and that all creatures suffer, heal, and even learn and grow. He tells me that we repeat this cycle until we don't anymore. He says, "The very *best* part of us—our hearts—can be cracked wide open and become even bigger and better. You see, in this deep hole of missing is *remembering*, the place where you'll find the pieces of your love for what you've lost."

Pooh's message could be maddening to the cracked parts of me that grip too tightly: judgment, withholding of love and forgiveness, and the desire to fix things *now*. But his matter-of-fact monotone words of wisdom resonate, soothe, and calm my spirit. The gaping wounds left by Grizzly begin to close again, leaving scars visible only to him and me.

We lie quietly for what seems like a long while but isn't. There's nothing more to say about Grizzly, knowing he will return again and that there will be more carnage and suffering. But there's nothing to be done about it—no way to avoid the attack.

I often forget that Grizzly's visits are survivable, and the next time he comes, I may believe I am dying again. But I don't think I will. What I will remember is the longing inside the sadness and the love inside the missing. And thanks to Pooh, I'll do my best to remember that love is much, much bigger than the biggest and strongest grizzly.

Mortality is the state of being mortal—susceptible to death. We live, we love, we experience loss; it is the way. We must live well and love deeply and be mindful that loss is only a heartbeat away.

Mary Oliver sums it up beautifully in this poignant excerpt from her poem "In Blackwater Woods":

> you must be able
> to do three things:
> to love what is mortal;
> to hold it
>
> against your bones knowing
> your own life depends on it;
> and, when the time comes to let it go,
> to let it go.[2]

This is the journey. The way we relate to our own mortality and the mortality of our loved ones—the way we relate to the vulnerability of loss—directly affects our capacity to love. When we hug another and have the awareness that we are going to die, it can change the quality of the connection. You may actually fall in love in that moment, transcending the fear of mortality and giving an astonishing redemptive quality to being fully capable of living, loving, and losing.

---

1   Benjamin Hoff, *The Tao of Pooh* (New York: Penguin, 1982).

2   *The Journalverse*, Mary Oliver > Quotes, accessed June 12, 2014, http://journalverse.com/poem-of-the-month-sept-2014-in-blackwater-woods-mary-oliver/.

Misty and Terri

Terri DeMontrond, LLC

Terri DeMontrond, owner of DeMontrond Wellness and Consulting, has been supporting others in their journey to well-being for over 20 years. The tools and skills she has accumulated include Life Coach Certification (LCC) with the Martha Beck Institute and studying Holistic Nutrition with Clayton College. She is a Yoga Therapist trained by Phoenix Rising, a Reiki Master utilizing mindfulness and energy balancing, a trained facilitator for NEA-BPD's "Family Connections," and has extensive experience with emotional regulation techniques using DBT practices developed by Marsha Linehan.

Terri recently completed the course for Compassionate Bereavement Care taught by Dr. Joanne Cacciatore, granted by the MISS Foundation, the Elisabeth Kübler-Ross Family Trust, and the Center for Loss and Trauma. Her personal experience as a bereaved parent has led her to passionately endeavor to repurpose her own traumatic loss and grief into a source of presence, love, and support for other families on that same journey. Terri is also a Hope volunteer within the MISS Foundation.

Personally, Terri continues to seek awareness for wellness and spiritual growth. She loves her daily yoga practice, painting, and writing. She is an avid reader, hiker, and traveler. Most of all she loves to be inspired by people and their life experiences and to share inspiration with others.

> *"No farewell words were spoken, no time to say goodbye. You were gone before we knew it, and only the Divine knows why." —Author Unknown*

Contact Information:
e-mail: demontrond@aol.com

PART III

Faith (and Nonfaith) Perspectives

HUMBLE REFLECTIONS ON GRIEF

An Agnostic Christian's Perspective on Mortality

James W. Stovall, DMin

THE GREAT ENGLISH minister and theologian Leslie D. Weatherhead wrote a book called *The Christian Agnostic*. In it, he states his intent "in complete loyalty to Christ and what I believe to be essential Christianity, to win back some of the best men and women I have ever known who are estranged from both because, being intellectually honest, they cannot 'sign on the dotted line' that they believe certain theological formulas."[1]

Weatherhead says he is agnostic in regard to some of the theological creeds that are presented as irrefutable truths in many Christian pulpits. In using the term "agnostic," he means that there are items of faith that he chooses to believe but cannot claim to "know." The book provides a wonderful affirmation of the authenticity of an "agnostic Christian faith," whereby a person hopes and believes and, at the same time, is intellectually willing to entertain questions and doubts regarding belief.

As a Christian minister for more than four decades, I fit well into the mold of an agnostic Christian. As the apostle Paul observed about the nature of faith, "we work it out in fear and trembling."[2] Preachers who utter faith language in terms of absolute certainty are well intentioned in their attempts to pull people into their churches: "You don't have to do any thinking—just believe!" For many believers, however, those words have just the opposite effect. They want their tenets of faith to appeal to the mind as well as to the heart.

In 1998, I was pastoring a church in Macomb, Illinois. In early February, family and friends were experiencing the death of Dr. Dick Longwell. Dick was an elder in the congregation and former head of the Geography Department at Western Illinois University. Two words that could be used to describe Dick's nature and character are "intelligence" and "wisdom."

A few days before he died, a caring friend went to visit him. She asked, "Dick, are you going to heaven?" He said, "I hope so." She replied, "You don't hope so. You know so." Later Dick told me this story and followed it with this comment: "I would rather hope." He considered hope, rather than certainty, to be the cornerstone of his faith.

In late April 2015, my wife, Luann, and I were in Illinois visiting our daughter, Holly; her husband, Tom; their daughter, Maya; and their son, Mathew. We received a call from Brittany Hall, who was taking care of the animals at our farm while we were gone. We had known the Hall family for about ten years and recognized them as wonderful neighbors. Brittany told us that her little twelve-year-old sister, Chelsea, had died suddenly. Chelsea was a sweet, kind, affable, active child whose presence was always a gift to others. The Hall family was immediately caught up in the grisly grind of grief.

One incident, however, stood out in their minds. Two days before she died, Chelsea reported to her mother that her precious deceased grandmother had come to her room during the night. The family pondered this communication from Chelsea, seeing it in a different light after Chelsea entered the same state as her beloved grandmother.

The Hall family was inundated with all the banal clichés that people typically offer to deeply grieving families. Many well-intentioned people feel that they must say something meaningful to a bereaved family. Meanwhile, families like the Halls reluctantly join a fellowship of other people who understand the value of a "quiet presence" in times of severe loss. Simply being present with bereft family members often conveys compassion and empathy more deeply than mere words.

I recently listened to a lecture from a humanist regarding the nature of a prescient dream—such as Chelsea's vision of her dead grandmother— that is coupled with the soon-to-follow death of the dreamer herself. He said that it falls under the category of coincidence. He said that there may be many such coincidences relating to one's reflections coupled together in the mind, but they are still coincidences and not facts. We can't deny the phenomenon of coincidence. Nevertheless, an encounter with transcendent mystery, such as that experienced by Chelsea, provides a pondering hope—a hope that many of us cherish and hold on to as a dear friend. Dreams are born of the unconscious mind and are hard to fit into the category of consciousness. So they stir hope which mere coincidences cannot.

It is not my desire to undercut science or religion when it comes to matters of faith, especially in regard to items like grief and death. However, blithely explaining away transcendent experiences is akin to what is known as reductionism, or reducing something down to naught. It relegates every unexplainable event as being a coincidence. I think that there are times when it is more appropriate to simply say, "I don't know." While good science can be helpful, so can good hope in attempting to make sense of the unexplainable.

Dr. Charles Kemp, one of the most notable pastoral psychologists of the twentieth century, once gave a sparkling lecture about the psychology of Carl Jung. In closing he said, "If religion wishes to have an ally from the world of psychology, Carl Jung is the most likely candidate."[3] Dr. Jung spent thousands of hours listening to people from places ranging from university think tanks to the psychological backwaters of mental institutions. His respect for the human personality was like that of other great lovers of people, such as Jesus, Gandhi, Carl Rodgers, and Erik Berne. For Jung, there are no codes or data to be derived from dreams, but rather reflections of the inner self, which can inform a person about what is happening in one's body, one's relationships, and perhaps, one's best nature and destiny.

Back to Chelsea's dream: Chelsea's subconscious mind knew what was going on in her body even though she was continuing her daily routine with smiles and laughter and performing her daily chores at home and at school. Inwardly, however, she was engaged in a seminal visionary experience, dealing with what theologian Rudolf Otto called "the tremendous mystery."[4] Coincidence is not enough! When confronted with the ultimate realities of living and loving and dying, cannot our inner selves provide us a glimpse into the awesome mystery whereby spirit reaches out to touch spirit, expressing love in ways that transcend our present ability to comprehend? And cannot that great mystery continue to animate our spirits beyond physical death? As an agnostic Christian, I affirm that hope.

And yet hope alone is not sufficient to heal our souls when confronted with the loss of a Chelsea. I agree with the apostle Paul, who said that faith, hope, and love are what truly matter and that the greatest of these is love.[5] In a poetic masterpiece of song written by Tomy Arata, "The Dance," singer Garth Brooks beautifully uses the word "dance" as a metaphor for love and points out that where there is love, there is always the potential for loss. However, the joy of the dance far outweighs the pain of separation:

> And now I'm glad I didn't know
> The way it all would end.
> The way it all would go.
> Our lives are better left to chance.
> I could have missed the pain,
> But I'd of had to miss the dance.[6]

I have experienced the pain that accompanies the loss of someone incredibly dear to my heart; but like Garth Brooks, not for all the world would I have passed on the immeasurable joy of that dance. Love not only gives meaning to the pain but also provides the process for transcending it. It's what "good grieving" is all about.

In 1988, my son, Chad, and I went fishing at Bernadotte Dam on the Spoon River in Illinois. We were not really adept at getting up early, so we got to the dam too late for the big catch period when the catfish were making their run up the river. That morning I caught only one thing: I somehow hooked a dead catfish about eight inches long. We had a great time together that day on the river. I tell that story with a sense of negative irony. In February 1997, Chad and a friend, Paul Klasner, planned a canoe float down the Spoon River. It was the season of La Niña, and the snow had melted and filled the river to overflowing earlier that winter.

While floating down the river on a nice Sunday afternoon, Chad and Paul saw that the dam they intended to float through was too dangerous, and they tried to paddle ashore, but it was too late. Paul's end of the boat drew near the shore while Chad's end churned in the middle of the torrent. The dam sucked the boat down into a giant vortex. Paul was able to find the shore only because he was a college-level swimmer. Chad, however, went down, as had twelve others since the dam was built by the Army

Corps of Engineers in WWII to provide water for German prisoners of war. Thereafter our family began a long sentence of hard labor and pain inflicted upon us by that terrible tyrant called grief.

Grief dissects hearts in a variety of ways, and everyone responds differently. While caring family and friends, observing our suffering, would like the grieving process brought to a quick end, it cannot be hurried. My wife suffered deep depression that tormented her far beyond the classic seven-year period of brutal grief following the loss of a child. The redeeming time came for her when we moved to the country and raised sheep, goats, a llama, two alpacas, three Highland cattle, and other fiber animals. She took up the art of spinning and weaving to have her hands on these gifts of fiber from living creatures. She has felt Chad's presence around her country home while observing the beauty of nature's panorama of shapes and colors. She found her own way to heal and continues to thrive in it.

As for me, I began to keep a diary of my deepest feelings, addressing Chad in most of my notations. I started writing poetry too. As time elapsed, I also read a lot of poetry, plus some brief biographies of poets and others. And I became aware of an intriguing detail: grief is a common element in the biographies of many people who have been prompted to become creative and to make a difference in this world.

Here are some people whose grief over the loss of a child moved them to become courageously creative: Theodore Roosevelt, James Longstreet, Ben and Deborah Franklin, Mark Twain, James Garfield, John Hancock, Johann Sebastian Bach, Joseph Auslander (America's first poet laureate), Bishop James Pike, Eugene O'Neill, Mary Wollstonecraft, Thomas Jefferson, William Seward, Abraham Lincoln, Tolstoy, Roy Rogers and Dale Evans, Don Rickles, Walter Mondale, John and Abigail Adams, Franklin Pierce, Dietrich Bonhoeffer, John L. McClellan, Archibald Macleish, John Winthrop, Jackie Robinson, John F. Kennedy, Martin Niemöller, Bobby Burns, Victor Hugo, David Grossman, Ben Jonson, William Wordsworth, Beaumarchais, Dwight and Mamie Eisenhower, Calvin Coolidge, Immanuel Kant, Voltaire, Queen Anne, Virginia Woolf, Glenn Wilkerson, and King David of Israel. Additionally, a host of other bereaved people from the fields of art, music, theatre, science, politics, mathematics, economics, and a surfeit of other disciplines have suffered

153

loss and left rich, positive tracks in its wake. They have taken the dark hole of grief and filled it with love and a dedication to life.

Pesach Krauss, the former chaplain at Memorial Sloan Kettering Cancer Center, wrote a book titled *Why Me? Coping with Grief, Loss and Change.* It is among the best and most touching proclamations of faith and hope I have ever read. One story he told was about a woman who came to the hospital where he was a chaplain. She met with an oncologist who told her she had only a few months to live. She responded with calm, as if she had been told, "The movie starts at noon." He asked her why she received this terrible news so serenely. She replied, "Doctor, I have lost a child. Once you lose a child nothing else is a great threat."[7] Indeed, intense grief can expose latent courage, open vistas of yet-to-be-tapped love, and unleash a kind sensitivity far beyond what the bereaved had previously known.

Luann and I have been in a lot of grief groups, mostly for parents who have lost children: Bereaved Parents Share, Compassionate Friends, SOHG (Sojourners of Healing Grief), and several weekly gatherings of folk who simply knew they needed one another. Being with others who share the same type of loss—and who understand the almost unbearable pain that results from that loss—can be very therapeutic. For some people, that "being with" is a lifetime challenge. Many others can go and talk and listen for weeks or even a year and then go it alone. I suppose it depends upon the preference of the introvert or the extrovert. Extroverts get energy from others, while introverts are energized by being either alone or with a few friends. Sometimes grieving is so intense that we may need to get a little help each day. No two people grieve the same.

The talented Shel Silverstein wrote a little illustrated book called *The Missing Piece.* Silverstein speaks of the manner in which we are like a vehicle with a missing portion of a wheel. Wherever we go, we leave tracks of what we have lost![8] Grief can render those tracks wobbly and unstable. However, it is important to make the effort to improve, to progress or to heal, though healing will never be pure or complete.

Those who have walked that walk unanimously agree that the grieving process is hard work. It involves taking one or more steps, which in turn empowers us to keep on stepping. In *Tracks of a Fellow Struggler,* minister and author John Claypool speaks eloquently about losing his beloved ten-year-old daughter to cancer.[9] Claypool uses a passage from Isaiah (3: 30–31) to describe his grief journey:

> Even youths will faint and be weary,
> and the young will fall exhausted;
> but those who wait for the LORD shall renew their strength,
> they shall mount up with wings like eagles,
> they shall run and not be weary,
> they shall walk and not faint.

Sometimes grieving wears us down, leaving us feeling faint and weary, other times we are able to gather our courage and walk with halting steps through the process, and occasionally we may experience one of those transcendent moments of faith and hope whereby we can run or rise up like an eagle. The important thing in the journey toward healing is to not lose hope and to keep on stepping.

One way to do that is to keep a diary of daily thoughts and feelings. In order to do so, it is important to have a broad emotional understanding developed through a growing vocabulary of "feeling" words. One guru of the emotional vocabulary is psychologist Thomas Gordon. He encourages people to identify feelings in sophisticated ways—instead of falling back on the root words of "mad," "glad," and "sad"—because that identification and subsequent expression can serve as a release valve for those feelings. One's vocabulary of grief can include a variety of terms, such as "emptiness," "shame," "forlornness," "lost," "aloneness," "the need for achievement," "the need to care for others," "the need to remember," and so on.[10] A diary offers an opportunity for a person to express her intimate self. Then she may go back later and read recollections in order to feel a sense of where one has one has been and where one is going.

I have a word of counsel for men (and women) who feel they have to be strong for the sake of their grieving family. That counsel is this: tears can be very therapeutic. There is a profound difference in the chemical makeup of tears as compared to a watery eye. Tears have a chemical ingredient that helps drain the pent-up feelings of desperation and pain or (ironically) gratitude and joy.[11] An important part of the healing process is to let your feelings of grief pour out naturally as they occur.

When my daughter, Holly, joined the church in 1981, I could not receive her into the church, because I was too tearful and speechless. An elder in the church, Howard Nutt, came forward and listened to her words of faith. I was able to baptize her with joy on Easter morning. Then the reverse happened in 1986, when my son, Chad, came forward. I received him on behalf of the church with no sign of joyful tears; however, those tears flowed when it came time for him to enter the waters of baptism. My tears of joy were symbolic of the tremendous love I have for my children. Then, when Chad died, I discovered the healing properties of tears of sorrow.

Grief is a holistic challenge. The great biblical scholar Rudolf Bultmann wrote that human beings do not have a body; we *are* a body.[12] We tend to divide up the self into parts such as soul, spirit, mind, and body. But our holistic existence does not fall neatly into such categories. Every category we might use to describe parts is always consumed by the whole.

Grief engages the entire body. It is such a profound and complicated encounter with one of life's most terrifying challenges that we may want to say, "The hell with it!" and disappear in a bed or recliner. This is the time for courage and determination to become effective components of grief and loss. Walk, run, lift weights, go! A lethargic body impacts directly those entities we call brain, spirit, and soul. Utilize physical exercise as a positive means of releasing the body's natural "pleasure chemicals" (such as endorphins) and helping soothe our feelings of emotional pain.

Talking helps too. A professional counselor, empathetic friend, clergyperson, or family member who is a good listener, and who will not discount our emotions, can play a valuable role in the healing process. Our son died eighteen years ago. My wife and I are now are in the process of telling our grandchildren about their uncle, as we speak over the lumps in our throats. And we are finding solace in the telling.

Gene Pitney was a famous vocalist in the 1960s. His signature song contains these words written by Hal David with musical score by Burt Bacharach: "Only love can break a heart. And only love can mend it again."[13] The first line is easy to understand. Intense grief is a product of intense love. The more we love someone, the harder it is to lose him or her; thus, "Only love can break a heart."

But what about the second line—"Only love can mend it again"?

Here's how I think that works. The loss of Chad has made me acutely aware of the fragility of life and has rendered me much more appreciative of the preciousness of those around me. The result is that my love for Chad has increased my capacity to love others. It has also prompted me to *better* love others, and that loving helps mend my heart.

Nicholas Wolterstorff discusses this phenomenon in his literary gem entitled *Lament for a Son*. The book deals with his experience of losing a son who died much like our Chad, drowning in a Colorado river. He maintains that grief can challenge us to become living instruments of the one we lost who seeks to "transcend absence" through our loving of others on his behalf.[14] Because Chad is not physically present to love those around him, more and more do I experience this wonderful compulsion to honor his memory by caring for people whose lives are broken. In other words, Chad—who possessed an extraordinary gift for caring—continues to love others through me. It is called vicarious love, and over the years it has provided my life meaning and joy in a rainbow of ways.

In the musical *Fiddler on the Roof,* an epic moment features Tevye standing on a steeply slanted roof, playing his violin, shifting from one foot to another, and sounding out his song as he desperately seeks to maintain his balance.[15] Many times, I have felt like old Tevye, seeking to achieve spiritual balance in a world where both great joy and great loss walk hand in hand. However, after seven decades of stance-shifting and thinking and hoping, I humbly submit to you what I have learned through my journey with grief.

I think that one way loved ones we have lost can experience immortality is through our honoring of their memories by caring for those in need. Their love and compassion can continue to live through us. It is one of those components of hope that I, as an agnostic thinker, hold deeply in my reflections. This hope comforts my sense of loss, calls me to live more lovingly, and gives meaning and purpose to my life.

---

1   Leslie D. Weatherhead, *The Christian Agnostic* (Nashville, TN: Abingdon, 1978), 32.

2   Philippians 2:12. 1. All Biblical or allusions to passages in this article are taken from the New Revised Standard Version Bible (NSRV), copyright

1989, Division of Christian Education of the National Council of the Churches of Christ in the United States of America.

3   Charles Kemp, lecture at Brite Divinity School, Texas Christian University, February 6, 1967.

4   Rudolf Otto, *The Idea of the Holy* (Oxford: Oxford University Press, 1958), 13.

5   1 Corinthians 13:13.

6   Garth Brooks, "The Dance," on *Garth Brooks*, Capitol Nashville, first released in 1989.

7   Krauss Pesach, *Why Me? Coping with Grief, Loss and Change* (New York: Bantam Books, 1988).

8   Shel Silverstein, *The Missing Piece* (New York: Harper Collins, 1976).

9   John Claypool, *Tracks of a Fellow Struggler* (Harrisburg, PA: Morehouse Publishing, 2004), 52f.

10 Victor M. Parachin, *Healing Grief* (St. Louis, MO: Chalice Press, 2001), 6.

11 From lectures in *Parent Effectiveness Training*, developed by Thomas Gordon.

12 Rudolf Bultmann, *Theology of the New Testament* (New York: Scribner, 1951–1955), 192f.

13 Gene Pitney, "Only Love Can Break a Heart," on *Only Love Can Break a Heart*, Musicor, first released in 1962.

14 Nicholas Wolsterstorff, *Lament for a Son* (Grand Rapids, MI: William Eerdmans, 1987), 59.

15 Joseph Stein, "Fiddler on the Roof"; Notes from a sermon by Dr. Jim Moore, Minister of St. Luke's United Methodist Church, Houston, Texas, May 11, 1986.

Note: In order to delve into the world of the unconscious one may refer to the works of Robert A. Johnson, especially his book, *Inner Work*. In addition, Morton Kelsey offers the following books for the skills of experiencing the unconscious: *Set Your Hearts on the Greatest Gifts: Living the Art of Christian Love*; *Dreams: A Way to Listen to God; God, Dreams and Revelation*; and *Companions on the Inner Way*. I think of these writers as the continuing school of Karl Jung. One does not find doctrinal creeds in these writings but nurture that points to realities beyond the dogmatic pale.

James (Jim) William Stovall, DMin

Born in 1943 in Poplar Bluff, Missouri, James W. Stovall grew up in a southeast Missouri town of about fifteen thousand people. On the west side of Poplar Bluff were the Ozark Mountains, dotted with small villages. To the east was the Mississippi delta. He lived on the boundary between the lands of the scorching sun to the shaded hills. This boundary boy left at age eighteen and sojourned to Texas Christian University (TCU) in Fort Worth, Texas, where he majored in religion and philosophy. He then obtained a Masters of Divinity at TCU, focusing on biblical theology and pastoral care. He continued his education at the University of Central Arkansas concurrent with serving disadvantaged children in the impoverished areas around Little Rock.

Jim settled in as pastor of the First Christian Church of Camden, Arkansas, where he also served for seven years as a Title I reading supervisor. Growing weary of two jobs, he attended Phillips University and acquired a doctorate of ministry while pastoring an Oklahoma congregation. Thereafter he served as a pastor for forty-eight years, during which time he busied himself with preaching, fitness-training, teaching, and serving congregations from Texas to Illinois. He was accompanied by his wife, Luann, his daughter, Holly, and his now late son, Chad, for whom grief has been his challenging companion.

In his life, the subjects of salience are history, spirituality, pastoral psychology, literature and social ministry. As an avowed progressive, he is devoted daily to growth via learning. It makes for a good life.

Contact Information:
e-mail: diegodoggerel@yahoo.com

ANXIETY AND DEATH

A Buddhist's Perspective on Mortality

Paul Foxman, PhD

SOME 2,500 YEARS ago, a privileged Indian prince named Siddhartha Gotama, seeking to understand the cause of human suffering, left his wife and family to sit in meditation under a Bodhi tree in an area now known as Nepal. He emerged six years later with four simple, powerful insights that he taught as the Four Noble Truths. Siddhartha was subsequently named the Buddha, meaning "awakened one," and these insights have become the foundation of a now-popular philosophy of life as well as a sophisticated psychology of the mind.

In this chapter, I will use the Four Noble Truths as a framework for addressing the bad news and the good news about mortality. I will start with the bad news: mortality in its many manifestations (loss, aging, sickness, decay, and death) is a source of anxiety, unhappiness, and emotional suffering. I will then turn to the good news: with the requisite insights and practices, mortality can serve as an ally for living more fully, transcending suffering, and awakening to joy and happiness. You will find that Buddhism offers a process by which we can live gracefully in the face of mortality and experience happiness even knowing that life is brief and death is a certainty.

The First Noble Truth: Mortality and Suffering

The Buddha's first noble truth is that life invariably involves suffering.

We each live in a temporary span of time between birth and death. In the larger scheme of history, a lifetime is a brief and transient moment. Suffering arises from our efforts to deny the passing of time and the inevitability of personal death; suffering can also be traced to our human desire to hold on to what is good and sweet in life. We want positive experiences and nice things, and we strive to make them last. At the same time, we are naturally averse to unpleasant experiences and try to avoid them. We do not realize that joy and sorrow are two sides of the same coin; we do not recognize that we appreciate the sun precisely because sometimes it rains.

The Buddha recognized that suffering comes with the territory of living in a body that is subject to aging, illness, decay, and eventual death. Physically we are in a continual state of need for food, warmth, sleep, movement, shelter, and sexual release. In addition, we are constantly fighting the pull of gravity, which will get us down if we fail to counteract it with exercise and good posture. Living in a body can be challenging, if not exhausting, as we strive to maintain homeostasis in the face of a never-ending cycle of needs. When we do succeed in achieving a state of peace and contentment, such a moment is fleeting, as yet another need soon presents itself. As a result, we frequently experience discontentment, frustration, and dissatisfaction.

The first noble truth deals primarily with emotional suffering. The Buddha used the Sanskrit word *"Dukkha"* in reference to suffering. "Dukkha" is best translated as "pervasive emotional dissatisfaction" or as "chronic emotional discontent." There are many forms of such suffering. We suffer when …

- we lose a friend, loved one, or family member;
- a pleasurable experience comes to an end;
- our hopes are dashed or our expectations are not met;
- a love relationship ends or when we feel alone;
- we believe that the grass is always greener on the other side; and
- we experience existential despair—the type of suffering that leads us to question our place and purpose in life.

Of course, there is suffering associated with illness and physical pain. All of these forms of suffering involve loss of companionship, love, satisfaction, joy, health, and, ultimately, life itself. Mortality fits into this category of suffering in that it involves so many losses.

There is yet another dimension of suffering that I feel personally as I watch and read world news. This is the pain I feel regarding man's inhumanity to man. Whether it is ethnic cleansing, genocide, police brutality, racism, or war in the name of God or economic competition, I suffer for both the victims of violence as well as for those whose suffering causes them to perpetrate violence. I also suffer when I realize I have done things that have hurt others—especially those I love.

The Buddha identified three sources of Dukkha. The first is the suffering associated with knowing that aging, sickness, decay, and death are inevitable. We may resist this truth and wish for immortality, but deep down we know our time is limited and death is certain. Second, our likes and dislikes contribute to suffering. Many students of Buddhism have interpreted this source of suffering as desire. To not have what we like, to not like what we do have, and to lose what we once had all lead to suffering. The third source of suffering is our narcissism—that which causes us to believe that our self-identities or personal narratives are important, irreplaceable, and resistant to the passing of time and the effects of aging. Psychologists call this a defense mechanism—a way of dealing with unpleasant awareness, typically of painful or uncomfortable thoughts and emotions. We each construct an ideal self-identity—a false ego—to help cope with the awareness of vulnerability, insignificance, fragility, and uncertainty. But suffering is inevitable when self-identity conflicts with reality, which often and in so many ways unfolds beyond human control.

Considering the many sources of suffering, a Buddhist-inspired psychiatrist, Mark Epstein, suggests that we could use the term "trauma of everyday life."[1] He asserts that trauma happens to everyone because it is part of the precariousness of human existence. Trauma may be explicit—such as loss, death, accidents, disease, and abuse—or trauma may be subtle, as in the emotional deprivation of an unloved child. These forms of suffering can be traumatic in part because they are humiliating. Life can humiliate us by throwing curveballs that can take us by surprise, strip us of dignity, break our hearts, threaten to crush our spirits, and remind us of our cosmic insignificance and ultimate personal demise.

For most of my life, I have denied my mortality because I enjoy life and my fun tools for living fully—my sporty car, my kayak, my guitar, my bicycle, my skis, my motorcycle—and I want to hold on to the good feelings they engender. I want my love relationships to last indefinitely. I want my vitality, sexuality, and health to pass the test of time. I want to be forever young. I want to believe that death happens to other people but does not apply to me. I enjoy life, and I don't want it to end. I don't want to die. I want to be immortal.

Yet I am reminded repeatedly of loss and the passing of time. I have seen friends and relatives die, some seemingly before their times. Richard, for example, was a close friend—like a brother—with whom I had enjoyed skiing, bicycling, and social activities. He appeared to be a healthy, athletic man, but two days after one of our Sunday bicycle rides, Richard died unexpectedly in a locker room after a workout at a health club. He was an energetic forty-eight years old at the time.

I had already lost both of my parents when, during the past year, my younger brother, Marc, died unexpectedly. As administrator of his estate, I was confronted once again with mortality as well as many questions associated with life and death. I was left thinking, "What is the value of Marc's material possessions—including his exquisite sound-recording equipment and high-quality woodworking tools—and what do I do with them? Where do I scatter the ashes that are the only physical remains of his body? How do I reconcile outliving a younger brother? Is it acceptable to enjoy my blessed and successful life when a brother is denied a chance to live out his dreams?"

As a parent, I had to learn how to accept impermanence as my children grew up. In parenting, time moves both slowly and quickly. What seemed like an endless stage of young family life, when my children were little and dependent on me for virtually everything, became a high-speed chase through high school sports, educational trips to Europe and the Middle East, driving lessons, a valedictorian speech, college applications, foreign exchange programs, summer internships at the United Nations and *Seventeen* magazine, college graduations, and two magical marriages in Vermont that launched them into families of their own. I fathered them, I delivered one of them, I dedicated my life to them, I invested in them, and I love them. But there came a time when I had to let them go.

Parenting is all about loss and letting go. Letting go begins at birth; first we have to let our babies out of the womb. Loss continues as our children go to day care, school, summer camp, driver's education, college, and study-abroad programs. And, if they are lucky enough, they go on to find a life mate, get married, and start families of their own. In the backs of our minds as parents, we hope our children will outlive us when we face the ultimate letting-go moment—our own deaths. These loss experiences are the basis of both joy and sorrow for parents. We can only hope there is a way to move gracefully through these letting-go experiences and the losses they represent. Can Buddhism help us to live more gracefully with loss and mortality?

As a psychologist and therapist supervisor, I deal daily with loss, suffering, and impermanence. I counsel clients facing health challenges, broken hearts, and losses of jobs. I see marriages ending in divorces, and I work with children from broken and abusive families. All too frequently, clients have lost parents, beloved pets, or, perhaps most painfully, children. I train and supervise therapists in preparation for licensure, only to see them move on professionally. Loss seems to be a fact of life.

In one of my therapy cases, an adult patient named Rhonda, who was deeply connected to her active eighty-nine-year-old mother, presented this mortality dilemma: "How do I tell my mother that it is time for her to give up her driver's license? How do you tell someone you love that, for her safety as well as the safety of others, it is time to give up a significant source of freedom and mobility?"

In that therapy session, we exchanged stories about how liberating it was as adolescents when we learned to drive. She recalled that, as a new driver, she eagerly volunteered to go grocery shopping so that she could experience the freedom of driving a car. But then, in reference to her aging mother, Rhonda said, "I feel like my mother is *dying in pieces*."

Her words resonated with me as I thought, "We are all dying in pieces."

Indeed, science dictates that our bodies typically begin to decline about age thirty. At a snail's pace of 1 percent per year, the human body starts to become unhinged: wrinkles appear, the skin loses its tone and freshness, and muscles start to sag. The ratio of muscle to fat shifts. Auditory and visual acuity taper off. Bones become thinner and more brittle. Stamina and endurance decline, while blood pressure and cholesterol rise, marking the beginning of heart disease. Cellular mutations create malignant tumors that strike one in three people, mostly after age sixty-five.

And yet, from an Eastern medicine point of view, aging may account for only a small percentage of the total changes taking place inside the body. Because our thoughts and feelings influence every cell in the body, aging is a fluid and changeable process that can speed up, slow down, stop, and even be reversed. Deepak Chopra, a noted Eastern physician, describes the mind-body relationship this way:

> Our cells are constantly eavesdropping on our thoughts and being changed by them. A bout of depression can wreak havoc with the immune system; falling in love can boost it. Despair and loneliness raise the risk of heart attacks and cancer, thereby shortening life. Joy and fulfillment keep us healthy and extend life. This means the line between biology and psychology can't really be drawn with any certainty.[2]

This is a compelling and hopeful premise—and one that reinforces my priority on health and my attitude toward mortality.

I awakened to mortality at age nine, when I had a near-death experience. I was sick with croup, an infection of the upper airway that results in a cough and labored breathing, particularly at night. Although it occurs in only 5 percent of cases, I developed an airway obstruction and awoke one night unable to breathe or call for help. I remember banging on the wall of my bedroom in a desperate attempt to alert my parents to my breathing crisis, before I lost consciousness. My next memory is from the following morning, when I awoke strapped to a hospital bed after an emergency tracheotomy, which began in the ambulance. I later learned that our doctor rushed to our house, got in the ambulance, and performed the tracheotomy by cutting my throat with his pocketknife and inserting the cut-off cap of his fountain pen to open up my airway. I spent two weeks in the hospital hooked up to a phlegm-extraction machine that used a tube inserted into my throat. Restraints were used to keep me from instinctively pulling the tube out of my throat. Those two weeks in the hospital seemed like an eternity; I had plenty of time for reflection on the fragility of life and on gratitude for surviving a close call with death.

As intense as that near-death experience was, I experienced several other threats to my life. At the age of thirteen, for example, I was violently assaulted by a man who threatened to smash my head open with the brick in his hand if I did not do what he told me to do. At twenty-one, I was drafted into the military service at the height of the Vietnam War, when more than fifty-eight thousand young American men ultimately lost their lives.

When I was age ten, my parents separated and subsequently divorced. From my perspective as a child, I got the message that marriages do not necessarily last and that love can dry up like morning dew. In families of divorce, there is almost always loss, including loss of the intact family structure, loss of emotional and financial security, and typically a loss of consistent contact with at least one parent. As one of my child patients worded it in a poem about her parents' divorce, "Divorce seems like it chops you in half and you lose your pride as it floats off into space."

I look back now and see how these painful and frightening experiences have helped me appreciate life and not take it for granted. Since childhood I have been on a mission to make the most of life, use time wisely, and achieve my highest potential. Among other gifts, my adverse childhood experiences resulted in a high priority on health. My highest priority, second only to love, is health and energy. Am I just trying to live at my highest potential, or am I denying my mortality?

Carl Jung, a psychoanalyst and one of my virtual mentors, was interested in working only with patients who were at least thirty-eight years old or seriously committed to the work of liberation from suffering. His explanation was that until we reach the threshold of midlife, we have no sense of urgency about time. Before middle age, we can deceive ourselves into believing that we are immortal, that we have plenty of time to accomplish our goals in life, and that the future is wide open. However, as we become aware of the early signals of aging, such as those telltale gray hairs in men and women or receding hairlines in men, our motivation to make the most of our lives becomes more urgent. At that point, we become more interested in addressing our personal signals of suffering: stress symptoms, addictions, lack of fulfillment, depression, anxiety, marital discontent, and so on. When we awaken to the passing of time, our willingness to do the work of living fully reaches a new level of commitment. Our symptoms are wake-up calls to address the underlying suffering, and therefore, suffering is a gift that leads us to the possibility of happiness and fulfillment.

The Second Noble Truth: Desire and Attachment

In the second noble truth, the Buddha identifies desire and attachment as significant contributors to unhappiness. Desire and attachment are revealed in our efforts to hold on, preserve, and control our positive experiences. Desire and attachment can also be described as clinging, grasping, craving, and expecting, all of which contribute to frustration, disappointment, and unhappiness.

We not only seek and hold on to positive experiences, but also we want to reject and avoid negative experiences. Of course, this does not apply to actual danger or threats, which our survival instincts are wisely designed to avoid. But life and death are intertwined, and if we really understand this, we can flow more gracefully through the ups and downs, the joys and sorrows, and the hellos and good-byes of human experience.

Among our attachments is the phenomenon of clinging to self-identity. We hold on to who we think we are and who we know ourselves to be even in the face of contradictory evidence. This is a core source of Dukkha. We suffer because who we think we are so often conflicts with our life experiences. Mortality leads to suffering when we realize that nature will have its way with us no matter how smart we think we are.

The term "ego" has often been used to describe the self-identities we construct to help us cope with uncertainties and the traumas of everyday life. Whereas Sigmund Freud referred to the ego as a mediator between our primal urges—such as sexuality and aggression—and our consciences, ego has come to refer to the concept of a constructed self-identity. We invent narcissistic self-identities to help cope with death-related anxieties.

In a spiritual guidebook titled *The Four Agreements*, Miguel Ruiz uses the term "personal importance" in discussing attachment to one's ego. He explains that personal importance is the reason we tend to take things personally and suffer as a result. In Ruiz's words, "Personal importance, or taking things personally, is the maximum expression of selfishness because we make the assumption that everything is about 'me.'"[3]

Our ego causes us to resist change, including aging. To the ego, change is threatening because it implies a shift from what is known and familiar to what is unknown and unfamiliar. Our egos resist acknowledging the aging process and other life changes that challenge our self-identities.

Mortality is the ultimate threat to our egos because it involves letting go of how we see ourselves and who we think we are. Mortality results in the end of individuality and the beginning of nothingness. We defend against mortality through various mechanisms, such as denial, keeping busy, fantasies of invincibility, and using food, drugs, cosmetics, shopping, hoarding, and other addictive behaviors for comfort and reassurance.

Terror management theory (TMT) suggests that religion and belief in an afterlife were invented to ease our anxiety about mortality. TMT is derived from anthropologist Ernest Becker's 1973 Pulitzer prize–winning work of nonfiction, *The Denial of Death*, in which he argues that many human actions are taken to ignore or avoid the inevitability of death. On a cultural level, we create religions and belief systems to cope with mortality. We soothe ourselves with the promise of heaven to ease the anxiety of suspecting that there are no second chances when we die.

Implied in the second noble truth is that our suffering is largely self-induced. We contribute to our own suffering by going against nature when we deny mortality as we keep busy, engage in addictive behaviors to soothe our suffering, and hold on to our fictional self-identities. We need to see the cause-and-effect relationship between our thinking and our suffering. As we will see in the third and fourth noble truths, the way out of suffering is through using our brains to change the way we think.

My work as a psychologist gives me an opportunity to help my clients live fully and enjoy their lives even with the backdrop of mortality. To do this work effectively, and to avoid burnout and compassion fatigue, I must find the balance between supporting and letting go. I can be an inspiration, a friend, a witness, and a wise counselor, but I can't stop the flowing river of life. I must accept my limits to alter the cycle of life and death unfolding before me. I need to work through my own losses and find a way to remain buoyant in the sea of my patients' emotional turmoil. I must maintain optimism and a sense of humor so I can laugh with my patients and my staff as part of healing and dealing with despair. And I must know how to be at peace with my own mortality. How do I accomplish this? What personal work is required, and which practices do I need to implement? Does Buddhism offer any help with this?

The Third Noble Truth: Relief

Based on the idea that much of our suffering is caused by desire and attachment, the third noble truth advises that suffering can be transcended through wisdom and insight into the sources of suffering. We can step back from our habitual daily activities and witness, without judgment, the nature of our own minds, emotions, and actions. We can understand how we create distorted self-identities to cope with uncertainty, aging, and death. We can know that self-identity is a defense mechanism to cope with mortality and lack of control. These insights open the door to liberation from emotional suffering.

What the Buddha seems to be saying in the third noble truth is that nature has endowed us with the ability to train our minds to bring us higher levels of satisfaction and relief from emotional suffering. Our capacity for self-awareness, wisdom, and insight is an evolutionary inheritance and a gift we can use to transcend suffering.

Buddhism has become increasingly popular in the mental health and psychotherapy fields for just this reason. The promise inherent in the third noble truth is that by changing how we think, we can overcome the very emotional disorders and symptoms that bring people to therapy. Research shows that cultivating a positive and optimistic attitude about life promotes better health, lower cardiovascular disease, and longer life expectancies. A 2004 study, for example, looked at life expectancy among nine hundred older adults and discovered that those with optimistic outlooks had a 29 percent lower risk of early death than pessimists, and they were 77 percent less likely to die of heart attack, stroke, and other cardiovascular diseases.[4] In a large Mayo Clinic study, pessimists had a 30 percent greater chance of dying during a forty-year period than optimists.[5]

The third noble truth asserts that we can reduce suffering by recognizing its self-induced sources—desire and attachment—followed by meditative practices that help us let go of our egos. The result is more inner peace, contentment, and happiness. I find this assertion both liberating and discomforting. I like the idea that I can be happy, but I resist the idea that I must stop identifying with my own thoughts—that I must see my emotions as the result of my own thinking style and accept that I am not who I think I am. In other words, I do not like the idea that I create my own suffering, but I am pleased to know that I have the power to reverse this pattern.

The Buddha's instructions on how to heal from suffering and achieve emotional well-being dovetail with one of the most popular psychotherapy frameworks of today, namely cognitive-behavioral therapy (CBT). The CBT approach to therapy is based on an idea espoused in the 1980s by cognitive therapists Aaron Beck, Albert Ellis, and David Burns. Radical at that time, the idea was that how we feel is determined primarily by how we think: if we worry, we will feel anxious; if we think negatively, we will feel depressed. Based on this premise, CBT focuses on changing how we think. This is essentially the message of the third noble truth.

As I apply the third noble truth to myself, I realize not only that any emotional suffering I experience is self-induced but also that mortality can enhance my life. Mortality makes life precious, and I can use this awareness to savor my daily experiences and maintain a broader perspective. Seeing mortality as part of life enables me to keep myself in balance and cope more gracefully with life's unexpected curveballs.

I accept my mortality by understanding that living and dying are intertwined. I can see how death leads to birth as much as how birth leads to death. I expressed this insight in a poem that seemed to write itself.

Death and Rebirth

I die, and I am reborn,
Not just once,
But each night
And every day.

I fall peacefully
Into the dark unknown,
Losing consciousness
But trusting this nightly death.

Like a promise kept,
The dawning light awakens me.
My heart beats with joy.
And I am thankful for another birth.

Another birth?
Yes, another chance to live
And die again.
May this never end!

The third noble truth suggests that the process of overcoming suffering involves learning how to be with our thoughts and feelings, without judgment, to be neutral or curious without craving the good or rejecting the bad. This may seem passive, as though we have no control over our thoughts and feelings. However, this is an active process—hard work due to the force of habit. Buddhism teaches that we have a choice in every moment of behavior but that this requires awareness of our thoughts and feelings and the ability to witness them objectively, from outside our egos. Joseph Goldstein, a recognized Buddhist meditation teacher, puts it this way:

> If there's something pleasant, we want it; something unpleasant, we desire to get rid of it. But if instead of ignorance in the mind there is wisdom and awareness, then we experience feeling but don't compulsively or habitually grasp or push away. If the feelings are pleasant, we experience them mindfully without clinging. If unpleasant, we experience them mindfully without condemning. No longer do feelings condition desire; instead there is mindfulness, detachment, letting go. When there is no desire, there's no grasping; without grasping, there's no volitional activity of becoming. If we are not generating that energy, there's no rebirth, no disease, no old age, no death. We become free. No longer driven on by ignorance and desire, the whole mass of suffering is brought to an end.[6]

In other words, we have the ability to get off the stage on which we act from ego and step backstage, where we see life as a play in which we are the actors. From the backstage point of view, we can take off our masks and costumes and make choices as to how we will play our roles in our daily lives and how we will act each day in the world. From backstage, we can see that mortality is part of the story of life, and we can decide how we want to face it. As William Shakespeare expressed in *As You Like It*,

All the world's a stage,
And all the men and women merely players.
They have their exits and their entrances,
And one man in his time plays many parts.[7]

What happens when we see the true natures of our own suffering, and how can we define "relief from suffering"? Is relief the *absence* of suffering, or is there a more positive way of describing it? What will we have more of if we have less suffering?

As a psychologist and therapist supervisor, I have noticed that most patients are able to identify their problems, and most therapists are competent at diagnosing their symptoms. However, I find that both patients and therapists lack the vocabulary or imagery for vividly describing the goals or desired outcomes of therapy. Almost invariably, the goals are defined in terms of having less of the problem: to worry less, to be less depressed, to not be so compulsive, to not procrastinate, and so forth. My question is, what would you have *more* of if you had *less* of the problem?

This question of what will replace suffering is addressed in another innovative approach to therapy called solution-focused therapy. In this approach, something known as a miracle question is asked during the first therapy visit.

When you leave my office today, imagine that a miracle occurs. As a result you no longer have the problem we have been discussing. However, the miracle occurs tonight while you are sleeping, so you won't know that you have been relieved of the problem until you wake up tomorrow morning. What will you notice, what will be different, and how will you know that you have changed?[8]

The Dalai Lama, acknowledged as the contemporary global spokesperson for Buddhism, describes the alternative to suffering with terms such as "peace of mind," "inner strength," and "happiness." He asserts that these are birthrights, achievable through certain practices we will explore in the fourth noble truth. The Dalai Lama states that these qualities will be essential when it comes to facing mortality.

> When you grow old, or have an incurable illness, and when death finally comes, then your practice truly gives you some kind of inner guarantee. After all, death is part of life, there is nothing strange about it; sooner or later we all have to pass through that gate. At that time, whether or not there is a life after, it is very valuable to have peace of mind. How can we achieve peace of mind at such a moment? It is possible only if we have some experience in ourselves that will provide inner strength, because no one else can provide this for us—no deities, no gurus, and no friends. This is why the Buddha says you must be your own master.[9]

The Buddhist assertion that happiness is the purpose of life synchronizes with a recent movement in my profession known as positive psychology. Positive psychology is defined as the scientific pursuit of optimal human functioning. In this approach, it has been found that physical health and mental health can be enhanced by positive emotions, such as optimism, hope, gratitude, compassion, and awe. One finding is called the undo effect, which postulates that positive emotions seem to undo the physiological effects of stress and lead to greater happiness as well as better health and longer life.

The Fourth Noble Truth: The Way Out

The Buddha experimented with many approaches to the way out of suffering, including asceticism or living simply, deprivation of physical comforts and pleasures, and fasting. But the one practice he experienced as most helpful was meditation. Therefore, while there are multiple paths to overcoming suffering, the fourth noble truth emphasizes meditation as a path to liberation. No practice is as beneficial in facing mortality than sitting still and learning to be at peace with oneself in each present moment. With such practice, we become more comfortable with the quiet emptiness associated with death while simultaneously focusing on the now rather than on what is to take place in the future.

One of my psychology interns at the Center for Anxiety Disorders has a sign in her office bearing a quote attributed to Robert Frost: "The best way out is always through."[10] This simple statement is the essence of Buddhism and the fourth noble truth. In psychotherapy, we advise facing and moving through emotional suffering in order to transcend it. In the same way, meditation is a process of being with and moving through. Meditation helps us to experience, understand, and heal from our emotional suffering. Meditation helps us know our true essence and move through the tunnel of suffering to find peace and happiness on the other side.

The purpose of meditation is to discern or analyze the workings of the mind for the purpose of ending the production of self-induced suffering. But meditation as a path to liberation is not a single practice; it is a way of life. In fact, the Buddha articulated eight dimensions of meditative practice—a synergistic set of skills and attitudes that have become known as the Eightfold Path. The eight dimensions of meditation are:

1. right view (seeing things objectively),
2. right intention (having motivation and knowing where to aim, like a rudder on a ship that keeps us on course through the many distractions of daily life),
3. right speech (the quality of thoughts are expressed through speech; so honest, kind, and caring speech is most helpful),
4. right action (living by ethical principles, such as not killing or stealing),
5. right livelihood (making a living ethically, in a way that does not involve exploitation or harm),
6. right effort (willing to do the work),
7. right mindfulness (adopting a nonjudgmental approach to moment-to-moment experience), and
8. right concentration (regularly stepping away from habitual daily activities and responsibilities to make time for meditation).

The last two steps in the Eightfold Path are at the heart of meditation practice. We are advised to regularly practice meditation, which consists of focusing on one object of concentration, such as breathing or a special word or sound, while adopting a witnessing attitude toward intrusive thoughts. In this process, we learn to view our own thoughts as cognitive habits or patterns and not identify with them. Meditation also involves nonjudgmentally observing the role of desire and attachment in suffering. And finally meditation aims at allowing practitioners to let go of thoughts altogether so as to experience mental quietude and the eternal now.

Meditative practices involve psychological mechanisms called "exposure," whereby we confront the sensations of a feared experience in order to master it. By sitting still and doing nothing, we are, in effect, confronting the death experience. As we take time out of our daily activities to sit still, we detach from our egos and our habitual ways of thinking and defining ourselves. We trade doing for being. We exchange something for nothing. We go gently behind our thoughts to a timeless realm while transcending our separateness. Research on meditation finds that such practice renders us more able to accept change and ego loss without anxiety.

The exposure phenomenon in meditation desensitizes us to silence, stillness, and detachment. This is good practice for dying. We die each time we let go of separateness, hopefully finding this to feel safe and comfortable. The more accomplished we become at this, the more comfortable we can be with mortality.

Meditation does not prevent death, but it does counteract the *fear* of death. By practicing silence and detachment, we find ourselves in a simulated death state, where we aim to do nothing other than to experience the quiet, empty space between thoughts. If I had to guess what death is like, I would say that sounds like it.

At the same time, meditation helps us appreciate our aliveness. By focusing on a single point, such as breathing, a nature sound, or a special word or phrase, meditation sharpens our powers of concentration. This allows us to experience life more fully and with greater sensitivity. We become more able to engage in our moment-to-moment experiences, and as long as we are alive and well in the now, there is no death. There is only life *or* death.

One stumbling block in gracefully accepting mortality is when there is physical pain associated with acute illness or disease of the body. In such cases, modern medicine offers palliative care in the form of narcotic drugs that keep us more comfortable until death takes over. Theoretically, then, we can live without fear of death or dying. We are alive until we die, and if we are in pain from diseases common in old age, we can at least be comfortable. Logically, there is nothing to fear.

What if we can experience this consistently? What if we can go through life with an attitude of wonder in which every moment is new, when there is only now, and there is only life and no death until the moment we die? How would that change the quality of life during the time between birth and death? It seems to me that we would be happier, less stressed, and healthier. We might even live longer while having more energy for enjoying the life we have.

Scientific research on the effects and benefits of meditation has been extensive. Meditation has been shown to have widespread benefits in mental, emotional, physical, interpersonal, and spiritual realms. Mentally, the benefits include improved concentration, attention, focus, and peace of mind. Meditation helps clear the mind, much as a disk-repair program reorganizes a computer hard drive to render it more efficient and capable. Meditation is also an effective psychotherapy tool because the practice involves increased awareness of the relationship between thoughts, feelings, and behavior. Meditation is a powerful process for treating emotional conditions, such as anxiety and depression, as well as for personal growth.

Physically, meditation has documented benefits for reducing a multitude of ailments and illnesses, including high blood pressure, insomnia, chronic pain, epilepsy, premenstrual syndrome, fibromyalgia, psoriasis, eating disorders, and cancer. For our purposes in this chapter, the most compelling findings are that meditation slows down the aging process and increases longevity. This is good news for those of us who want to live longer and better. While it may not be desirable to simply add more years to our lives, meditation can help add more life to our years as well as improve quality of life.

There are many variations of meditation practice, but mindfulness—a concept from Buddhism—is now in vogue in the mental health field. I define "mindfulness" as "awareness of present experience without judgment." However, mindfulness, in my view, is not a practice. Rather, mindfulness is the outcome of various practices. Mindfulness is a way of being and interacting in daily life. There are many practices that can cultivate mindfulness, including techniques such as transcendental meditation, insight meditation, witnessing, flow, savoring, and yoga. I have practiced these methods and found that, among other benefits, they have helped reduce my fear of death and have enhanced my ability to live vibrantly in the present. I discuss them in detail in my book *Dancing with Fear*,[11] which I recommend as a next step for readers interested in exploring these practices.

Conclusion

In this chapter we explored the Four Noble Truths of Buddhism as a framework for addressing mortality. We saw that life involves suffering due to aging and the inevitability of decline and death. We found that meditative practices help us face mortality and aid us in living vibrantly and experiencing happiness.

We recognized the many ways in which we deny the anxiety associated with mortality, including the construction of self-identities—personal egos—that we rely on to cope with change, uncertainty, and the dark unknown of death. We found that there is a path to peace and happiness but that this requires accepting the truth and working through it in a new way. We found that the way out of emotional suffering is through meditative practices that train us to do away with ego and immunize us to the fear of death.

It is apparent to me that at the end of my life it will be easier for me to say good-bye if I have lived well. Will I be able to do this? I have had many chapters of life experience. I have fulfilled many of my dreams. I hope I have made a difference. I hope that I will leave behind something of value to others and that I will leave the world better than I found it. Meditation practices have allowed me to live in the present with less fear and more happiness. These practices have involved a kind of death rehearsal and ability to live more comfortably with impermanence. I accept mortality but focus attention on being alive and enjoying the now in each and every day.

1   Mark Epstein, *The Trauma of Everyday Life* (New York: Penguin, 2013).

2   Deepak Chopra, *Ageless Body, Timeless Mind: The Quantum Alternative to Growing Old* (New York: Harmony Books, 1993); E. Becker, *The Denial of Death* (New York: Free Press, 1973), 5.

3   Miguel Ruiz, *The Four Agreements: A Practical Guide to Personal Freedom* (San Raphael, CA: Amber-Allen Publishing, 1997), 48.

4   Michael Miller, ed., "Two-way street between depression and heart disease: Lifting depression can help the heart; exercise is essential," Harvard Mental Health Letter 25, no. 12 (June 2009): 1–3.

5   Beverly Brummett et al., "Prediction of all-cause mortality by the Minnesota Multiphasic Personality Inventory Optimism-Pessimism Scale scores: Study of a college sample during a 40-year follow-up." Mayo Clinic Proc. 81, no. 12 (December 2006): 1541–4.

6   Joseph Goldstein, *The Experience of Insight: A Simple and Direct Guide to Buddhist Meditation* (Boston: Shambala, 1976), 120.

7   William Shakespeare, *The Complete Works of Shakespeare* (New York: Barnes and Noble, 1994), 622.

8   Linda Metcalf, *The Miracle Question: Answer It and Change Your Life* (Bethel, CT: Crown House, 2004), 5.

9   Dalai Lama, *The Four Noble Truths* (London: HarperCollins, 1997), 128.

10 Robert Frost, "A Servant to Servants" (poem), *North of Boston* (New York: Holt, 1915), 66, line 55.

11 Paul Foxman, *Dancing with Fear: Controlling Stress and Creating a Life Beyond Panic and Anxiety* (Alameda, CA: Hunter House Publishers, 2007).

Paul Foxman, PhD

Paul Foxman was born and raised in a New York City neighborhood known at the time as Hell's Kitchen, a violent multicultural community where he suffered a traumatic childhood and adolescence. His first book, *Dancing with Fear: Controlling Stress and Creating a Life Beyond Panic and Anxiety*, begins with his personal recovery story and details the steps that can be taken to overcome trauma and live a vibrant and fulfilling life.

Paul became the captain of his public high school track team, marking the beginning of a lifelong commitment to health and fitness. His success as an athlete resulted in his recruitment by the Yale University track and field coach, who led the United States team at the 1964 Olympics in Tokyo. Paul never stopped training and stays in shape for his favorite outdoor recreational activities, which include skiing, kayaking, bicycling, hiking, and motorcycling.

After earning a bachelor's degree in psychology at Yale, Paul earned a PhD in clinical psychology at Vanderbilt University. Paul's professional training has included predoctoral internships at the Department of Psychiatry of Mount Zion Hospital in San Francisco and the Kennedy Child Study Center in Nashville, and training seminars at the San Francisco Psychoanalytic Institute.

Paul is the founder and director of the Center for Anxiety Disorders, a private outpatient practice and therapist training center in Burlington, Vermont. His books—*Dancing with Fear, The Worried Child, The Clinician's Guide to Anxiety Disorders in Kids and Teens*, and *Conquering Panic and Anxiety Disorders*—have resulted in an international speaking business in which he lectures on the topics of stress and anxiety at an average of thirty cities each year. As a speaker for the past fifteen years, Paul is known for his knowledge, sense of humor, and engaging speaking style. Paul's commitment to education is also reflected in cofounding the Lake Champlain Waldorf School in Shelburne, Vermont, which is now flourishing from kindergarten through high school.

Paul lives in Vermont, where he and his wife, Sheryl, raised two daughters. In addition to enjoying outdoor recreation, he appreciates the benefits of yoga and meditation. Paul's hobbies include writing and playing the guitar. If there is life after death, Paul hopes to be reincarnated as a successful musician and performing artist.

Contact Information:
e-mail: paulfoxman@aol.com
website: drfoxman.com

The Graves's a Fine and Private Place …

A Philosopher's Perspective on Mortality

David V. Mason, DMin

THE YORKSHIRE METAPHYSICAL poet and sage writer Andrew Marvell makes his case "To His Coy Mistress" by stating that in his pursuit of her he would take one hundred years "to praise thine eyes, 200 to adore each breast and 30,000 years" to extol the rest of her body and spirit. Alas, the pace of the seduction is damnably slow because his refined, desirable lady seems unable to recognize this fact: "Time's winged chariot [is] hurrying near."

Yes, even in the 1850s there were romantic hurdles. In our vernacular, he's telling her that both their romance and seduction are faltering, so "Let's get this show on the road. We're not getting any younger!" At their present snail's pace, their bodies will be food for the worms before they ever consummate their love. Though we only hear his voice, the presumed virgin has been acting as if time were of no concern to her and as though they could love more purely if their living, fleshy bodies weren't in the way, as if they could somehow transcend bodily functioning. Marvell disagrees, stating boldly that for his purposes, dead is dead.

> The grave's a fine and private place,
> But none, I think, do there embrace.[1]

Well, who wouldn't choose the vitality of life, romance, and sex over waiting for death? He writes in the formal manner of his day, but we know he's telling her, flatteringly, "Let's get with the program, dear. The bedroom awaits."

After nearly thirty years of teaching literature, philosophy, and religion at the college level, it's clear to me that the topics of death and dying are among the most thought-provoking and poignant issues for our students to explore. In a recent classroom discussion on this topic, one bright-eyed young coed, a math major, stated, "Wow! Talk about a common denominator." How right she is. Death awaits us all, and ignoring or postponing contemplation of this reality will not make it any less real when our time comes.

And we all know this, do we not? But how to approach this seminal topic (no slight to Marvell's lusty efforts with his lady) for our twenty-first-century sensibilities? Let's consider William Cullen Bryant's thoughtful poem "Thanatopsis," which literally means "one's view of death." Herein he urges us to view our own demise as a reward we have earned, and in this 1817 American romantic poem, Nature itself is speaking at the outset, and Nature takes the long view of both life and death. All who have lived in the ancient past have also died; it is the human estate, and so it is with all living things. Mortality means just that—we live, and then we die. Immortals, if such exist, are so different as to be beyond our ken. They are not what we are. Nature counsels us and claims all, from the pauper to the prince, because death is no respecter of persons. We are not being singled out by death for this special horror or our morbid anticipation of it. The "Solemn brood of care" shall pass for all that knew us. We are invited to, in Bryant's words, take our places in "that innumerable caravan," which ceaselessly moves toward "that mysterious realm" to which we all are headed.

Nature harvests all of us in due time, and no process could be more expected or natural. Yes, it brings up within us "Darker musings," but it does so "with a healing sympathy" despite the images that frighten us: "Of that last bitter hour … of the stern agony, and shroud, and all, and breathless darkness, and the narrow house (coffin)." If you begin to shudder and grow sick at heart when facing death—don't. Listen to the voice of Nature, for you will be embraced by the very soil that bore Adam and nourished you. Soon you will be resolved to the earth to "mix together with the elements" and be joined with the very ground, which then will be pierced by new living things: roots, leaves, grasses. The cycle of life will continue as it always has. Furthermore, you will not be alone. You will join all others in the great cortege of those who have died down through the ages. "All that breathe shall share thy destiny." You will not lose dignity in death; you could not ask for a more magnificent or serene resting place.

So then, Nature's instruction to us is to take our places in "the silent halls of death" and join the grand procession; others we know and love will follow shortly. Live so that you are not a captive or tormented slave; you should and will be "sustained and soothed by an unfaltering trust." Go to your grave as one going to sleep and pulling the blanket over you and lying down to "pleasant dreams."[2]

Beautiful, even calming, isn't it? It also reminds us of old Walt Whitman's injunction for people who may read his work or remember him after his death. "If you want me again, look for me under your boot soles."[3] That is, beneath the leaves of grass, of course.

Compare this outlook with the thanatopsis of the hard-drinking Welshman Dylan Thomas as he renders these famous lines:

> Do not go gentle into that good night,
> Old age should burn and rage at close of day;
> Rage, rage against the dying of the light.[4]

Yes, death is the common enemy, but Thomas urges us not to accept it but to instead defeat it. But how? Old age and decrepitude overcome us, or death may strike quickly; and as one radio sports commentator in Houston quipped, "Father Time is undefeated." Driving to the local funeral home and punching the proprietor in the face is probably not going to help, though Thomas might have tried it. We learn in the sixth and final stanza that the speaker has an immediate and personal stake in the matter: His own father is dying. He is less belligerent toward his own death than that of his dad, it seems. Wistfully, he admits, "… wise men at their end know dark is right …" The night is somehow "right," but its darkness surely symbolizes death. Seems contradictory, doesn't it? Even the carousing Welshman acknowledges that acquiescing to the inevitable is wiser than adolescent raging against it.

Since this battle cannot be won, could this have been John Donne's motivation for writing "Death be not proud …"? Is death arrogant in its ceaseless laboring, undefeated in its extinguishing of all life? At the end of Holy Sonnet 10, he stands his ground as an Anglican clergyman, declaring,

> One short sleep past, we wake eternally,
> And death shall be no more; Death, thou shalt die.[5]

And what of Shakespeare's melancholy Dane who mused, "To die, to sleep—to sleep, perchance to dream—ay, there's the rub, for in this sleep of death what dreams may come …"? Here Hamlet seriously contemplates suicide, as if living were barely worthwhile in his present state. "To be or not to be, that is the question …"[6] Let's recall also Keats' magnificent "Ode to a Nightingale." Written in 1819, two years before his death at the age of twenty-five, he knew death was coming for him; he could feel it in his tuberculosis-ridden body. He both envied and feared the short-lived nightingale while listening to its dark, entrancing song. The poet then addressed the nightingale: "Darkling, I listen; and for many a time I have been half in love with easeful death." And further, "… now more than ever seems it rich to die."[7] The allure of ending it all is strong, but herein we also see fear as a pervasive theme, as in many of these poetic musings.

When we consider our own deaths, is the major issue really fear? Is it true, as Freud contended, that the foundation of our personal and communal religion is our fear of death as well as the need to be cleansed of the dirtiness of life? Anaïs Nin has said, "People living deeply have no fear of death."[8] My own experience has been different, frankly. People can and do fear death no matter how accomplished, famous, wealthy, or spiritually profound they may be.

Writing during the American Civil War but oblivious to it, reclusive poet Emily Dickinson had a deep-seated preoccupation with death and dying; one of her curious poems on the subject is "I Heard a Fly Buzz When I Died." With loved ones gathered around her, as she lies on her imagined deathbed with sharply diminished perception, her last will and testament completed, a common fly interposes itself between her and "the light" from the window. She writes,

> And then the windows failed—and then I could not see to see....[9]

Upon rereading this piece, I thought of the many hospice chaplains and workers who deal with imminent death on a daily basis. One told me that so many people think (and hope) that death will be an expansive, transcendent experience akin to the oft-spoken "I saw my whole life flash before me" comment. He said that in the hospice bed at the actual moment of dying, the person about to expire, so limited in sight and hearing, can sense only the immediate and miniscule right before they pass, if they can sense anything at all. There is no Panavision, no fanfare—just the organs giving up, the relaxing of the bowels and bladder, and, soon, rigor mortis.

Not much that's romantic in that, is there?

In college classrooms, responses from both younger and older students have left lasting impressions on me over the years. Generic secular phrases such as "the great beyond" and "the other side" are common. The "RIP" on tombstones seems innocuous to many, but it belies the fact of actual death by stating that the deceased are merely resting, not stone-cold dead. There are always some who say that we should not contemplate death until we have to; "Concentrate on living this day, this moment," they say. "Carpe diem!" one sophomore offered in an American literature class. When I asked her if she knew what that phrase meant, she paused and said, "Seize the damn carp, right?" Others say that because we are the only animals on this planet that believe and hope, our believing and hoping is, finally, self-serving while attempting to be life-affirming. Death, that problematic common denominator, may be our natural estate, but it's unhealthy, even morbid, to dwell too much upon it. These are outlooks I've heard from quite a few literature and philosophy classes over the years.

This reminds me of film critic and social commentator Susan Sontag's purview: "Death is the obscene mystery, the ultimate affront, the thing that cannot be controlled. It can only be denied."[10] In other words, change the subject. Euphemisms now abound even in newspapers, which readers in the past viewed as objective, unvarnished purveyors of the facts. One supposes that the editors are trying to be upbeat even about death. Note that today the word "obituary" often does not appear; nor does the archaic word "necrology." Today, the *Houston Chronicle* uses the title "Life Tributes" for its listings of those who have just died. You know, like the life tributes given recently to comedians Jay Leno and Steve Martin. They attended their own gala ceremonial tributes because they are alive, not dead.

When a comedian flops on stage, he "dies." Where there should be laughter, there is the silence of the grave. One of my students mentioned Woody Allen's quip: "I'm not afraid to die. I just don't want to be there when it happens."[11] Even after all these years, the Woodman is still good for a few chuckles. As experienced teachers know, with all the electronic gadgets the kids try to use in class today, it's a constant struggle to keep their attention. Modern technology and virtual reality have led some students to wonder if "virtual death" might be interesting to explore. They don't want to actually "go there," but simulating the death experience, they opined, would be cool. Medical flatlining and near death experiences (NDEs) have been hot topics for the last four decades, and such interest is still afoot among students. The appeal seems to be that NDEs allow you to put your foot in the water without diving in, and the NDE doesn't really put the student at risk. But as one large, rustic fellow, a basketball player in my Philosophy 1301 class, stated succinctly, "Yeah, but near death ain't death." Quite right.

Several students have mentioned Joseph Campbell, who is fond of telling the tale of the Sioux Indians who would ride into battle shouting, "It's a good day to die."[12] They knew they could be facing death momentarily, but they weren't hanging on. George Orwell stated his humanistic attitude that life's struggle must continue and that "death is the price of life." Franz Kafka, that troubled Czech philosopher and tormented man of letters, said simply, "The meaning of life is that it stops."[13]

The rejection of death and roadmaps for life after death go back even further in Western culture than Pythagoras (circa sixth century BCE) who taught that your immortal soul, the real you, lives on by taking another form via transmigration of the soul; one could wind up in the next life as an animal or another human. And thus he was a vegetarian, because he couldn't stand the thought of possibly eating his mother. He also believed that he was at least part divine, fathered by no less than Hermes (Mercury in his Roman garb), and he often wore a diadem when teaching. It was said of him that he had a thigh made of pure gold—don't ask how that worked. He was not merely a mathematician; along with his wife, he was the undisputed leader of his own deeply religious sect on the island of Samos in the Aegean—the Pythagoreans. He was really good with triangles, too.

Then along came Socrates, the great father of Western philosophy who told his students, "To fear death, gentlemen, is no other than to think oneself wise when one is not, to think one knows what one does not know. No one knows if death may be the greatest of all blessings for a man, yet men fear it as if they knew that it is the greatest of evils."[14] He also believed in the immortality of the soul, which his greatest student, Plato, expanded and deepened into the tripartite soul (reason, spirit, appetite). This strongly influenced Freud twenty-three centuries later and helped form the model for his ego, superego, and id as the psychological breakdown of the human psyche.

Aristotle, Plato's young genius at the Academy, also believed in the soul; but unlike his teacher, Aristotle stated that your soul dies when you die. All living things have a soul (animus, anima); that's what animates us; and when we die, it's because our soul has lost its vitality and cannot keep our bodies or itself alive. In Near Eastern cultures, we learn of the soul's journey in the afterlife; it is usually tortuous and fantastic, and the soul usually heads toward judgment by the gods. The rejection of death as final has been widespread for many centuries; so has the hope, even presumption, of an afterlife. Death is not really death but a transition—a continuation of the path ahead that can't be seen although it's there.

One ancient Hellenistic philosophy that directly addresses death and dying is Stoicism. The best-known exemplars are a former slave, Epictetus, and none other than Marcus Aurelius, Roman emperor from 161–180 CE. While not all Stoics can be characterized neatly and quickly, it's accurate to say that their emphasis was on self-reliance and duty. An important duty Roman Stoics felt they had near the end of life was to die with integrity and dignity. Their outlook on death was shaped by their model for dying the good death—none other than Socrates. He did not fear death, and he was ready for it; he even prepared his friends and students for the ending of his life. He accepted the state-mandated death sentence even though his friends, including Plato, would have gladly paid off his jailer and sent their beloved teacher into life-saving exile.

But of course, Socrates would have none of it. He refused to play fast and loose with the truth, and he would not dishonor himself or his beloved Athens by escaping the judgment against him. He drank the hemlock and died a sickeningly slow death as his friends watched in horror. Was it suicide? A state-sanctioned execution? The debate continues.

One heralded twentieth-century work that has directed my personal development is Victor Frankl's important book *Man's Search for Meaning*. Herein the famed Viennese psychiatrist puts forth his theory of logotherapy.

189

He states that the primary and most therapeutic purpose of our lives is to find meaning. Doing this can cure neurosis and make life bearable—even fulfilling. He survived a Nazi concentration camp but watched many of his fellow prisoners die from malnutrition, disease, torture, or the gas chamber. He understood that finding meaning in suffering was essential for his own survival and that the practice of seeking meaning was a deed in itself. It's your responsibility to determine the meaning of your own life by utilizing hyperintention and hyperreflection. To find meaning in your suffering is to find meaning in your experience of living and dying. Life, death, and meaning are inextricably linked.

The term "Meaning," in Frankl's estimate, refers to a very down-to-earth concept and practice. In his essay "Case for a Tragic Optimism," he states that we will benefit from an optimistic perspective on life no matter how unbearable our hardships might be. Accomplish something, experience something, or encounter someone—these are the three ways to find meaning and turn personal tragedy into triumph. Suicide can be the result when no real meaning, and thus no hope, exists in someone's life. Both meaning and purpose can be found in your suffering if you choose to search for it. This path can overtake the "tragic triad" of pain, guilt, and death, which is common to us all.[15]

A real-life example of this comes from the world of Hollywood and Louis B. Mayer, movie mogul par excellence. There has been no more powerful personage in show business history, and he was the acknowledged star-maker and megaproducer of the famed MGM Studios. He was both powerful and highly accomplished, but on his deathbed in October 1957, with family members surrounding him, his last spoken words were these: "Nothing matters … nothing matters."[16]

Victor Frankl would likely respond, "Find the meaning. Make it matter."

By the way, I've also been an ordained progressive Protestant minister for the last thirty-five years. During this time span, I've presided at more than fifty funerals and memorial services—some for people I've known but also some for people I'd never met: relatives, friends of family, and referrals. In my experience, the most common thing spoken by those at a memorial service is "He made his peace."

You've heard this too, but what does it mean? He cleared his personal debts? He forgave those who wronged him and asked forgiveness from those he'd wronged? He made his peace with God, having repented of his sins? All the above? Many, it seems, say this intending to mean that Ol' Joe in the coffin had somehow readied himself for death.

The second most common utterance at funerals is "We know he's in a better place now." To that some will add "Right, Padre?" (Well, what can the minister say to that? *No, I know what kind of life Ol' Joe lived, and he's probably roasting on a spit in Hell right now*?) You tell me that he's in a better place, but that's not really our call, is it? Of course, I play my ministerial role properly and offer an understanding nod, adding an expression of sympathy. Saying these things to the presiding clergyman seems to help family and friends engage their grief and cope with their loss. Such statements may also be their own declaration of faith in the face of death.

A service for the dead is not the time for levity or hypocrisy. Done well, the ritual is usually a time of hushed awe as mourners huddle together against the presence of death before them. And, of course, no one wants to speak ill of the dead. Why? Is it because we fear the dead one might hear us and haunt us if we do? Even today superstitions and folkloric tales of ghosts or the spirit of the newly deceased hovering nearby are told. To me this smacks of more rejection of death and its powerful claim on us. Such tales usually grow out of an inability to accept that the loved one is really gone, never to return. Marcel Proust put it this way: "People do not die for us immediately, but remain bathed in an aura of life which bears no relation to true immortality but through which they continue to occupy our thoughts in the same way as when they were alive."[17]

But, of course, they are not traveling abroad. They are dead. Pardon my cynicism, but religious faith usually offers a sweet afterlife if we join the believers' private club/church and follow their rules. Only then will God open the gates of heaven for us; so their creeds usually state. Quietly but skeptically, I've wondered if those who weep and grieve at a loved one's memorial service aren't actually grieving for themselves and their own impending deaths. The memorial service done well allows people to grieve yet hold dear their memories of the departed. It expresses, at least in a Christian context, the hope and promise of heaven. Clergy performing the memorial or funeral service *must* proclaim the words of John 11:25,26

(RSV): "I am the resurrection and the life; he who believes me, though he dies, yet shall he live." This is not optional for Christian clergy. Like it or not, the clergyperson must proclaim this boldly even if he or she has personal doubts of its veracity.

Wouldn't we all like to live peacefully, if not excitingly, after we pass through this vale of tears? Notions of eternity, with its unendingness beyond our ken, are scary to ponder—even more so the eternal torments of hell with which the church has horrified and goaded believers for centuries. There may be more comfort in simply believing that "It is finished,"[18] to borrow that well-known saying from the cross. You're done. No more worries or striving for tomorrows. But resting in peace is not resting as you and I know it; it's literal nonexistence—the obliteration of our identity, of our very life force, if you will. And so we ponder and worry, do we not? An example from my own life might help here.

Carmine Infantino, a renowned comic book illustrator, left this world in 2013 at age eighty-seven. Three years ago, he treated me to a fine Italian lunch near his home on East Forty-Sixth Street in Manhattan, and during our time together we discussed a wide range of topics. I am interested in truly artistic people and their creative processes, which he knew. After a while, we talked religion; and he mentioned that he was a lapsed Catholic, which I knew. Near the end of our meal together, he paused over his crème brûlée and looked at me. I must admit I was taken aback by what he asked: "What happens when we die?"

He was curious, sincere, and somehow innocent. His health was failing, and he simply wanted to know, so he asked the clergyman sitting across from him. His face searched mine. I swallowed hard and then muttered that I didn't *know* but only believed and hoped. I told him I believed that what we are now—how we live and know ourselves today—is not the final term of our existence. After giving him this honest, off-the-cuff response, I wish I could have lunch with him again and respond differently to his question, but I can't. Now my friend Carmine does not need to ask that question anymore.

To speak with certainty about afterlife now, in my mature years, somehow seems the height of presumptuousness. Some twenty-seven years ago, Billy Graham was a guest on the *Tonight Show* with Johnny Carson, and the evangelist boldly stated that he would be happy to die right that moment; he was ready, and he knew beyond any doubt that he was headed for heaven. Carson had no clever rejoinder, and the audience gave Graham a light, awkward smattering of applause. My response? It set my teeth on edge to hear him say that—enough to say aloud to the TV screen, "No, Billy, you don't know. You believe and you hope, just like the rest of us." I'm not sure why my revulsion at his statement has stayed with me, but it has. How odd that I've spoken with the same certainty at memorial services, as have the clergy at all the memorial and funeral services I've ever attended. Such internal contradictions linger within me; and I've learned to accept them, bowing to the complexity of the issues at hand.

We live on through our children, through our legacies, and in the memories of those who knew us well. We want our efforts and our lineages to go forth, to live on in this world and do good things: uphold the family name and reputation, and live on proudly as long as life endures. But still we are personally left alone and tormented with the stark reality of death. Anxiety about our deaths is the inescapable human condition. We are the only living creatures on the earth who contemplate our deaths and fear our mortal ends. Though his calm eyes seem so wise, my four-year-old Irish setter, McStinko, doesn't seem concerned at all with his impending death, though I've explained it all to him several times.

So what are my own views on death and dying? Should we fight against death? How, and how much? Rage, Rage? Battling the inevitable seems an adolescent response. One of my students said, "Each of us will die. Deal with it." Life is surely bound up with meaning, and so is death. Anticipating, even embracing, death as the final natural step in life's journey should bring a depth of meaning to our lives and help us to engage our deepest human and spiritual yearnings. Dealing with life leading to death, the way things really are, should finally give us more satisfaction than avoidance offers.

I like to return to one of my favorite dramas of the American theatre, Thornton Wilder's *Our Town*. The stage manager serves as folksy philosopher, raconteur and narrator, stating:

> We all know that something is eternal. And it ain't houses
> and it ain't names, and it ain't earth, and it ain't even the
> stars ... everybody knows in their bones that something

is eternal, and that something has to do with human beings. All the greatest people ever lived have been telling us that for five thousand years and yet you'd be surprised how people are always losing hold of it. There's something way down deep that's eternal about every human being.[19]

I cannot state it any better. It's a mystery to us—perhaps the ultimate mystery among many mysteries and miracles in this world. Mainline Protestants, in my experience, don't care much for miracles. We prefer rational explanations, yet I'm convinced that miracles and mysteries loom around us and within us. Accepting this, my thoughts now move to a statement from the former homiletics professor of Union Theological Seminary in New York City, the great Harry Emerson Fosdick: "I would rather live in a world where my life is surrounded by mystery than live in a world so small that my mind could comprehend it."[20]

You and me both, Harry. While miracles and mysteries abound, it may simply be that our faith is a bridge across the gulf of death—a narrow, rickety footbridge between two mountains with a great, yawning chasm beneath—one that each of us must traverse alone. I do not know; how could I know? This image frightens me, and I wonder if others feel this same fear. Am I truly alone on that bridge, or are others with me? Maybe they too are deciding whether it's better just to jump off that bridge and be done with it.

---

1   Andrew Marvell, "To His Coy Mistress," *The Oxford Book of English Verse, 1250–1900* (Oxford University Press, Arthur Quiller Couch, ed. 1919), 357.

2   William Cullen Bryant, "Thanatopsis," *American Literature: The Makers and the Making,* Vol. 1 (St. Martin's Press, Inc., 1973), 214–215.

3   Goodreads, Walt Whitman, > Quotes, accessed September 15, 2015. https://www.goodreads.com/quotes/256900-if-you-want-me-again -look-for-me-under-your-boots.

4   Dylan Thomas, *Norton Anthology of English Literature,* Vol. 2, Revised (New York, 1968), 1914.

5   John Donne, "Death Be Not Proud," *The Holy Sonnets of John Donne* (London: J. M. Dent and Sons for Hague and Gill, 1938), 10.

6   William Shakespeare, "Hamlet," Act 3, Scene 1, *The Complete Illustrated Shakespeare* (New York, W. H. Smith Publishers, Inc., Gallery Books, 1989).

7   John Keats, *Norton Anthology of English Literature,* Vol. 2, Revised (New York, 1968), 532–535.

8   BrainyQuotes.com/quotes/authors/a/Anais_Nin.html.

9   Emily Dickinson, *American Literature: The Makers and the Making, Vol. 2* (St. Martin's Press, Inc., 1973), 1249.

10 BrainyQuotes, Susan Sontag > Quotes, accessed July 23, 2015. http://www.brainyquote.com/quotes/authors/s/susan_sontag_2.html.

11 BrainyQuotes, Woody Allen > Quotes, accessed September 4, 2015. http://www.brainyquote.com/quotes/quotes/w/woodyallen148186.html.

12 Moyers and Company, Joseph Campbell > Quotes, accessed October 2015.   http://billmoyers.com/content/ep-4-joseph-campbell-and-the-power-of-myth-sacrifice-and-bliss-audio/.

13 Reddit, Franz Kafka > Quotes, accessed September 30, 2015. https://www.reddit.com/r/quotes/comments/1xt9xy/the_meaning_of_life_is_that_it_stops_franz_kafka/.

14 Proverbia, Socrates > Quotes, accessed September 24, 2015. https://En.proverbia.net/citasautor.asp?autor=16836.

15 Goodreads.com/work/quotes/Man's Search for Meaning quotes/Victor Frankl.

16 AZ Quotes, Louis B. Mayer > Quotes > accessed September 24, 2015. http://www.azquotes.com/author/28531-Louis_B_Mayer.

17 Goodreads, Marcel Proust > Quotes, accessed September 24, 2015. http://www.goodreads.com/quotes/31680-people-do-not-die-for-us-immediately-but-remain-bathed

18 Gospel of John, *Revised Standard Version of the Holy Bible* (Oxford University Press, Inc., 1973), 1304.

19 Goodreads, Thornton Wilder > Quotes, accessed September 24, 2015. https://goodreads.com/work/quotes/3119231-ourtown.

20 BrainyQuotes, Harry Emerson Fosdick > Quotes, accessed September 12, 2015. https://*brainyquotes.com*/quotes/author/h/harry_emerson_fosdick.html.

David V. Mason, DMin

Dr. David V. Mason is originally from northeastern Ohio but then moved to the Washington, DC, area, where he earned his BA from George Mason University in Fairfax, Virginia, in 1976. He earned his master of divinity degree from Union Seminary/Columbia University in New York City in 1979, and his doctor of ministry degree was granted by the San Francisco Theological Seminary in 1985.

He has lived in the Houston, Texas, area since 1979 and taught both literature and philosophy at the University of Houston, the University of St. Thomas, Houston Community College, and Wharton County Junior College.

He has served several churches in the greater Houston area and also worked as a Protestant chaplain jointly at the University of Houston and Texas Southern University. His specialty has been ministry with singles in churches and pastoral care. Dave has served Disciples of Christ, United Church of Christ, and Presbyterian churches throughout his thirty-six years of ordained ministry.

Dave is also the author of four ethical mysteries for young adults, and he has enjoyed speaking across the nation at schools, churches, and business settings on decision ethics for youth and for life.

Contact Information:
e-mail: davidvmason@yahoo.com
website: www.davidvmason.com

LIFE, DEATH, AND THE LIFE AFTER

A Muslim's Perspective on Mortality

M. Javed Aslam MD, FRCP(C)

FOR EVERY BIRTH that we rejoice, there is a death that we mourn. Death is inevitable, but death is also indispensable. The old must wither and die to be replaced by the young and new; that is the law of God, the law of His universe. For some death comes way too soon, like a heartbreakingly painful nightmare both for the one who is dying and for those who are left behind. For others death is like a long-awaited friend who's come to take one's hand to help one across the threshold into the unknowable void. In some ways, death is a dreadful enemy, relentless in her pursuit, inescapable, and merciless. In other ways, death is the elixir that kills pain and suffering, and that ends the misery when life can no longer be cherished or even desired.

Soldiers and medical professionals share the unenviable task of watching death and the dying from up close—soldiers fighting to kill before they themselves are killed and physicians thrashing around to save the dying. Victory for one means coming back home alive; victory for the other, to send someone back home alive.

Some medical specialists never encounter dying patients; others make a living caring for those who have already found out how much of life remains. People certainly die from all sorts of causes. Even a bite from the wrong kind of mosquito can kill. But specialties like hematology and oncology, the latter of which was my practice area, and a few others deal in large part with illnesses that have no cure. Being thankful for small and temporary miracles is often the only joy available to those who work in these fields.

Medical professionals, including physicians, often get emotionally attached to their patients. There is always great joy in walking into the exam room to tell a patient about the shrinkage of a tumor or the disappearance of abnormal cells. At the same time, one cannot help but feel the pain and disappointment of a course of treatment that made the patient deathly ill without producing a discernable benefit.

Sharing with a patient the abnormal results of a test—a biopsy, perhaps—is never easy; but to tell a young person, who is just beginning to visualize life's great potential, of a diagnosis of a malignancy is like changing one's dream into a nightmare. It is a fine line—one that is always hard to walk. On the one hand, there is a duty to be utterly frank and honest; on the other, there is an obligation as a human being to be comforting and humane. Physicians slowly learn how to deliver the bad news gently to lighten the jolt. Patients quickly learn to read the physician's face like an open book. Somewhere in the middle, the minds do meet; what needs to be said gets expressed, with or without words; and what needs to be heard does reach its mark.

Physicians offer words of comfort and encouragement, citing cases of other patients with similar illnesses having great results. It is like trying to open a window in a dark and stuffy room. It is merely a ray of light, but more often than not, it does work to provide a glimmer of hope. One marvels at the human spirit as it rises from a state of gloom to reach out to hope with courage and determination.

"When can we get started, Doc?"

"As soon as we get all your blood results." The physician feels a genuine wave of determination. For a few moments, at least, one can sense joy returning. There is effort to be made, work to be done. We are not giving up. We are soldiers in battle, ready to step out. We shall fight; we shall overcome.

Physicians are taught to be professional—a term that is usually well understood by physicians but hard to define in concrete terms. Physicians must be honest with their patients, no doubt; but as with many things, truth can be conveyed in many different ways. A friend of mine going for surgery on his spine asked the surgeon if he should be aware of any complications. Most surgeons I know would voluntarily discuss with the patient the possible complications as well as the expected positive results. The surgeon's honest but terse response to my friend was "Well, you could die." That response, in my judgment, was not just cruel and condescending; it was unworthy of a medical professional. Patients certainly ask questions that may be difficult to answer without saying something cruel, but usually there are ways to be both truthful and kind. For most surgeries, there can be complications short of death that can be shared with the patient to start with. Finally one can add that, of course, there is always a chance that a patient may die. It is also possible that physicians have not had comprehensive training or discussions on the art of answering patients' questions truthfully, kindly, and humanely.

It is the grace and mercy of almighty God that the times of our deaths remain hidden from us. Even when we are deathly ill, we hope to go home as soon as we are well. This hope of waking up the next day, day after day, is what distinguishes us from a person on death row. How miserable life would be if we were not totally oblivious to the time, place, and manner of our death!

Whenever a patient with a malignancy asked me how long he or she had to live, I usually told him or her that any number I could offer would likely be too far off the mark to be of any practical value. I would then share with the patient what I knew to be a known range in patients with the same illness, usually starting with the longest end of the range. And I would often end with a question, such as "And how about trying to add a few months or years to that statistic—wouldn't that be an effort worth making?"

Right after being diagnosed with a terrifying disease, the patient is often in a rather fragile state of mind. That usually is not the time to start talking about how long a patient has to live, which is something a physician cannot know for certain anyway. Just as in other calamities, the first obligation, as a physician and as a human being, is to provide hope and encouragement without giving unrealistic expectations. The natural processes of the human mind will usually allow the patient to arrive at a balance between optimism and pessimism.

Sometimes a patient will bluntly ask about survival and insist on knowing the chances of success of treatment. Those questions ought to be answered truthfully, of course.

Any oncologist in practice for a decade or more will encounter patients whose reactions span the entire range of human emotions after the diagnosis of a life-threatening illness. Some malignancies, because of the body parts they involve, can cause severe and intractable physical pain.

Others, while not physically painful, can be just as hard to endure because of the malignancy's reputation of dismal outcomes. Most oncologists can narrate stories of great courage and endurance exhibited by their patients—some more than others.

Lessons Learned

Having been retired for a very long time, the details of my patients' illnesses are somewhat hazy, but I remember some who showed strong demeanor and courage under very difficult circumstances. A lady, possibly in her fifties, was referred for the treatment of a malignancy. She came accompanied by her husband. Both she and her husband were the kind of people one would like to have living next door—kind, soft-spoken, amicable, churchgoing people. Her family said they had been told she had only a few months to live.

After discussing the different options, I suggested a course of treatment. We started the therapy, and the patient responded very well. A few years passed, and during follow-up visits, she was relatively well. There were recurrences, but they were brought under control. But as is usually the case, the malignancy came back with a vengeance. She tried staying at home as long as possible; but, as expected, she ended up coming back to the hospital with severe difficulties.

I stood next to my patient's bed as she lay there breathing with difficulty in spite of the oxygen. Apart from asking her if she was comfortable or if she needed something for pain, I did not have much to say. The expression on her face was more like that of someone who had stopped to rest after a run than of someone who was at the end of her life. She reached out to touch my hand, and I could sense that she wanted to say something. I bent down so I could hear; I thought perhaps she needed something. What she said I was totally unprepared for.

"Don't be sad," she said. "I know you have done your best. It's my time to go." Thoughts went racing through my head, but not one that I could share with her. Of course I was thankful for her kind words. I am certain she could see that in my face. All I could think to do was take her hand in my both hands and hold it, perhaps providing some warmth. I mumbled something and then quickly asked if she was comfortable. She said she was, under the circumstances. Not long after that, she passed away.

People may not know this, but physicians, especially in specialties like oncology, do share the ups and downs of their patients—elation at the success of a course of treatment, and a sense of loss, defeat, and helplessness when all seems to be failing. As human beings, we cherish relationships. A mother and her child, a father and daughter, brothers and sisters—these are not mere biological ties. They are also ties of closeness; of having laughed and cried together; of sharing each other's circumstances; of knowing each other's vulnerabilities, weaknesses, and strengths; and of mutual competitions with fair dealings and unfair advantages. The physician–patient relationships, especially when the life of a patient is at stake, have their own moments—some happy, some sad. There are defeats as well as victories; sometimes far too brief a victory is followed by an inevitable defeat.

Almost twenty years after the passing of the patient who told me not to be sad, I was invited to speak at a church. As I was standing and watching the audience file in, a young lady walked up and asked me if I had my oncology practice in a certain part of town long ago. I answered in the affirmative. She said that she had been a child then and that I had taken care of her mom. When she started to tell me the details of her mother, the episode came rushing back to me. I vaguely remembered seeing a child in the room when I went to talk to the family—the hard task that every physician has to perform when the patient dies. In the few minutes we had before my presentation, we talked about her mom. I told her how special her mom had been—how gracious as well as courageous. She told me that her mom appreciated the care I provided, and I could see that grace and courtesy certainly ran in the family—like mother, like daughter.

We all live and die. While the times, places, and manners of our deaths always remain hidden from us, how we spend the time we have is usually pretty much in our control. Many measure the success or failure of a life by the fame and fortune achieved. Others may use different measures, such as professional recognition. All of those are fine achievements worth commemorating. The vast majority of us, however, live our lives in quiet anonymity, with love and honor within our families; and when we die, the memories in the hearts and minds of our children, grandchildren, friends, and relatives are just as precious and satisfying and reflective of lives well-lived.

The worst mortality-related circumstance for a physician has to be when the physician can almost certainly cure the patient and send him home but the patient's religion forbids the treatment. Most religions have prohibitions of one kind or another. Muslims and Jews, for example, are not allowed to consume anything that comes from swine. But in Islam, a person lost in a jungle and dying of starvation is allowed to eat the meat of a pig to save his or her life. A Muslim is also allowed to—possibly even required to—break fast during Ramadan if faced with injury or death from dehydration, which can happen commonly in hot countries when Ramadan comes in the summer months.

When I was in training in hematology, a man was admitted because he had blood in his urine. His low blood count made clear this had been going on for some days before he came. The cause of the bleeding was a problem with his blood, possibly associated with some pathology in his urinary tract. The hematology consultant's recommendation was to give the patient transfusions of blood products to correct the deficiencies and to raise the blood hemoglobin level. This appeared to be a rather routine order until the nurses called a short time later saying that the patient refused to receive a transfusion because of his religion. The consultant sent me to talk to the patient to try to convince him of the need. I tried my best and thought I was finally getting through to him when fate intervened—in the form of his faith.

Two or three members of his family walked in as the visiting hour started. My first reaction was that of relief. "Surely," I thought, "they will help me convince the patient, who is clearly not thinking straight." I was so wrong. The visiting family members asked if they could talk to me privately. Outside the room, they told me that their religion absolutely prohibited the use of any blood or blood products. I told them that without transfusions, he would continue to bleed and would most likely die.

"So be it," they said.

For the next week or two, the visitors sat with the patient around the clock to make sure he did not receive any blood. They were always very polite when the nurses, the house staff, the professors, and probably even the orderlies asked the family to reconsider. In the meantime, the patient continued to get weaker and weaker, paler and paler. He finally died.

For most of the medical staff at the time, it seemed a senseless death and was hard to understand. Now, reflecting back, I am not so certain it was senseless. Those were his relatives. From what I could see, they loved and cared for him. They treated him tenderly, fed him with a spoon, and wiped his face with a napkin. They talked to him as long as he was able to listen and respond, and they were clearly sad to see him go. But surely they went home believing that what they had done was the right thing, even when the price they had to pay was the life of their brother, husband, or father.

Most people would consider life as the most precious gift of the Creator—something to cherish and preserve at all cost. Even life itself comes packaged with the strongest determination and desire to hang on, no matter what the circumstances and regardless of how feeble the prognosis may be. This strong desire to survive is something we share with all other forms of life. Simply allowing life to terminate, especially when there is a clear pathway to evade death, is rather incomprehensible in terms of why and how.

It also appears to be a purely human phenomenon. Because we are sentient beings, having been given the gift of reason, perhaps a few questions are in order. What does our creator, our God, expect us to do under those circumstances? Should I embrace His most precious gift by choosing the path He has opened for me to stay alive, even though I have been told that the pathway is forbidden? Or should I be willing to sacrifice my only real possession—my life—in order to obey my Creator even when it means I am throwing away His precious gift? How certain am I that the pathway is, in fact, forbidden?

Some would argue that the pathway might not be forbidden after all. We believe things, we cherish our beliefs, our beliefs become sacred in our lives, and we are ready to lay down our lives for those beliefs—even fight and kill for them. We believe things our parents believed. Does not the vast majority of humanity inherit its beliefs?

On one level, the physician is merely a professional whose job entails, among other things, observing other humans' trials and tribulations in their final days and hours. But physicians go much further than being mere observers. They are active participants in life-and-death struggles. They are charged with the responsibility of bringing patients back from the brink, sometimes reaching down over the precipice and, with every ounce of strength they can muster, pulling patients back. Alas, it is sometimes for no more than a few additional breaths.

Physicians are also experts in proclaiming when someone has gone over the brink, when a line has been crossed, when the event that can never be undone has already taken place. Prior to that moment, there is a patient—a father or mother, a brother or sister, or a son or daughter—after that, there is merely a body to be respectfully disposed of. A change has taken place. Life is gone, but to where? Physicians are never asked that question. When physicians talk about death, they are generally talking about life—with death as a mere epilogue.

The Limitations of Books

Medical books have nothing more to offer when a patient's life ends. At that point, religious scholars and their books take over. There is usually a satisfactory consensus in the medical books; the books of religions and their keepers, on the other hand, differ on just about everything.

There are those who believe in their hearts that death is truly the end, after which there is nothing but an empty void; for them, there is nothing more to explore or discuss. But some of the great religions of the world propose otherwise.

God has given the human being a tremendous capability of intellect, reason, and logic, as has been demonstrated through the ages. But there are two areas that our creator has kept completely hidden and out of our intellects' reach. One, we have no clear knowledge of God, and two, we have no means of learning what happens after we die. There is no scientific method that can be applied to find answers in either of those two areas. Both are matters of belief. Interestingly, of the five elements of Muslim belief, called *Iman*, the first two are a belief in God and a belief in life after death. What follows is one Muslim's understanding, based on the teachings of the Koran.

For Muslims, life on earth is merely a very tiny initial part of human life that shall continue after death regardless of the wishes of a given human.

The quality of this second life, which will last for a very long time, depends entirely on how one spends earthly life. The life in this world is merely a period of test and trial in terms of one's beliefs, one's obedience to God's commandments, one's worship of Him and Him alone, one's honesty and integrity, one's behavior and truthfulness in one's dealings with other human beings, one's sense of justice, one's gratitude to God for all His blessings, and one's patience and perseverance in difficult times. All are essential qualities that civilized societies value in human beings. They are also among the values that have been specifically stressed in the teachings of all three Abrahamic faiths. Interestingly, the differences between the three religions are mainly in the two areas of which we can never have a definitive knowledge (i.e., the concept of God and the understanding of life after death). Because this is a discussion of death and dying, I will limit my remarks to Islam's teaching concerning life after death.

When making a presentation at an interfaith gathering, if I made a statement such as, "For a Muslim, life on earth is merely a period of test and trial, the results of which we shall see in the next life," I would most likely be asked why that is so. My first answer would be that this is the teaching of the Koran. While this theme of human accountability in the next life—accountability based on beliefs, attitudes, and behavior in this life—runs throughout the Koran, there is no better illustration or more explicit explanation of this concept than in the very story of human creation through Adam and Eve. But talking about human creation in this day and age, when every child knows for a fact that we simply evolved from the chimp, is no easy task. So here is a bit of explanation as to where I stand on this issue as a Muslim.

Having spent my life as a physician—and having dissected cockroaches and frogs as a student to discover anatomical and physiological similarities to humans, and having learned how similar the structure of human genome is to the genomes of other forms of life, and having studied the evolutionary process up close—I can see and recognize sound evidence supporting the concept of evolution. The Koran does not argue against it. It is clear that the universe itself has evolved from the moment it was created. There is also good reason to believe that life forms have evolved. In any case, it is hard to imagine an Adam and Eve for every one of the billions upon billions of life forms in the oceans, on land, and in the air. Hence, I do believe in the evolutionary process.

I do not, however, believe that humanity came into existence as a result of evolution. All Muslims believe in God, and as we look at His creation, whether on earth or in the cosmos, we get a glimpse of the Creator's infinite powers. Yes, our logical minds tell us that if life began from a single-cell organism and evolved all the way to the chimpanzee, then it would likely continue to evolve into a human. For those of us who are of one Abrahamic faith or another, whose books have taught us just about everything that we believe in and live by, why would we not believe when the same books tell us that humanity began with Adam and Eve? God, our creator and sustainer, can create us from Adam just as easily as creating a single cell and then having it evolve into a chimpanzee billions of years later.

In Islam's view, death is an option only here on earth. The Koran teaches us that the human being has been created with certain specific attributes that, qualitatively and quantitatively, greatly surpass those given to any other creature that ever lived on earth. That is not to say that the human surpasses the animal in every which way. A dog's hearing, a monarch butterfly's ability to migrate thousands of miles without instruments, an eagle's vision, an ant's ability from outside my house to sense the presence of a few grains of sugar on my kitchen counter, and even a donkey's strength, are all unquestionably better than corresponding abilities in a human. Unprotected by our walls and weapons, we are mere morsels for most animals. But the Creator gave us the gifts of intellect, reason, logic, language, and immensely inventive minds. We call ourselves sentient beings. We look up and wonder where we came from and who created the universe. Yes, we and other forms of life do have similarities, but we also have monumental differences.

Here, briefly, is the story of human creation as narrated in the Koran. The numbers in parentheses are chapter and verse references. If the corresponding text is in quotation marks, it represents an approximate translation of the verse. Otherwise, it is my understanding in plain language.

A bit of an explanation is needed when talking about the Koran's translation. Unlike the Bible, there is no "authorized" translation of the

Koran. In fact, there is no universally recognized central authority to authorize translations of the Koran. As long as the translation includes the original Arabic text, Muslims tend to look upon any minor errors of translation as the result of an expected human failing.

In choosing the words of the following translation, I have consulted four different English translations. They include original renderings by Abdullah Yusuf Ali, Marmaduke Pickthal, Muhammad Asad, and the translation known as the Noble Koran. I have also consulted Urdu translations by Abul Ala Maududi, Ibn Kathir, and Mohammed Shafi.

What I have presented below is based on my best understanding. There are individual verses for which the translation may have come from more than one source. For example, the translation "Behold thy Sustainer said to the angels [Asad], I will create generations after generations on earth [Noble Koran]" (2:30) comes from two different sources. To keep the text easier for the reader, no further references will be provided. In most cases, I have copied the translation from the most widely used and respected work by Abdullah Yusuf Ali.

"Behold thy Sustainer said to the angels, I will create generations after generations on earth" (2:30). The Arabic text in the verse makes clear that this new generation of beings—the humans, not yet created—were being created to live on the earth. In other words, our placement on earth was not a punishment for a sin but a part of the original design. God also tells the angels, "After I have fashioned him, and breathed into him of My spirit, fall ye down in obeisance unto him" (15:29). Adam, having been created, "God taught Adam the nature of all things" (2:31). God demonstrated this capability to the angels by first challenging them to describe some of those things, which the angels could not but Adam readily could (2:32–33). This tells us that Adam had a very special genome—one that would create a very special progeny with unparalleled intellect and all the capabilities to rule this earth. From Adam, Eve was created.

Next the almighty God added another character to the mix—an adversary to man. This one did not need to be created from scratch, since he already existed. All that was needed was to unmask him, perhaps with a little coaxing; perhaps this is a reason for jealousy—the same kind that gets us all worked up every day. The Koran talks about two types of existing creation: angels, who, we are taught, have been created from "light," and jinni, who, the Koran teaches us, have been created from the "fire of a scorching wind" (15:27). When God brought Adam before the angels, among those present was a member of the jinni by the name of Iblis.

Now, when Adam's exceptional capabilities had been demonstrated and God had asked all those present to prostrate before him, all angels submissively prostrated, but

> not so Iblis, he refused to be among those who prostrated themselves. God said, "O Iblis! What is your reason for not being among those who prostrated themselves?" Iblis said, "I am not one to prostrate myself to man whom Thou created from sounding clay, from mud molded into shape." … Iblis said, "I am better than he, Thou created me from fire, and him Thou created from clay." God said, "Then get thee out from here, for thou are rejected, accursed. And My curse shall be on thee till the Day of Judgment." Iblis said, "O my Lord! Give me then respite till the day the (dead) are raised." God said, "Respite is granted thee till the day of the Time Appointed." Iblis said, "Then By Thy Power, I will put them (Adam's progeny) all in the wrong, except thy servants among them, sincere and purified." God said, "Then it is just and fitting, and I say what is Just and Fitting, that I shall certainly fill hell with thee, and those who follow thee—every one." (15:31–33; 38:76–85)

Iblis from that point on became Satan, unmasked by God as an adversary to humans, born out of jealousy and with a promise of life until the Day of Judgment, an enemy with the freedom and an avowed desire to mislead and misguide us at will.

Adam and Eve, while apparently fully grown, were like newborn human children, innocent and not yet ready to be sent to the earth. Adam and Eve were now allowed to roam free in the garden but were commanded not to go near one specific tree. They had seen the rebuke of Satan and his vow to misguide them. They were also warned to be wary of Satan, whom they were told was their avowed enemy (20:117). It has been said that God works in mysterious ways. This time God's mysterious way was to accomplish all that remained to be accomplished with a single, inevitable misstep on the part of the two humans. "Satan whispered evil to him: he said, 'O Adam! Shall I lead thee to the Tree of Eternity and to a kingdom that never decays?' As a result, they both ate of the tree, and so their nakedness appeared to them. They began to sew together, for their covering, leaves from the garden. Thus did Adam disobey his God and allow himself to be seduced ... He (Adam) forgot, and We found, on his part no firm resolve" (20:120–121; 20:115).

In effect, what they ate completed their development to adulthood. It also made them realize that they had disobeyed God and awakened in them a feeling of remorse. It was God who now reached out to them. "But his Lord chose him for His Grace. He turned to him, and gave him guidance" (20:122). He taught them the words to repent. "Then received Adam words of guidance from his Lord; and his Lord accepted his repentance for verily He alone is the Acceptor of Repentance, the Dispenser of Grace" (2:37). They were now ready for earth, not as a punishment but as a fulfillment of the original plan, to begin procreating and populating the earth as its newest inhabitants. "We said, ... Get ye down all from here, with enmity between yourselves. On earth will be your dwelling place and your means of livelihood, for a time. ... And if, as is sure, there comes to you guidance from Me, whosoever follows My guidance, on them shall be no fear, nor shall they grieve. But those who reject belief in Me and belie Our Signs, they shall be companions of the fire, they shall abide therein" (2:36, 38–39).

We have been given the smarts to look into and discover the secrets of the universe that are absolutely beyond the understanding of anything that might evolve from the chimp, at least within humanity's lifetime. We have been given the ability and the freedom to explore just about everything on the earth, whether it is on the surface or inside, on dry land or in the depths of oceans. We have the ability to understand mathematics, physics, chemistry, and biology, and most importantly, we can communicate using appropriate languages in all those disciplines, thereby building on each other's discoveries, inventions, and ideas. This has led to an ever-increasing speed of discovery on earth as well as in the rest of the universe. All of that is with the permission of God and with the abilities He has blessed the progeny of Adam and Eve with. "O Ye assembly of Jinn and men, if it be that ye can pass beyond the zone of heaven and earth, then pass. Thou shall not pass without authority" (55:33).

As a creation of God, a human being is a perfect specimen—one that can never achieve perfection. We can never be flawless or infallible. It appears that the intellect we have been blessed with has the ability to guide as well as misguide us. We are marvelous creatures, in a sad kind of a way, with any of us having simultaneous abilities of being good and bad, miserly and generous, selfless and selfish, honest and dishonest, cruel and merciful, dumb and smart, and caring and aloof. We feeling the pain of some while, at the same time, inflicting pain on others. We can see the same phenomenon and draw totally different conclusions; read the same text and see different meanings. It is a struggle for the righteous and God-fearing—for others, perhaps a mere distraction. The best we can hope for is to fall at least a little bit on the side of the good. That is what it is to be human—all of that having been built into our genome by the Creator in a marvelously delicate balance. Why?

One answer that the Koran provides is summarized in the following verses.

> Verily We created man from a drop of mingled sperm in order to try him. We gave him the gifts of hearing and insight. We showed him the way. (It is up to him) whether to be grateful or ungrateful. For the ungrateful, We have prepared chains, yokes and fire. As to the righteous, they will drink of a cup—from a fountain where the devotees of God do drink, flowing in unstinted abundance. (These righteous people) perform their vows, and they fear a Day whose evil flies far and wide. They feed the indigent, the orphan, and the captive, for the love of God, saying, "we feed you for the sake of God alone: no reward do we desire from you, nor thanks." (76:2–9)

The behavior of most animals appears to be guided by hunger, the need for procreation, and a strong desire for survival. Most of what they do in life appears to be intended to satisfy those needs. Whenever one sees an odd behavior on their part, like the transformation of the grasshopper into a locust swarm, one cannot help but wonder if there isn't a mighty hand behind the creation of that tornado of insect creatures to serve a different purpose.

Human behavior, on the other hand, is driven by much more than hunger and a desire to procreate. We want to conquer and subjugate others. We want to be the biggest, the tallest, the strongest, the richest, and the best looking, and we are never sure that we are any or all of those unless the rest in our surroundings humbly bow before us in recognition. Whether it is a tennis racket or a sword in our hand, we must prove that we are the best at wielding it; otherwise, we are merely a human holding a gadget, ordinary and inconsequential. It would not be an exaggeration to postulate that humanity may not have survived even one millennium without the guidance that we received from our creator in the form of His prophets and His books—prophets and books that awakened within us values like humility, kindness, generosity of heart and wallet, and the ability to feel the pain of the weak, the hungry, the homeless, the persecuted, the hunted, and the terrified. They taught us to feel a sense of joy when there is peace in the land, when we share our blessings willingly with others, when one human's belongings are safe without locks and chains, or when a person walking alone at night is not fearful of being mugged, robbed, raped, or killed. Those books and prophets taught us how to be the best that we can be as human beings.

The Koranic verses I quoted above tell us that God values goodness in a human being and hates evil. The Creator has made it clear that while we appear to have unlimited freedom to live as we please in this life, being good shall have its rewards and being bad its consequences in the life to come. The choice is ours to make.

Javed Aslam, MD, FRCP(C)

Dr. Javed Aslam received his medical degree from King Edward Medical College, Lahore, Pakistan. KEMC had the distinction of being the oldest medical school in Asia, having had a centennial celebration a year earlier. After a year of postgraduate training, he decided to see the world while at the same time pursuing further studies. On June 27, 1963, he found himself sitting at the airport in Norfolk, Virginia, waiting for a ride to DePaul Hospital, his first employer. It was his birthday. He had twenty dollars in his pocket.

For additional training he traveled to Baltimore; Pittsburgh; and Winnipeg, Canada, finally joining the Winnipeg Clinic as a hematologist/oncologist. Life was good. Winters were unbearably cold. He started watching American football just to see people walking around in short sleeves in Miami. Then came the breaking point. The month was February and the temperature forty below. The family started traveling south in a straight line. Reaching Houston, they realized they could not go any farther. The year was 1977. Dr. Aslam is board certified in internal medicine, hematology, and pathology and is a Fellow of the Royal College of Physicians, Canada.

He is an active member of the Islamic Society of Greater Houston and has held various positions in the society over the past three decades. He delivers sermons at Friday congregational prayers in the Houston-area mosques. During the past twenty years, he has been a speaker in churches and educational institutions. He and his wife, Tasnim, are regular participants in many interfaith activities in the Spring and Woodlands areas. By the grace of God, all three of their children have families of their own and live nearby. They have eight lovely grandchildren; the oldest enrolled in UT this year.

Contact Information:
e-mail: Jav0627@iCloud.com

FINDING COMFORT IN
MY LOSS OF FAITH

A Humanist/Atheist's Perspective on Mortality

Bracha Y. Etengoff, JD

I T WAS THE second night of Rosh Hashanah, the Jewish New Year, and I was in a cab. That may sound unremarkable, but for most of my life, it never would have happened. Until I turned thirty, I was strictly observant, and Orthodox Jews don't ride in cars on the Sabbath or most Jewish holidays. My parents are not just Orthodox; my father is a rabbi. Growing up, I spent long days in yeshiva (Jewish day school), devoting every morning to Jewish studies. Our religion was a fully immersive experience that colored and dictated every aspect of my life.

But a few years ago, there I was in that cab, on my way to my friend's house for a festive dinner. Like many Jewish atheists, I still like to mark the New Year. My friend and most of the residents of her neighborhood are Orthodox, and over the years, the cabdriver had seen many noteworthy behaviors that resulted from the myriad Sabbath prohibitions observed by Orthodox Jews. He was very eager to share his knowledge with me. I listened for a while, but eventually I told him that I was familiar with them because I used to be Orthodox too.

"Oh," he said, sounding deflated.

I felt guilty. He'd really been enjoying himself. But he brightened when he realized that in fact, I'd just given him another opening.

"So what are you now?" he asked. "Reform? Conservative? I know about all of them!"

"No," I replied calmly. "I'm an atheist."

His hands jumped off the steering wheel. "Oh! I'm sorry. I didn't mean to pry."

His apology made me feel even guiltier. (You can leave God behind, but there is no escape from Jewish guilt!) I assured him that I'd taken no offense, which I hadn't. After all, I'd brought up the subject of my religious anti-journey first.

Once he'd recovered from his shock, he told me about people he knew who were very close to one another, despite their religious differences. I get this kind of response a lot. Another cabdriver once told me that his wife frequently went on religious pilgrimages. While she was off on those, he went on pilgrimages of his own—to the best golf courses in the country! It's encouraging to know that every day, everywhere, people are bridging the divide that religion can create.

When we arrived at my friend's house, he told me he hoped I'd enjoy the dinner.

"Oh, I will!" I responded.

"I know," he said. "Otherwise you wouldn't be here."

He'd hit the nail on the head. Orthodoxy demands constant observance of hundreds of commandments, whether you like it or not. Now I choose which rituals to integrate into my life, based on what I find valuable and personally satisfying.

I told my friend about the cabdriver's reaction to my lack of faith, and I asked for her insights. I was sure the man didn't think he was prying when he asked about my current affiliation. So what changed when he learned I didn't have one? My friend suggested that to some people, a declaration of atheism is tantamount to an admission of murder. But it was clear from the rest of our conversation that although my cabdriver had been shocked by my response, he wasn't horrified.

Perhaps he was afraid he'd hit a nerve. It's almost impossible to execute a religious 180 without significant angst and pain, as I know from my own experiences and my discussions with others who have "gone off the path" (i.e., left Orthodoxy). An innocent question about religious identity may come at a time when someone is in the midst of turmoil, or when her memories are still raw. Thankfully, my own pain is now in the past.

When I put the question to the dinner guests, one suggested that perhaps the driver thought he'd insulted me by assuming I was still religious to some degree. Now, in my opinion, if you've just told someone you used to be Orthodox and you're on your way to a Jewish holiday dinner, you can't blame him for asking what kind of Jew you are now.

But I can imagine that *some* atheists might find his assumption insulting, because there are times when *many* atheists find the assumption of faith hurtful—myself included.

One such time is when society faces especially tragic encounters with mortality. Although atheists generally believe that there is no afterlife and therefore no suffering after death, this doesn't eliminate the heartache we feel following school shootings or mass terrorist attacks any more than the belief that the dead are in a better place does. And when exclusionary faith-based language is used at these times, insult is added to injury. For example, after the horrific 2012 school shooting in Newtown, Connecticut, in which twenty children and six staff members lost their lives, one atheist bemoaned, "The endless talk about faith in God as the only consolation ... Some of those grieving parents surely believe, as I do, that this is our one and only life. Atheists cannot find solace in the idea that dead children are now angels in heaven."[1]

Language that is meant to be all-inclusive, but which in fact excludes us, can be hurtful even when it is less overtly religious. We've made some progress on this front. Many public figures now say that the victims of these tragedies will be "in our thoughts and prayers"—not just "our prayers." I hope that soon our leaders will also say "Americans of all faiths and none," instead of "Americans of all faiths," especially during difficult times. Although this may seem trifling, to me, it's similar to the need for gender-neutral language. We now speak of "humankind" instead of "mankind." When making general statements, we replace the old default male pronouns with plural ones to avoid the need to choose a gender, or sometimes we take affirmative action and use feminine pronouns instead. In short, we've already recognized that a phrase which purports to include everyone but which excludes a minority group is hurtful and perpetuates the belief that the group is unworthy of mention.

So much for the source of comfort that atheists lack. What sources of comfort *do* secular people have in times of loss?

I know that we have at least one source in common with religious people. We also remember the happy times we shared with those we mourn, the highlights of their lives, and the satisfaction they got from their accomplishments. True, these memories are a double-edged sword. They bring us grief as well because we know there will be no more. But they also bring us comfort. They remind us that while our loved ones lived, they found joy and meaning in life.

When the loss of life is tragically unnecessary and intentionally inflicted by human hands, as in a mass murder or a terrorist attack, I also find comfort in my belief that people's capacity for good equals their breathtaking capacity for evil. I try to focus on the selfless acts that we invariably learn about afterward: the people who ran back into the Twin Towers to save others, the teacher who died shielding her students in Newtown, the Danes who rowed more than 90 percent of their Jewish citizens to safety in Sweden during the Holocaust.[2] And I reaffirm my commitment to take these heroes as my models.

This source of comfort also transcends religion—as long as you stop here. But as an atheist, I take it one step further. When I consider humanity's capacity for good and evil, I also recall my belief that what we make of this world is completely up to us. No god will save us, but no god will punish us either. Personally, I find this comforting. I'd rather be left alone to make a complete muddle of things than be subject to meddling.

Phil Zuckerman, a secular sociologist who has studied atheism extensively, expressed this idea eloquently: "Humanity is certainly a major source of much brutality, suffering, and destruction, but at the same time, humanity is a major source of kindness, compassion, and reparation. We have no gods to appeal to for help, no avatars, no saviors, and no prophets to do our work for us. Just our all-too-human selves: our minds, our reason, our bodies, our love, and our camaraderie."[3]

Finally, I find comfort in a third source that may surprise some. I find comfort in my *loss* of faith. God was always a burden to me in times of tragedy, not a blessing. Theodicy, the problem of why a good and just God allows evil to exist, troubled me from an early age. Jews often raise this question in the context of the Holocaust, and I was no exception.

"How could six million people have sinned so badly they deserved to die?" I asked my father. One million of those victims were children, and in Jewish law, girls under twelve and boys under thirteen aren't even accountable for their sins yet. And how could *anyone* have deserved such tremendous suffering?

My father made a beeline for a tome in his extensive library and said, "Read this, and then we'll talk." He handed me a compendium of attempts by theologians throughout the ages to answer this question. Most of the authors were Jewish, but Saint Thomas Aquinas made an appearance too. I read them all, fully confident I'd find the answer *somewhere* in a book that big. Until then, I'd always found a chest of gold at the end of my father's pedagogical treasure hunts. But this time, I was disappointed.

I brought the book back to my father and said, "None of these really answer the question." My father didn't try to argue, which in retrospect is not surprising. Our theological discussions were always quite frank. Even when we talked about the existence of God, he didn't claim we have proof. Instead, he talked about a leap of faith. But I never really understood why we should make one. Why believe in a God, let alone a good God, and spend our lives observing hundreds of dubiously divine commandments, in light of contradictory evidence or simply a lack of any evidence at all?

I continued to struggle with theodicy intellectually for years, but in my early twenties, it suddenly became very real. My close friend's baby, born just two weeks before his due date, was stillborn. Soon after my friend went into labor, the doctor told her that he couldn't find a heartbeat. She had to continue anyway, knowing that her pain would bring no joy but only more pain at the end.

When she told me what happened, I couldn't find the right words. Maybe there weren't any. But I wanted to do something, anything, so I offered to cook. I remember asking her, "Do you like lasagna? Plain or vegetable?" I can still hear her answering that her husband didn't like it with vegetables. I'd never felt so helpless. One of my dearest friends had lost her baby, and all I could do was make lasagna.

Looking back, I think that was the beginning of the end for me—but not for my friend and her husband. They both still lead strictly Orthodox lives. I couldn't understand how their loss, which I'd experienced only secondhand, could shake the pillars of my faith but not theirs.

But when I mourned the deaths of the Newtown schoolchildren, I "only" had to grieve for the loss of innocent lives with so much potential, and for the children's and parents' suffering. When terrorists kidnapped three Israeli children in the summer of 2014, they were missing for weeks and ultimately found murdered. Afterward, some of my religious friends poured out their theological pain on Facebook. They asked why God had allowed this to happen, where all the prayers of Jews around the world during those agonizing days had gone. I pitied them. We were all devastated, but at least faith had not added to my pain.

It follows that atheists, particularly with backgrounds like mine, may find it very hurtful when religion is forced on us, especially during encounters with mortality. But pressing religion on another is wrong no matter what kind of background we come from. For example, pressuring a known nonbeliever to accept last rites or recite the Jewish confession when death is imminent is nothing less than cruel. Telling an atheist whose wife died that she's in a better place now will certainly not comfort him, and it may well cause him more pain. But although many of us would agree that proffering unwelcome religion is wrong, at the very least when people are suffering and vulnerable, I recently encountered someone who disagreed completely.

One day last fall, I was sitting in the phlebotomy waiting room in Memorial Sloan Kettering Cancer Center. Six years earlier, I had thyroid cancer. My thyroid was removed, and I underwent radiation therapy. Now I take a synthetic thyroid hormone pill, and periodically I have blood drawn to make sure the dosage is correct. Sometimes they include a panel of tests to check whether the cancer has returned. These blood tests have gotten easier for me, but they can still prompt worries about the future and awaken memories of a difficult time in my past.

Some doctors refer to thyroid cancer as "the good cancer." I, and many other thyroid cancer survivors, hate that term with a passion. For the patient, there is no good cancer. The words minimize our experiences and seem as oxymoronic as the phrase "a just genocide." But I understand what doctors mean by it. The survival rate for thyroid cancer is very high, and its physical effects and treatments are nowhere near as bad as those of many other cancers. Nonetheless, a thyroidectomy is often very painful; and the radiation protocol is difficult and traumatic. Equally important, the physical severity of cancer does not necessarily correlate with its psychological impact, which is highly individual.

For me that impact was tremendous, probably because the timing couldn't have been worse. I had just quit my job to *escape* cancer. For three years, I'd represented people who had developed mesothelioma and lung cancer from working with products containing asbestos. Several clients of mine passed away while their cases were ongoing, one after trying to complete his deposition in a hospice. Besides litigating my own cases, I oversaw the distribution of settlement funds to the families of deceased clients, which meant I was constantly speaking with the bereaved. On behalf of hundreds of clients, both living and deceased, I also supervised the filing of thousands of claims with trusts that compensate victims of asbestos exposure.

The sheer weight of so much death was overwhelming. The more time passed, the heavier it grew, until eventually I was in danger of being crushed beneath it. I left my job right before Thanksgiving in 2008. Then, in January 2009, I got the news of my diagnosis. The fallout in my life was intense. My marriage had long been fragile, and thyroid cancer was the last straw. I filed for divorce soon after my surgery. I also finally left religion.

My parents sometimes wonder what they did wrong. Why didn't their upbringing and my twenty-one years of Orthodox education keep me on the path? After all, most people who are raised Orthodox remain Orthodox. I think the answer is that although my parents taught my siblings and me to be strictly observant, they also taught us to be critical thinkers, even in the realm of religion.

I've found that people who are critical thinkers and remain or become religious Jews fall into three groups. The first group simply does not think critically about religion. Whether this is a conscious or subconscious choice, the result is the same. They keep these aspects of themselves dichotomized and thereby preserve the tenets of their faith.

The second group thinks critically about religion and must wrestle with questions that shake the foundations of their faith. For example, religious Jews who think critically about theodicy may accept or continually struggle to accept the idea that because the human mind is limited, we cannot see the full picture or the grand scheme. When tragedies like genocide and the murder of innocent children threaten their belief in a good and just God, they try to hold on to the idea that if we could understand God, we would be Him.

The third group, to which I used to belong, engages in the same intellectual struggle but concludes there are no good answers. Nevertheless, they choose to remain or become observant.

There are many reasons that people choose to remain religious. (In listing them, I don't mean to ignore the role of faith. But after speaking with many people, I've found that there are almost always additional motivators.) Some feel that religion brings meaning and morality to their lives, or that it provides a good framework for raising children. Often people stay because of social pressure or because they value or need the warmth and community support that is so much a part of Orthodox Judaism. A good friend told me that she chose to remain Orthodox in part because she simply couldn't fathom who she'd be without this major part of her identity.

There are also strong family pressures. People may feel bound by unspoken commitments made to their spouses when they married to live observant lives. Some parents don't want to disrupt their children's lives by taking them out of religious schools. Family pressure can also work top down: people are loath to hurt or disappoint their own parents or to break a chain of tradition that goes back many generations.

In addition, it's hard to overestimate the effectiveness of a strictly Orthodox upbringing. There's no time off, whether at home, in school, in summer camp, or on vacation. Many people really *don't* cheat and try bacon just once. As impossible as it sounds, many people don't have premarital sex, and some won't even touch their fiancées before marriage.

Once, a Catholic friend asked me how Orthodox Jews achieve such impressive compliance rates. He suggested that they must do a really good job of putting the fear of hell, quite literally, in their children. I told him that wasn't it. In Jewish tradition, heaven and hell certainly exist, but the afterlife doesn't come up much in a typical *yeshiva* education. Only one Orthodox person has ever told me that he remains observant because he's afraid of going to hell when he dies.

I had to think so hard about his question that I realized my effort itself pointed to an answer. A strict Orthodox education can dye you so deeply in the wool that you don't *need* the fear of consequences to keep you in line. To illustrate with an analogy from secular law, often people don't refrain from murder because it's illegal and they're afraid of going to prison. Rather, they don't murder because it is shockingly immoral and goes against their very natures. For many Orthodox Jews, eating bacon is a ritual sin equivalent to homicide. The taboo against it is so strongly ingrained from such an early age that they just cannot put it in their mouths, however good it smells.

On a more positive note, some people stay because, despite their doubts, they *feel* God in their hearts. They "know there has to be something more." When they pray with intense concentration, they sense a listening presence. My parents do. But I never did, no matter how hard I concentrated.

So why did I pray twice a day since junior high if I never sensed anyone listening? Why did I observe hundreds of commandments for thirty years, despite weighty doubts ranging among such fundamental concepts as theodicy, the divine nature of the Bible, and the very existence of God? Why did I keep pouring my psychological energies into a futile attempt to reconcile my religious and personal values when they were so often diametrically opposed? These are all good questions, and in fact, now that I've left, I can't believe I stayed so long myself.

But the answer to all of them is simple: some of the motivators I've listed were strong enough to keep me in. My upbringing, familial and social pressures, and the implicit commitment I'd made to my ex-husband to lead a religious life made for a powerful combination. Therefore, when I think about my ultimate decision to leave Orthodoxy, I don't think in terms of why. The real question is, why then? What changed?

Three things changed all at once. First, as long as theodicy remained an abstract problem or a concrete but secondhand experience, I could banish it to the back of my mind. But when it became personal, it suddenly leaped onto center stage. My own thyroid cancer was detected because my sister had been diagnosed a few months earlier, and her doctor recommended that the rest of our family get screened. Her diagnosis was a total shock. The doctor offered so much reassurance, but in the beginning, the C-word blocked out everything else. And even when I realized she'd be okay, watching my sister go through so much pain that I couldn't protect her from was heartrending.

And then it was my turn. I wasn't shocked this time, because I tend toward cheerful pessimism. I honestly would have been surprised by a *clean* pathology report. But of course, that didn't make it easy. And two of us at once?! I remember thinking we were good people—not saints, but no worse than many families who hadn't been visited by cancer. In my mind, we'd done nothing to deserve this.

Second, I left then because my decision to divorce absolved me from any obligation, real or perceived, to continue living a religious life with my ex-husband. My divorce freed me to redefine myself. I had no children, and although I knew my parents would feel hurt by my choice, they agreed I had the right to make it. I love my parents very much, but I couldn't live an inauthentic, limited life because of that love.

And third, I left then because cancer forced me to confront my mortality. Although I'd encountered so much death in my job, only firsthand experience with serious illness taught me that *I* was vulnerable, that cancer or the like could strike again—and that next time could be the end. My mind had known that life is finite, but it took my own thyroid cancer for me to really believe it. I'll always remember thinking, "What if I have only ten years left?"

The answer came with the same force as the question. I knew I didn't want to spend another minute constrained by religious restrictions I didn't believe in. Whether I lived another ten years or another fifty, I didn't want to spend one more Saturday not driving to the beach on a beautiful day if I wanted to. Nor did I want to go through the hassle of bringing kosher food on vacation and eating it while longing to be in a nearby restaurant that smelled heavenly instead.

No, I wanted to be free: free to make my own choices about how to live my life, however long it might last—free to soak up all the goodness I could from it. I was overcome by the desire to live richly, fully, passionately. But I decided to decrease my observance gradually. When people become fully observant in the space of a few weeks, it never turns out well for them. Breaking every religious taboo that had been deeply ingrained in me for thirty years at once also seemed like a recipe for psychological disaster. So I took it slowly, but I got there.

Now my religious anti-journey lies firmly in the past. I've never regretted my choice, and I've never regretted my divorce either. And my thyroidectomy scar has healed so well that even I have to look hard to find it. But going to Sloan Kettering will never be easy.

So that was my emotional backdrop on that fall day in the Sloan Kettering waiting room. When a woman in an orange sweater gave me a pamphlet, I accepted it reflexively, not realizing what it was. People let their guard down in a hospital, and rightly so. You shouldn't have to fend off proselytizers in hospital waiting rooms in the same way you do in the public square. After all, you don't have to wait for the light to change when you walk down hospital hallways.

When I did realize what that pamphlet was, I jumped up and handed it off to the receptionist like a hotcake. Of course, now I wish I'd saved it. But since it was entitled *What Cancer Can't Do to You* and my two-second scan revealed the words "love" and "Jesus," we can extrapolate from there.

I began speaking to the receptionist in a calm, quiet tone laden with subtext.

"Excuse me, that woman in the orange sweater is distributing these pamphlets. I don't know if you're aware of this. [But now you are.] I don't know if the hospital has a policy about this. [But you should!] Personally, I don't think it's appropriate to distribute religious tracts about cancer. [I'm upset, but I'll restrain myself from making a scene … for now.]"

This gained me a sympathetic nod from the receptionist and a request to point out the offender. I happily complied. I was pretty sure I'd won her over, but I like to cover my bases.

"Maybe you should escalate this. [Or I will!]"

The receptionist left the desk. I saw her speak with another woman while showing her the pamphlet. A few minutes later, another employee began discreetly gathering up the ones that other ungrateful recipients had left on the coffee tables. Then the phlebotomist called me in, so that was the end of that.

I was so angry with that evangelist. It infuriated me that she was preying on people when they were at their most vulnerable. Later I realized that, from her perspective, she was sharing the most valuable gift in the world with the people who needed it most. But I still find her actions reprehensible.

People often ask if my parents and Orthodox friends disowned or excommunicated me when I left religion. Nothing could be further from the truth, and I know how fortunate I am to be able to say that. But some of them are sad that I've given up this valuable gift we used to share. I can understand that. There's a part of me that wouldn't mind standing in Times Square opposite the evangelists and calling out, "There is no God! Find the peace and freedom that comes from escaping the shackles of religion!"

But I won't. Unless people initiate religious debates with me, I won't challenge their faith. Some atheists will do so every chance they get. Recently, researchers at the University of Tennessee who classified atheists into six categories dubbed the militants "Anti-theists."[4] Reading about them brought to mind the comedian Bill Maher, who often pokes fun at religion. In one routine, he asked why people always say that we must respect everyone's religious beliefs. Why are they off limits? Why should we treat personal religious beliefs any differently than anything else?

To me the answers are obvious. I may agree with Mr. Maher that religious beliefs are unsupported or illogical, and that looking at history as a whole, religion has done more harm than good. But history has also taught us, time and time again, that when people's religious beliefs are ridiculed, persecution and bloodshed follow. That alone seems like a good reason for a hands-off policy to me. I also know that many people have religious experiences that are the polar opposite of mine. Religion helps some survive the most difficult times of their lives and comforts them in their times of death. Who am I to try to take it away from them?

Our attitudes toward others' faiths are hardly the only ways in which atheists differ. But we do share "certain key traits and values, such as self-reliance, freedom of thought, intellectual inquiry, cultivating autonomy in children, pursuing truth, basing morality on the empathic reciprocity embedded in the Golden Rule, accepting the inevitability of our eventual death, navigating life with a sober pragmatism grounded in this world (not the next), and still enjoying a sense of deep transcendence now and then amid the inexplicable, inscrutable profundity of being."[5]

Likewise, many of my thoughts on mortality are similar to other atheists', although my story is my own. Most of us believe that "(1) this life—miraculous, rich, and fleeting—is the only life, (2) we must seize it, savor it, and be open to it, and (3) there is nothing to fear when it comes to the end."[6] Finally, we find nothing depressing in the belief that this life is the only one we have. To the contrary, "the reality of mortality renders life all the more urgent, and all the more precious, and all the more wonderful."[7]

---

1 Susan Jacoby, "The Blessings of Atheism," *New York Times*, Jan. 5, 2013.

2 Leo Goldberger, *The Rescue of the Danish Jews: Moral Courage Under Stress* (New York: NYU Press, 1987), xx–xxi.

3 Phil Zuckerman, *Living the Secular Life* (New York: Penguin Press, 2014), 222.

4 Christopher F. Silver and Tommy J. Coleman, "Non-Belief in America Research," accessed February 12, 2015, http://www.atheismresearch.com.

5 Phil Zuckerman, *Living the Secular Life* (New York: Penguin Press, 2014), 6–7.

6 Ibid., 169.

7 Ibid., 197.

Bracha Y. Etengoff, JD

Bracha Y. Etengoff is a writer, attorney, and mediator living in New York City. She received undergraduate and graduate degrees in psychology from Yeshiva University and Queens College, respectively. She then attained a JD from the Benjamin N. Cardozo School of Law. Bracha is currently editing an anthology of essays by patients, caregivers, health care professionals, and attorneys that addresses the psychological aspects of illness and the importance of patient advocacy. She also muses about life's chance encounters on her blog, www.allmywanderings.com, and her stories have been syndicated by literary publications.

As the principal of Law & Mediation Offices of Bracha Y. Etengoff, PLLC, Bracha collaborates with her clients to create life plans, including wills and health care directives. She draws on her own experiences and advanced training in psychology to enable them to address the sensitive issues of incapacity and mortality. In her mediation practice, Bracha helps families resolve conflicts related to living arrangements for elderly members, the distribution of inheritances, prenuptial agreements, and divorce. She also provides legal services to support small businesses.

When not writing or practicing law, Bracha may be found singing, exploring the great outdoors, or communing with her cat, Dakota. She also works diligently to maintain her MFA (Most Favorite Aunt) status among her nieces and nephews.

Contact Information:
e-mail: brachalaw@gmail.com
website: www.brachalaw.com
website: www.allmywanderings.com

FREED FROM THE FEAR OF DEATH

A Hindu's Perspective on Mortality

Ramesh Patel, MD
(As told to B. Glenn Wilkerson)

I WAS BORN IN India and came to the United States in 1972. I am a cardiologist. My practice of medicine and my approach to daily living are heavily influenced by the knowledge and beliefs I have acquired through my immersion in Hinduism. My religion has also profoundly influenced my feelings regarding death and dying and life after physical death.

Hindus believe that, while there are many gods, they are all manifestations of the one God Almighty. He is the God of all religions and the entire universe.

Among God's creations is the element of nature, or maya. The word "nature" refers to all the material aspects of God's creation: trees, animals, stones, stars, planets, and humans. Through God's creative process, the human body evolved over the millennia as the highest form of nature. Nature is both outside the human body—in the form of the world around us—and also inside the body in the forms of human consciousness and reason. Our human nature dictates how we act and behave.

More specifically, the human body has three elements:

1. The visible, physical body
2. The invisible body, which is the mind
3. The reason

Reason is our inner nature; it determines our behavior. Reason tells the mind what to do, and the mind tells the physical body what to do. These three elements—reason, mind, and physical body—compose the human body. Then we must add to these a fourth element, the soul, which is different from the body, though it resides within the body. The soul is the guiding force of the other three elements.

There are two kinds of people as far as facing imminent death is concerned. One group does not want to die. They die in emotional pain and without a sense of fulfillment. They have plenty of desires left to work on. The second group feels they have nothing more to do or achieve. They are ready to return home with a sense of accomplishment and with no regrets, and they are very, very joyous about leaving this world.

My mom requested her doctor, "Please let me go home. I want to go to Heavens from my home, not from the hospital." She was discharged to go home, and she happily went to Heavens two days later. It was an enjoyable ending on Earth and a happy landing in Heavens. I and my family witnessed this second type of dying in my mother.

There is an illustrative example in Hindu scriptures that describes the relationship between the body and the soul. It pictures two birds sitting in a tree—the tree of life. One of the birds is living life and enjoying it, and the other bird is watching that bird. The first bird represents the body, and the second symbolizes the soul.

Our bodily nature dictates our behavior, and the soul has to observe it and work with it. Soul transcends the body. While the body is mortal, the soul is the spirit of God and is therefore infinite and immortal. When the body dies, the soul continues to exist and is reborn in another life form.

Many people confuse this concept of rebirth with the term "reincarnation." In American dictionaries, reincarnation and rebirth typically appear as synonyms. In Hinduism, the two terms have vastly different meanings. Very simply, rebirth (*punarjanm*) applies to the human soul, whereas reincarnation (*Avtar*) has to do with the appearance of God here on earth. When conditions on earth deteriorate, God will descend and walk the earth in human form to bring peace and harmony to the world. Appearances of the Lord here on earth are called "reincarnations" of God. Among the important reincarnations of God are the Lord Rama, the Lord Krishna, and the Lord Shiva.

Over 230 years ago, a reincarnation of the Lord called Swaminarayan appeared on earth. He was said to have mastered sacred Hindu scriptures by age seven, and he wrote the *Shikshapatri*—a book of social principles that summarizes those scriptures. He was a great spiritual leader and was venerated as a champion of women and the poor.[1] My denomination (and there are many denominations in Hinduism) follows the teachings of Swaninarayan, and the principles I share in this chapter are derived from Him. That is the concept of reincarnation: the Lord God himself coming to earth in human form with the intent of reforming the culture and making the world better.

Returning to the concept of rebirth, it is important to remember that reincarnation occurs with God, while rebirth has to do with the human soul. Rebirth occurs when the body dies and the soul is reborn in another form, depending on the type of life that has been lived. There are an estimated 8.7 million living species in the world.[2] All these species have souls, which is why Hindus consider all living things to be sacred, including viruses, bacteria, plants, and animals. The highest form of soul is found in human beings, and the soul does not die. When its body dies, the soul is reborn in another living form. If a person has not led a good life, it is possible that he or she could be reborn in the animal world. The determining factor in rebirth is how we deal with nature around us. How do we treat one another? How do we treat the living planet on which we live? Do we habitually succumb to the lusts and fears and greed that can negatively impact our relationship with nature, or do we rise above those lower forms of conduct?

Our behavior is important because it subjects us to the law of karma. The word "karma" refers to deeds and actions, and the law of karma is the law of moral causation. It embodies the concept that how we behave will have corresponding consequences, not just in this life but in future lives as well. Karma explains why misfortune and evil occur in the world— sometimes to people who do not seem deserving. Their misfortunes may be the results of their actions in previous lives.

Our karma dictates the destination of the soul's rebirth into a new life form. The better our behavior, the better conditions will be in the next existence. The opposite is also true; that's the law of karma. We reap what we sow. The ultimate goal is for our souls to become so enlightened with the fruits of our good behavior that they escape the cycle of rebirth and rise out of nature to be with God.

This concept of the rebirth of the soul can free us from our human fear of death. I see many people who are afraid to die. I once treated an eighty-year-old woman who was having a heart attack in the emergency room. She grabbed my hand and cried out, "Dr. Patel, please save me!" The prospects of dying were terrifying to her.

Contrast her reaction to that of another patient, my mother, who was an eighty-eight-year-old Hindu. She was sitting in a chair and recognized that she was having a heart attack. Her family members told her, "Let's call 911." She looked at a picture of the Lord Swaminarayan on the wall across from her, folded her hands in prayer, and said, "Lord, I want to be with you. Please take me." She felt assured that her soul would not die and would be reborn. So she approached the prospect of her physical death blessed with a sense of comfort and peace.

There are two kinds of people as far as facing imminent death is concerned. One group does not want to die. They die in emotional pain and without a sense of fulfillment. They have plenty of desires left to work on. The second group feels they have nothing more to do or achieve. They are ready to return home with a sense of accomplishment and with no regrets, and they are very, very joyous about leaving this world.

My mom requested her doctor, "Please let me go home. I want to go to Heavens from my home, not from the hospital." She was discharged to go home, and she happily went to Heavens two days later. It was an enjoyable ending on Earth and a happy landing in Heavens. I and my family witnessed this second type of dying in my mother.

It seems to me that, freed from the fear of death, people can not only make peace with mortality but can also embrace this existence with a greater sense of appreciation and joy. Instead of engaging in a frenetic, mind-numbing pursuit of youth, wealth, and personal achievement as a means of avoiding consideration of their eventual demise, they can pause in their activities to smell the roses and involve themselves in deeds that benefit others. I believe that God desires me to live this life as fully and joyfully as I possibly can. The Lord expects me to find great pleasure in the gift of this existence, and I am intent on doing so.

As a physician, one of the positive things I have observed over the years is a change in perspective regarding end-of-life care. When I was a young doctor, it was assumed that my colleagues and I would do anything and everything within our knowledge and skill sets to preserve human life. Even if it resulted in a medically assured terminal patient's untold suffering, many doctors would pull out all the stops and prescribe every possible drug or procedure as a means of denying the reality of physical death. In effect, the patient had little or no control over the actions of a doctor whose primary professional goal was to prolong life. I believe that was wrong. A patient should be accorded as much personal control as possible over the medical decisions relative to his or her own death and dying.

Thank goodness today's medical culture is pivoting in the direction of allowing patients who have been pronounced terminally ill to make their own decisions regarding the care they receive when they are dying. It is important that patients have the foresight to create written and signed documents that will direct the actions of the medical staff when the patients themselves no longer possess the cognitive ability to do so.

I am very comfortable with trying to honor, to the best of my ability, a person's end-of-life decisions regarding the treatment his body receives. However, unless directed to do so, I see no point in prescribing unnecessary procedures that unnaturally extend the physical life of a dying patient. I believe my role is to offer palliative care and to make a patient's transition through the dying process as comfortable and dignified as possible.

As a Hindu who believes in the infinite nature of the soul, I am not afraid to die. My soul will not be extinguished by my body's demise. As for how I am to live while occupying this body, God has provided reincarnations of Himself here on earth whose intent is to equip me with some clear directives. Those reincarnations reveal that love is the force of life from God himself. He is love, and his love permeates the universe. He loves me, and his love compels me to love others. God's love enlightens my understanding and knowledge of how I am to live, and He calls my immortal soul to ultimately free itself from nature—from this material entanglement—and rise to be with my Lord God.

In the meantime, like that first bird on the tree, I am to enjoy this life, experience its pleasures, and live as fully as possible in the present moment. My goal is to live a meaningful life and to be a good person. That which I have learned in this life will be carried forward. Then, when physical death comes, my soul will be ready to move on to the next adventure God offers.

1   "Swaminaryan," *Wikipedia*, last modified March 26, 2016, https://en.wikipedia.org/wiki/Swaminarayan.

2   Carl Zimmer, "How Many Species? A Study Says 8.7 Million, but It's Tricky," *New York Times* online, August 23, 2011, www.nytimes.com/2011/08/30/science/30species.html.

Ramesh G. Patel, MD, FACC, FCCP

Ramesh G, Patel was born in Bodal, Gujarat, India, in 1947 and was raised in Bodal until the seventh grade. He received his MB BS degree from Maharja Sayajirao University in Baroda, India, in 1972. He came to the United States in 1972 and is an American citizen.

Dr. Patel received his medical degree from Queens Hospital on Long Island, New York, at the Jewish Medical Center, in 1975. He received his American Board of Internal Medicine/Cardiology certification while serving as staff cardiologist at VAMC in Des Moines, Iowa, during 1980–1989. He is licensed to practice cardiology in the District of Columbia, Florida, Iowa, New York, New Jersey, and Texas.

From 1989 to the present, Dr. Patel has practiced cardiology at Bayshore Medical Center, South East Memorial Hospital, and St. Luke's Patient Medical Center in the Houston area. He also has operated a private practice since 1989 in Pasadena, Texas, titled the Universal Heart Center Association.

Central to Ramesh's life is his spiritual practice. As a practicing Hindu, his temple is the BAPS SHRI Swaminarayan Mandir Houston Temple, located in Stafford, Texas. The headquarters of this branch of Hinduism is located in India. He considers himself to be a spiritual lecturer rather than a teacher. When he speaks to groups, he is also the one learning. Once a year at the temple, he serves at a health fair; and, three times each year, he serves at the community help desk.

Contact Information:
e-mail: universalheart@aol.com

FROM DEATH INTO LIFE

A Catholic's Perspective on Mortality

Leon F. Strieder, SLD

I AM A CATHOLIC priest and seminary professor. I've been a priest for thirty-eight years and a professor for twenty-four. One of the courses I regularly teach is the core course on the Sacrament of the Anointing of the Sick, often still called by its older name, Extreme Unction or the Last Rites. While I do not have the full burden of the pastoral care of a big Catholic parish, I am privileged to minister to the families who know me or hear me preach on a regular basis and who ask me to be present to them in their times of suffering and loss. What follows in this chapter is the fruit of these two unique opportunities—one scholarly, one pastoral—of my priesthood.

As I write these words, I am freshly aware of a young woman, only twenty-four, whom I recently visited. She is suffering greatly from stomach cancer and is a patient at one of the best hospitals in the world—M. D. Anderson Cancer Center. The first round of chemo did not shrink the tumor, and she has just started on a second round with a new concoction of drugs—all most deadly. Even with this second round, the doctors give her a 10 percent chance of surviving. While stomach cancer is terribly painful, and the uncertain effectiveness of this new concoction of drugs can lead to desperation, she has actually found a whole new perspective on living, despite the human feelings of facing her mortality. She had, in her words, lost her faith and left the church, but now she believes again and has faith that God and the power of prayer will help her survive.

Her parents are trying to be strong for her and, in the good Catholic way, are asking everyone to pray for their daughter. When I agreed to come to visit her, her father was convinced that I could find the right words to help his daughter. I told him very simply that it would have to be God who would find the right words, if any were to be helpful. Suffering and death are human mysteries, and only the gift of faith can offer a response. A minister can only be present, speak what the Word of God and the rites of the Church celebrate, and let the power of God have its effect. Anything beyond this places too much emphasis on the person of the minister.

In the Catholic tradition, "suffering and illness have always been among the greatest problems that trouble the human spirit." These are the first words of the first paragraph of the general introduction to the ritual Pastoral Care of the Sick, which contains our present rite of the anointing of the sick. This paragraph proceeds to declare that Christians know that "sickness has meaning and value for their own salvation and for the salvation of the world." This statement is problematic for many people in our secular society, including many Christians of various persuasions, because suffering seems to have no value and can be seen only as a negative experience or as a punishment from God for one's personal sins or the sins of society. Witness some of the discussion from some churches that see HIV and other diseases as punishments. In the Catholic tradition, paragraph two of the aforementioned ritual states clearly, "although closely linked with the human condition, sickness cannot as a general rule be regarded as a punishment inflicted on each individual for personal sins." It makes reference to the man born blind in John 9, where Christ states it was neither his sin nor his parent's sin that caused his blindness.

While it is true that some illnesses and much suffering can be seen as at least partially caused by our actions or the actions of others, many people seemingly suffer for no evident personal reason, like the young woman with stomach cancer. The reality is that the effects of original sin—that sin of Adam that Paul so powerfully wrote about in Romans 5:12[1]—affect us all. "Therefore as sin came into the world through one man and death through sin, and so death spread to all because all sinned." Our mortality is the result of the original sin of Adam, and we are easily reminded of our mortality every time serious illness and death affect us.

As an example of human frailty, I remember this anecdote from teaching a group of permanent deacons—generally married men, many older—who are ordained to baptize, witness marriages, perform funerals, and help at Eucharist by reading the gospel, sometimes preaching, and serving as ordinary ministers of Holy Communion. I mentioned that elderly deacons did not have to kneel or genuflect during our rituals, and one deacon asked me to define "elderly," to which I quickly answered, "'Elderly' is when what used to work doesn't work anymore!" He got the meaning. It doesn't take us long to realize that our bodies are fragile. As teenagers we think we are invincible. By thirty-five, our bodies begin to remind us otherwise. Thus, part of our Catholic creedal teaching is that we will obtain new glorified bodies in heaven. While the Nicene Creed, the one commonly prayed at many Catholic and Protestant churches, declares that we look forward to the resurrection of the dead, the older Apostles' Creed states we believe in the resurrection of the body. Both declare faith in the resurrection, but the earlier creed emphasizes the image of our bodily presence in heaven.

The theological concept of body is essential for the Catholic understanding of church. Taking the Pauline image of the church as the body of Christ, what we are as a church is that mystical body of Christ, which is as real as both the Lord reigning in glory at the right hand of the Father and the Eucharistic elements we offer and receive in Communion. Paul proclaims, in his graphic description of the early Eucharist in 1 Corinthians 11:27–30, that "whoever eats the bread or drinks the cup of the Lord in an unworthy manner will be guilty of profaning the body and blood of the Lord … For anyone who eats and drinks without discerning the body eats and drinks judgment upon himself. That is why many of you are weak and ill, and some have died." Again we see the connection between sin and sickness; here the sin is the failure to recognize both the presence of Christ in the Eucharist and the presence of Christ in the body of believers, and this sin leads to illness and death.

Returning to the general introduction of the Pastoral Care of the Sick, in paragraph three we read that "we should fight strenuously against all sickness" and that "we should always be prepared to fill up what is lacking in Christ's sufferings for the salvation of the world." This latter quote is from Colossians 1:24, which causes some misunderstanding for some Christians. The full text reads, "Now I rejoice in my sufferings for your sake, and in my flesh I complete what is lacking in Christ's afflictions for the sake of his body, that is, the Church." Unless one understands that the community of believers is also the body of Christ and that "if one member suffers, all suffer together," taken from 1 Corinthians 12:26, then one will not understand that somehow mystically suffering is an ecclesial reality and that we can help one another in our shared tragedies and, since we also participate in the eschatological suffering of Christ, that we share in the ongoing salvation of the world.

One of the theological terms often used to wrestle with the question of why a good God allows good people to suffer is "theodicy." "Theodicy," which etymologically means "the justification of God," was coined by Gottfried Leibnitz around 1710 to try to prove the existence of God from pure reason. But it raised the logical point that if God is all powerful, then all things happen because of his will, including when bad things happen to good people. This question perhaps needs to be also seen in light of Boethius's sixth-century distinction between God's foreknowledge and his all-powerful will. Boethius was struggling with the notion of fate. While some Christian groups, following John Calvin, subscribe to the concept of predestination, based on reading Ephesians 1:11–12: "In him, according to the purpose of him who accomplishes all things according to the counsel of his will, we who first hoped in Christ have been destined and appointed to live for the praise of his glory." This is further supported by Romans 8:29–30: "For those whom he foreknew he also predestined to be conformed to the image of his Son, in order that he might be the first-born among many brethren. And those whom he predestined he also called; and those whom he called he also justified; and those he justified he also glorified." However, while salvation is the initiative of God, Catholics have always maintained the freedom of each individual to accept or reject the mercy of God.

Classic Catholic theology has at least two schools of thought regarding theodicy: an Augustinian theodicy of free will, which has been recently developed by Karl Rahner, and an Irenaean theodicy, which was the foundation of the thought of Teilhard de Chardin. Augustinian theodicy looks upon evil as a privation of good. The original harmony of the cosmos has been corrupted by the misuse of human freedom. This is the common understanding of Western Catholicism. The Irenaean theodicy of perfection puts the harmony of creation not at the beginning but at the end of history, proclaiming that somehow we are progressing, as John 1:16 states, "grace upon grace." This is more Eastern in its articulation, especially when viewed through the lens of the Eastern concept of the divinization of humans in God. But in either case, evil and death are real, and God has sent his Son to redeem us and free us from both.

However, Catholics have always struggled with the following question: if God knows what will happen, why does he not do more to prevent suffering, death, or damnation? The answer lies somewhere in the mystery of God creating humans with the ability to love him and others. If we are free to love, we must also be free to reject God and others. Thus, while the great human gift of the ability to return God's love is to be cherished, the opposite reality that God will leave us to our choices is perplexing. This returns us to the reality of original sin. This concept is not accepted or understood by many, both Christians and nonbelievers, and sometimes Catholics are confused by it. As stated above in the quotation of Romans 5, because of Adam's sin, sin and death have entered the world. Thus, our mortality is the result of original sin.

At the beginning, we were created to live forever in the garden without suffering, deprivation, or death. The theological teachings of the first chapters of Genesis are intended to give some inspired explanation as to why we die and why people can be cruel and murderous, as in the example of the brothers Cain and Abel. This is why we were in need of a savior, God Himself, who would assume our humanity and conquer our mortality by dying our death. This is most incredibly expressed in 2 Corinthians 5:21: "For our sake he made him to be sin who knew no sin, so that in him we might become the righteousness of God." This is what Catholics call the Paschal Mystery, which is the concept that Jesus took our humanity, died our death, and rose from the dead to give us hope of eternal life.

This is why Catholics baptize infants. While we no longer terrorize mothers with some fearful image of limbo for children who die without baptism, we must still teach that baptism, at least baptism by desire, is necessary for salvation. This is part of our teaching that there is no salvation outside of Christ. In the Rite of Baptism for Children, we continue the tradition of an exorcistic first anointing, taken from the early rites for adult catechumens, which was intended to protect adults on their journeys to baptism. It is now intended to rescue children from the kingdom of darkness and free them from original sin. Often in baptismal classes for parents, this concept is either skipped or quickly covered without explanation, mainly because to talk about a beautiful baby and sin is seen as somehow too cruel and medieval. Yet I have found that speaking of infant mortality—the fear of such a beautiful baby dying of anything, especially sudden infant death syndrome (SIDS)—is real in the minds of our parents. This makes original sin real. Death at any age is too young and is a consequence of original sin.

The theology of baptism also helps us to understand baptism as a dying to Christ. Romans 6:3–4 states, "Do you not know that all of us who have been baptized into Christ Jesus were baptized into his death? We were buried therefore with him by baptism into death, so that as Christ was raised from the dead by the glory of the Father, we too might walk in newness of life." Baptism as a first death to sin is given a specific hope in Revelations 2:11: "He who conquers shall not be hurt by the second death." In this case "death" refers to mortal death. This second death is further clarified as a damning death in Revelations 21:8: "But as for the cowardly, the faithless, the polluted, as for murderers, fornicators, sorcerers, idolaters, and all liars, their lot shall be in the lake that burns with fire and brimstone, which is the second death." Whoever is baptized and believes in him shall live forever. Death has no power over him. And to add a Eucharistic note from John 6: 53–54, "Truly, truly, I say to you, unless you eat the flesh of the Son of man and drink his blood, you have no life in you; he who eats my flesh and drinks my blood has eternal life, and I will raise him up at the last day."

One very profound experience in my priesthood was the case of the unborn son of some dear friends of mine. The father called me and told me that through ultrasound their son was discovered to have so many abnormalities, including halted development of the brain and lungs, that he would not be able to live outside the womb. The options were to abort, an option not acceptable to the parents, or to wait for the child to be born and die in a few minutes. He asked for my advice. I told him that since the window of life would be so short, he should prepare himself to baptize his son when he was born, a simple rite in danger of death. And as it happened, the little son was born, his father baptized him, and he let his wife hold their son as he died.

Then the task came to me to preside at his burial. What was I to say? Luckily my friend kept a journal that he allowed me to read. What I discovered in those pages was that this little son, who lived for such a short time, had become a catalyst for his parents to grow in their love. That became the basis for my few words that day.

Nonetheless, there is great need to articulate the reality of original sin in a way that can be better accepted today. The old Augustinian concept of concupiscence is somewhat corrupted when it is used to refer only to perverse sexual desires. In reality, Catholic theology understands this result of original sin as being that of many different desires—not only sexual ones. It is good to remember that there are seven deadly sins: pride, anger, hate, envy, gluttony, lust, and sloth. Some lists add an eighth one, despair. Any of these, if left without forgiveness and grace, leads to real death. We are flawed human beings with flawed natures. This is the war that Paul articulated so graphically in Romans 7:15: "For I do not do what I want, but I do the very thing I hate." To illustrate the effects of original sin as the cause of evil, suffering, and death, I have found the following triple concept helpful.

1. Some evil we bring upon ourselves by our poor choices. Of course habitual sin and addictions mitigate our culpability, but we are still responsible for fighting against them.
2. Much evil is perpetrated against us by the bad choices of others. We are victims of the evil actions of others, such as violence and war.
3. Finally, and most commonly, there is "cosmic evil"; that is, our world is also flawed. Our earth is flawed. Our bodies and their genetic makeups are flawed. This accounts for natural disasters and for the fact that, for the majority of us, we will not die of old age in our sleep, even though that too is the result of original sin. Instead, various ailments and sometimes dreadful diseases will ravish our bodies.

God did not intend all this when he first created humanity. This is the result of the sin of Adam and Eve, as the first chapters of Genesis explain biblically.

Thus, when we hear the question, where was God when the Twin Towers came down? the answer is that God was in those Twin Towers. The mystery of the Incarnation is that Christ is forever bonded to us, in birth and in death. There is no life outside of the love of God, who first created it and offered redemption to all who would seek life. Thus, God was present to all those who died on 9/11 and is present to all in their moment of death.

Tragedies are of course the most difficult realities to understand and to address with mere and humble words. But here are some basic Catholic approaches. First of all, we should never say a tragedy came about according to the will of God. God does not will evil or death. God wills the salvation of all and somehow mystically offers salvation to all, most vividly in the last moments of one's life. We hear often of the visions of light reported by those who have near-death experiences. Yes, there is judgment; we are held accountable for our deeds or lack of action. The final judgment scene from Matthew 25 is very clear. Those who've fed the hungry, given drink to the thirsty, welcomed the stranger, clothed the naked, and visited the sick and the imprisoned will inherit the kingdom prepared for them from the beginning. Those who have not done these things will depart into the eternal fire prepared for the devil and his angels. But it is God's will that all be saved. The words of 2 Peter 3:9 are perhaps helpful here: "The Lord is not slow about his promise as some count slowness, but is forbearing toward you, not wishing that any should perish, but that all should reach repentance." He offers, but we must accept.

One recent tragedy concerned a young couple. I met them when they were helping with youth ministry. They asked me to witness their marriage—always a lovely event. A year or so after their wedding, I got a phone call that the young woman had been abducted and was missing. After a day or so of searching, her body was found with a gunshot wound to her head and duct tape still on her mouth. This duct tape was to prove helpful in finding her killer, as it had his fingerprint on it. It turned out that this man was a high school classmate of hers; that is why she must have been willing to go with him when he approached her. As became evident, he was a very disturbed young man who had been stalking her.

Her funeral was traumatic for all involved, including me. My words, poor though they must have been in the face of this overwhelming loss, included the passage about the little girl that Jesus raised from the dead in Mark 5:41. The actual Aramaic words of Jesus are recorded: "Talitha Koum, little girl, I say to you arise." I used this text to talk about arising not to walk again in this life but to walk in eternal life.

Unfortunately her husband began to suffer from depression, a fairly expected result, and after a short time found comfort with another young woman, whom he married, and they had a son. But the depression went unabated, and in another year or so, he took his life. This was another tragic funeral at which I struggled to find some words. Luckily that young son, barely a year old, was present. I was able to use that young baby to remind us of renewal, of life, and of the promise of the future. While death had taken away so much, this baby represented the hope that would enable us all to continue.

Another phrase often used when a young person dies is that God had more need of the deceased than we did. While there may be some truth in the greater picture that somehow this young person was needed to join the interceding of the saints for us still on earth, heaven is not so much a place where God has need of us as it is a place where we can see God and enjoy his life. This concept of those in heaven interceding for us has its biblical basis in the description of the martyrs in Revelation 7 and 8—especially 8:3–4, where an angel "was given much incense to mingle with the prayers of all the saints upon the golden altar before the throne; and the smoke of the incense rose with the prayers of the saints from the hand of the angel before God." This concept of the intercession of the saints is problematic for some Christians, but is central for Catholic thought. When someone dies, he or she stands before the judgment seat of God, who is certainly all merciful, but the belief in the presence of the prayers of both the church on earth and the saints in heaven is certainly consoling. It is not that these prayers change God's mind or his just judgment; rather, it is that they stand in solidarity with the very body of Christ, both sacramentally on earth and gloriously reigning in heaven.

The checkered history of purgatory must be factored into a discussion about the judgment of God. This concept of purgatory, with its parallel concept of indulgences, has a history of misunderstanding and abuse. The history need not be discussed here, but still many Catholics do not understand what we teach about purgatory, and most non-Catholic Christians find the concept repugnant.

Basically there are two judgments: one at death and one at the end of time. In the history of public penance, people were given a temporal punishment—a certain time of penance: forty days, one year, three years, seven years, ten years, and so on. The issue is this time concept, which in the minds of many created a third place—a place of torment—between heaven and hell, in which this temporal punishment was to be fulfilled. This image perhaps comes from 1 Corinthians 3:13–15, which speaks of our lives and whether they are built on the foundation of Christ: "for the Day (of judgment) will disclose it, because it will be revealed with fire, and the fire will test what sort of work each man has done. If the work which any man has built on the foundation survives, he will receive a reward. If any man's work is burned up, he will suffer loss, though he himself will be saved, but only as fleeing through the fire."

The teaching is that most, if not all, of us will stand before the throne of God in need of further purification and perfection. This is the idea of purgatory. And this perfection is brought about by God's mercy, aided by the prayers of the church and the saints. This is the basis for the role of indulgences—prayers to aid "the poor souls in purgatory," as we called them. These prayers are not magical but are part of the mystery of our prayers having value in the face of judgment.

Pope Benedict XVI wrote clearly on the subject in his encyclical on hope, Spe Salvi, where he writes in paragraph 47, "At the moment of judgment we experience and we absorb the overwhelming power of his love over all the evil in the world and in ourselves. The pain of love becomes our salvation and our joy. It is clear that we cannot calculate the 'duration' of this transforming burning in terms of the chronological measurements of this world. The transforming 'moment' of this encounter eludes earthly time reckoning—it is the heart's time, it is the time of 'passage' to communion with God in the body of Christ." The issue is not about time, because in God, in eternity, there is not time as we know it. The issue is about forgiveness and transformation in love.

In Spe Salvi, paragraph 48, Benedict writes about prayer and praying for the dead: "So my prayer for another is not something extraneous to that person, something external, not even after death. In the interconnectedness of being, my gratitude to the other—my prayer for him—can play a small part in his purification. And for that there is no need to convert earthly time into God's time: In the communion of souls simple terrestrial time is superseded." Here we can see the idea of solidarity. We are all in this life together, and we all will die and are in need of God's mercy.

Sometimes people express the tragedy of a person's death with words to the effect that the person was too good for this life. This is often stated in the case of a young person, and perhaps this notion can bring some consolation to the family of one who died too young and innocent. I remember a funeral I performed some years ago for a young man who died of carbon monoxide poisoning. It was Thanksgiving; the first cold front came through, and being chilled, he lit his space heater, which was not properly vented. The young man fell asleep and died. His parents and three sisters were devastated. While I did not try to claim that somehow he was too good for this world—he was a typical student pursuing a college education—I did try to comfort his family with his basic goodness. We need to be careful and not use a funeral to canonize someone. However, we can trust that the basic goodness of a person counts.

When someone passes away after a long illness, people often say that the departed is now in a better place. This idea helps us take comfort that in heaven there will be no more suffering and somehow we will have new glorified bodies that will not fall apart. While this concept seems to make perfect human sense after a long illness, we need to be reminded that life here—even a life with much pain and suffering—can and must bear fruit. Paul put it simply in Philippians 1:21: "For to me to live is Christ, and to die is gain." I was recently reminded of this when I was asked to say a few words at the funeral of one of my cohorts here at the seminary. She had just retired and was looking forward to many years with her grandbaby and was hoping for a few more grandchildren. Shortly after retirement, she came down with Bickerstaff's encephalitis as part of Guillain-Barre syndrome. In a very short time, she was completely paralyzed; and while there were some small victories, after twenty months she died, perhaps aware that her daughter was pregnant with a second child.

Cognizant of the sadness of her family, thinking she would never know her grandchildren, I spoke of heaven as somehow being in God and, more specifically, as knowing the mind of God. Thus, whatever the future might bring could be known through the mind of God. I tried to console the family with the idea that she would not miss out on all the marvelous things her grandchildren would do.

Another relevant issue for many elderly people is that they feel useless. Unable to do what they once were able to do, they feel they are a burden to those who care for them. While these are true feelings, we have to remind the elderly of what they still can do—namely, minister by prayer and their own witness to those around them. The Pastoral Care of the Sick 56 puts it this way: "The minister should encourage the sick person to offer his or her sufferings in union with Christ and to join in prayer for the Church and the world. Some examples of particular intentions which may be suggested to the sick person are: for peace in the world; for a deepening of the life of the Spirit in the local Church; for the pope and the bishops; for people suffering in a particular disaster."

Those who minister to the sick may wish to bring along a bulletin of all the activities of the parish with perhaps a few highlighted for extra prayer. Certainly prayer lists of those who are sick or who have died are traditional. The power of prayer, even if that is all someone can do, is far more efficacious than we imagine. One of my professors, Fr. David Power, OMI, wrote an article in the *Heythrop Journal* 19 from 1978 entitled "Let the Sick Man Call," in which he suggests on page 262 that "What is at stake is the sacramentality of sickness itself, or, perhaps it would be better to say, the mystery which is revealed in the sick person who lives through this experience. In other words, the accent is not on healing, nor on forgiving, nor on preparing for death. It is on the sick person, who through this experience discovers God in a particular way and reveals this to the community."

This profound quote reminds us of the role that the sick person plays in revealing to the community that sickness and sick people have value. And their major value is to witness to the beauty of life at all stages and the great gift of suffering and dying well in Christ. These are not easy tasks. They are possible only with grace.

I'll close this chapter with the famous resurrection hymn of Paul at the conclusion of 1 Corinthians 15: 51–55:

> Lo! I tell you a mystery. We shall not all sleep, but we shall
> all be changed, in a moment, in the twinkling of an eye,
> at the last trumpet. For the trumpet will sound, and the
> dead will be raised imperishable, and we shall be changed.
> For this perishable nature must put on the imperishable,
> and this mortal nature must put on immortality. When

the perishable puts on the imperishable, and the perishable puts on immortality, then shall come to pass the saying that is written: "Death is swallowed up in victory."

"O death, where is thy victory? O death, where is thy sting?"

---

1   All Bible or allusions to passages in this article are taken from the Revised Standard Version Catholic Edition (RSVCE), copyright 1994, National Council of Churches of Christ in the United States of America.

Fr. Leon F. Strieder, SLD

Fr. Leon Strieder is presently the associate professor of liturgy and sacraments at the University of St. Thomas School of Theology in Houston, Texas. He was born and raised just west of Houston in Sealy, Texas. He finished a BA in classics at the University of St. Thomas in Houston before heading to Rome to earn an SLD, a doctorate in sacred liturgy, from the Pontifical Liturgical Institute at San Anselmo. He did Hispanic ministry in the Austin area and campus ministry at Texas A&M University in College Station before coming to Houston to do seminary work some twenty-five years ago.

His interests are liturgy and sacraments, but Dr. Strieder has a strong interest in interfaith dialogue issues and issues of evangelization. In fact, his life's work from these past years is presently at the publisher. It is a narrative history of evangelization from the standpoint of the conversion process: what was in the mind of the evangelizer and what was happening in the mind of those who became Christian in the various times of evangelization over the years. The working title is *Building and Rebuilding the Kingdom: Evangelization Revisited*.

What keeps him sane and happy are his musical and travel interests, which he partakes in so that all life may be a joyful noise before the God of all.

Contact Information:
e-mail: strieder@stthom.edu

THE IMMORTALITY OF NAME AND WORK

A Jew's Perspective on Mortality

Rabbi Rifat Sonsino, PhD

ON JULY 24, 2013, *Newsweek* published a cover article titled "You Can Live Forever." In this piece, the author, Andrew Romano, interviewed two American academics, Walter M. Bortz II, MD, and Aubrey de Grey, about their views on the aging process. Dr. Bortz, a past president of the American Geriatrics Society (AGS), teaches medicine and is involved with regenerative medicine. Mr. de Grey works as a researcher at Strategies for Engineered Negligible Senescence, a research and advocacy program that aims to develop a cure for aging.

Bortz states that we should be able to live to age one hundred, adding, "Maybe we can go on to one hundred twenty, through exercise and good nutrition." De Grey, on the other hand, appears more aggressive in his thoughts. He believes that by using special medical technologies, it will be possible to "cure" aging—not to stop it, mind you, but to repair and reverse it indefinitely. He stated, "People who are alive today are going to be able to live indefinitely." So we will not age at all; we will simply regenerate.

That, I believe, is a pipe dream. Yes, with good nutrition and sound medical care, we may be able to lengthen our lives, but I am doubtful that we will be able to live forever. Instead I would argue it is better to accept the fact that death is a part of life and to make the best of what is allotted to us here on earth. The Hebrew Bible states, "What man can live and not see death?" (Psalm 89:49).[1] Similarly, the ancient rabbis affirmed that "those who are born are (destined) to die" (Mishnah, Avot 4:22). In fact, it is the recognition that death is inevitable that compels us to view life as precious. Every moment counts. Every breath is a blessing. A limited life provides perspective and purpose. Thus the Psalmist said, "Teach us to number our days that we may obtain a heart of wisdom" (Psalm 90:12). Living forever is like living in paradise. After a while, it becomes monotonous and ultimately boring.

In the Ancient Near East

Death is a human crisis. Life ends either suddenly or slowly and, at times, painfully. Primitive people must have been baffled when they discovered that individuals they knew well and loved simply ceased to exist. Eventually they accepted the reality of death and argued that immortality is only for the gods, not for fallible human beings.

Ancient Near Eastern texts show that the idea of human aspiration for immortality, as well as the ultimate recognition of a limited life on earth, is very old. Here are two examples.

In the Gilgamesh epic, one of the oldest legends in the ancient Near East, which goes back to the first millennium BCE, a powerful king called Gilgamesh learns about eternal life from Utnapishtim, a hero who appears in the story of the deluge. Utnapishtim tells him that the secret of eternal life is found in a magical plant. Gilgamesh eagerly looks for this plant and finally locates it. However, just before he is ready to eat it, he sets it aside temporarily in order to bathe in cool waters. At that point, the text tells us, "A serpent snuffed the fragrance of the plant; It came up [from the water] and carried off the plant".[2] Gilgamesh is heartbroken. After so much effort, he loses the source of his eternal life to an animal that takes it away from him. Resigned to the idea that he will remain mortal, he sits down and weeps, sadly accepting what Siduri, the alewife, had previously told him: "When the gods created mankind, death for mankind they sat aside, life in their own hands retaining" (*ANET*, 90).

Similarly, in the Adapa legend, written in Akkadian and dated to the fourteenth century BCE, Adapa, the priest of the god Ea of the city of Eridu, is erroneously told that when he goes to heaven, he should refuse to eat anything given to him by the gods. When he arrives, the gods offer him the bread of life as well as the water of life, but he turns them down, thus failing to obtain immortality. However, he returns to earth as "the wise, who knows the heart of the great gods" (*ANET*, 102) and achieves a measure of consolation.

In the Hebrew Bible

The Hebrew Bible raises the subject of losing immortality in the early chapters of Genesis. Having eaten from the legendary Tree of Knowledge of Good and Evil—most likely a fig tree[3]—Adam, the prototype human being, readies himself to eat from the tree of life to achieve eternal life. At this point, God draws the line: "And the Lord God said, 'Now that the man has become like one of us, knowing good and bad, what if he should stretch out his hand and take also from the tree of life and eat, and live forever!' So the Lord God banished him from the garden of Eden, to till the soil from which he was taken. He drove the man out, and stationed east of the garden of Eden the cherubim and the fiery ever-turning sword, to guard the way to the tree of life" (Genesis 3:22–24 JPS).

In the above passage, the Israelite God appears to be concerned about His own status as the Eternal One and is worried that humanity might compete with Him by living forever. Therefore, God banishes Adam from a privileged place and imposes upon him some restrictions in life, including death.

The Bible, however, is not univocal. As critics have already noticed, a different opinion about the Tree of Life is expressed in sacred scriptures: "She is a tree of life to those who grasp her, and whoever holds on to her is happy" (Proverbs 3:18). Here the Tree of Life is not a threat to the divinity; it does not refer to the mythical Tree of Life in the garden of Eden, but rather it stands for something that every human being ought to pursue and possess—namely, wisdom. Later on, the rabbis interpreted "wisdom" as referring to Torah (Jewish law and teachings) and therefore saw no contradiction between the two biblical texts. (See Mishnah, Avot 6:7.)

In many Christian denominations, the act of eating the forbidden fruit and the expulsion from the garden of Eden are commonly referred to as "the Fall of Humanity." Thus, for example, we read in the *Catechism of the Catholic Church* that "by yielding to the tempter, Adam and Eve committed a *personal sin*, but this sin affected *the human nature* that they would then transmit *in a fallen state.*"[4] The term "Fall of Humanity" is not found in the Hebrew Bible, but it is in the apocryphal book of 2 Esdras 7:48, which was written at the end of the first century CE, probably by a Jewish Christian. Also, according to *The Wisdom of Solomon*, a book written by an unknown author in Alexandria circa the early first century CE, man's corruption was caused by the devil's envy (2:24).

In Judaism, the consumption of the forbidden fruit and the forced departure from the garden of Eden are mostly viewed as a means to convert the first humans into responsible human beings capable of choosing between alternatives and therefore cognizant of their full humanity. Adam and Eve, symbols of humankind, knew the blessings and limitations of life, and were able to survive by making use of the best that the world could offer. As Harold S. Kushner points out, "The Story of the Garden of Eden is a tale, not of Paradise Lost but of Paradise Outgrown, not of Original Sin but of the Birth of Conscience."[5] Similarly, Claus Westermann, a biblical scholar of our time, acknowledges the fact that Genesis 2–3 "does not speak of a 'Fall.' Neither, in the Bible, is sin something that can be inherited."[6]

The Hope for Resurrection

During biblical times, the Israelites believed that after death one is "gathered to his kin" (Genesis 25:2, 17) by going "down to *Sheol*." (See Genesis 37:35; Proverbs 5:5.) The etymology of the word "Sheol" is unknown, but the Bible often refers to it as a place that lies beneath the earth. (See Numbers 16:30.) It is described as a place of darkness (Psalm 88:13) enclosed by barred gates (Isaiah 38:10). There was no life after the grave, they said. The psalmist makes this clear: "There is no praise of You among the dead; in Sheol, who can acclaim you?" (Psalm 6:6). Similarly, Job maintains that "whoever goes down to Sheol does not come up" (7:9). It is told that King David, following his affair with Bathsheba, lost his son to death. At that point he gave up praying for him and, in fact, abandoned his fasting and weeping and began to take food. He reasoned, "Can I bring him back again? I shall go to him, but he will never come back to me" (2 Samuel 12:23).

It must be clearly stated that in the Bible, Sheol is not a place of punishment; it is not equivalent to hell. It is a place to which everyone goes after death, a place of no return: "As a cloud fades away, so whoever goes to Sheol, does not come up" (Job 7:9). The biblical idea that a dying person goes down to the underworld for good is derived from the religious life of ancient Mesopotamia. This place was called in Akkadian language *ertzet la tari,* a "land of no return," and it was described in "Descent of Ishtar to the Nether World" as "a house without exit for him who enters therein" as well as a dreary realm that is ruled by a ruthless divine king and queen, Ereshkigal and Nergal.[7]

However, a few literary texts hint that, in some unusual circumstances, one can come back from the realm of the dead. This concept of resurrection finds its origins in a myth known as "The Descent of Ishtar [in Sumerian it is *Inanna*] to the Nether World." In this Mesopotamian myth, the goddess of fertility goes down to the "land of no return" and is detained there by Ereshkigal, the queen of the Nether World. However, under duress, Ishtar (and Inanna, before her) is finally released, and she returns to the land of the living with hope that the dead there will rise and smell the incense again. Similarly, in the Bible, King Saul, who was threatened by the Philistines, forces the infamous witch of En-Dor to bring up the prophet Samuel from the grave in order to obtain some guidance, but the old prophet becomes angry and says, "Why have you disturbed me and brought me up?" (1 Samuel 28:15).

Among biblical Israelites, even though Sheol was considered to be the final destination for human beings, the hope of returning to life did not completely disappear from the Jewish consciousness. During the Babylonian Exile, the prophet Ezekiel started to talk about the resurrection of the people of Israel: "Thus said the Lord God: I am going to open your graves and lift you out of the graves, O My people, and bring you to the land of Israel" (Ezekiel 37:12). The prophet Daniel, in the second century BCE, narrowed it down to personal resurrection, but on a limited basis: "Many of those that sleep in the dust of the earth will awake, some to eternal life, others to reproaches, to everlasting abhorrence" (Daniel 12:2; cf. Isaiah 25:8, 26:19). It was only during the rabbinic times that resurrection from the dead became a major religious dogma. Early rabbis claimed that it was even derivable directly from the Bible itself (Talmud, Sanhedrin 91b).

The idea of resurrection was part of a larger view of Jewish Messianism that slowly emerged sometime during the exilic period (after 586 BCE) and got stronger in subsequent times. Even though the sequence of events is not always clear, it was believed that in the future, God would send the

Messiah (literally, "anointed one"), a king from the Davidic line, to bring back all the Jews to the land of Israel, establish peace and harmony among the nations, and usher in a period of renewal of life for the righteous, both Jews and gentiles. During his reign, the dead would rise from their graves on the Mount of Olives and submit to a final judgment. As Maimonides exclaimed during the medieval times, "In that era there will be neither famine nor war, neither jealousy not strife. Blessings will be abundant, comforts within the reach of all" (*Mishneh Torah*, Kings 12:5).

Many Western religions maintain a belief in resurrection at the end of time. As a medieval Jewish textbook, the *Sefer haHinnuch*, which dates to thirteenth-century Spain, states, "The matter of the world-to-come is known and apparent to every intelligent person."[8] The Catholic Church has a clear statement about this issue in its Catechism: "We firmly believe, and hence we hope that, just as Christ is truly risen from the dead and lives forever, so after death the righteous will live forever with the risen Christ and he will raise them up on the last day. Our resurrection, like his own, will be the work of the Most Holy Trinity."[9]

Judaism is primarily this-world oriented. Life is to be fulfilled in this world and not in the hereafter. For the rabbis, a Jew is expected to live by the Torah and carry out the Mitzvot, the divine commandment, here on earth. Yet rabbinic teachers realized that life does not end when the body ceases to exist and that there is an afterlife that every Jew must consider and prepare for. So Judaism—a historic religion practiced by Jews throughout the centuries in different parts of the world and under the influence of various cultures—has developed various and, at times, even conflicting views of the afterlife. Even though rabbinic Judaism advanced the belief of resurrection of the body during the first century CE; in time, different Jewish positions were maintained in various parts of the Mediterranean basin. The great scholar of rabbinic Judaism, G. F. Moore, clearly recognized that there is no systematic Jewish teaching on this subject when he suggested that "any attempt to systematize the Jewish notions of the hereafter imposes upon them an order and consistency which does not exist in them."[9]

Jewish Views of Life after Death Today

The concept of Sheol disappeared after the biblical period. The rabbinic belief in the resurrection of the body became the main view on this subject, and it is still the dogmatic teaching of Orthodox Judaism today. As one ancient rabbinic sage put it, "They that are born [are destined] to die; and the dead [are destined] to be brought to life again" (Mishnah, Avot 4:22). Even though its origin is obscure, many scholars maintain that the concept of resurrection came into full prominence during the Maccabean period, in the second century BCE, when, according to Louis Jacobs, "many good men were dying for their faith and the older view of reward and punishment in this life became untenable."[10]

The concept of resurrection was controversial among the Jewish sects of the first century CE. The Jewish historian Josephus tells us that the Sadducees rejected it, whereas the Pharisees, the group that eventually gave rise to the rabbis, accepted it and turned it into a dogma.[11] After the destruction of the second temple by the Romans in 70 CE, the concept became a fundamental teaching for both Jews and early Christians.

In modern times, Orthodox Jews accept resurrection on faith and praise God daily for the anticipated *tehiyyat hametim* (reviving the dead). Other Jewish denominations reject it. Reform Jewish teachers, in particular, speak of a "messianic age" that will be brought about by human efforts. As the Pittsburgh platform issued by the Central Conference of American Rabbis (Reform) in 1885 stated, "We reject as ideas not rooted in Judaism the belief both in bodily resurrection and in *Gehenna* and Eden (hell and paradise) as abodes for everlasting punishment or reward."

Today some Reform rabbis, such as Richard Levy, have started to speak once more of the possibility for bodily resurrection.[12] Other rabbis defend the belief in the immortality of the soul. Consequently, many contemporary Reform Jewish prayer books include two parallel conclusions in the second blessing of the Amidah (literally, "standing up"—a key prayer in the Jewish liturgy that asks God for personal and communal needs), stating either "You give life to all" or "Revive the dead." Within the modern Conservative Jewish movement, Neil Gilman, too, is reclaiming resurrection on the basis that "if God is truly God, if God's will and power are absolute, then God must triumph over death as well."[13]

Even though resurrection is a rabbinic dogma, Jews have always held different perspectives on life after death. There are those who, like Louis Jacob (d. 2006), a British rabbi, do not know what will happen to them after they die.[14]

Others believe that after death there is total disintegration—what Freud called a return to "inorganic lifelessness." Alvin Reines (d. 2003) puts it clearly: "When I die, my individual identity will be annihilated, and both my psyche and body will perish."[15]

In Jewish mysticism, Kabbalah, the concept of reincarnation, called in Hebrew *gilgul neshamot* (turning or rolling of souls), plays a major role. Here the picture is not uniform. Some mystics argue that reincarnation applies only to human beings. Others maintain that it includes animals as well. The purpose of reincarnation, many mystics say, is the cleansing of the soul, and this may occur in various cycles. The downturn of this rolling is that, at times, an evil spirit, or *dibbuk*, may enter the body, at which point an exorcism becomes necessary.

Over time, other Jews, such as Philo of Alexandria in the first century CE, the German Jewish philosopher Moses Mendelsohn in the eighteenth century, and, recently, many Reform Jews subscribed to the belief that the body disintegrates after death but the soul returns to heaven, where it rejoins other souls and remains eternal. Even though it is of Greek origin, early Jewish philosophers, like Philo and the author of *The Wisdom of Solomon,* defended this as a Jewish concept. Here, too, slight variations occur. Maimonides, in the twelfth century, spoke only of the immortality of the intellect. Others rabbis insisted on the immortality of the soul.

And other Jews believe that they will transcend death biologically through their children, through humanity in general, or through their deeds and influence on others.

My Personal Hopes and Expectations

As a congregational rabbi for more than four decades and now as an academic, I have been asked many times what I thought of life after death, and I was often expected to console the dying and the bereaved with words that spring from Jewish sources. In my experience, I have found that those who are afraid of death express their fears verbally or through their behavior primarily because they don't know what will happen to them once they are gone. In reality, no one knows with certainty what is beyond the grave. Most religious assertions are nothing but cultural and religious projections. No one has had an experience of death to tell about. (I do not believe in the so-called near-death experiences. You are either dead or you're not.) Being a religious rationalist, it is difficult for me to conceive that after dying one goes to heaven or is "with the angels" or, worse, "in a better place." Death is sad and final, and how we deal with it reflects on the values we hold regarding life here on earth.

As I get older—I am seventy-seven years old as of this writing—I become more and more aware of my mortality and, at times, fantasize about my afterlife. I do not believe in miracles that circumvent the laws of nature. Since I assume nature operates mostly in a predictable manner and that when it deviates from its pattern it does so because we do not always know the secrets of the universe, I find resurrection of the body an unbelievable concept, given the mechanics of the act (How? At what age? Where? Et cetera.) The idea of eternality of the soul may have been acceptable in the past, but in today's science-and-research-rich world, it is difficult to speak of souls or minds. The word "energy" would fit better. Matter (e.g., the body) turns into energy, and vice-versa. The concept of total disintegration leaves me cold. There has to be something more than that. Our lives, we hope, should have some meaning for others.

More and more, I am drawn to the idea that I will live on through my children, my deeds, and my influence on others, even if it is for a limited period. Almost everybody does. In some unusual cases, certain names stand out in our culture. For example, Einstein will be remembered for generations to come as a genius who contributed so much to science. So will Hitler be remembered for his infamous acts against Jews and others. In ordinary cases, however, memories are short-lived. After all, who else remembers my cherished maternal uncle, my special French teacher, or my rabbinic mentors who changed my life? After my death, memories of them will likely disappear with me as well. Some things may remain for longer periods of time—among them our teachings that changed the lives of others, and the physical objects of quality we fashion and preserve in a secure place. Michelangelo is immortal for the great work he created in his time. People who love literature will always remember Shakespeare. The names of Moses and Jesus are here to stay for the religious movements they are said to have launched.

In my case, I vividly remember how excited I was when my doctoral dissertation, *Motive Clauses in Hebrew Law*, was published in 1980 and a copy of it was placed in the Library of Congress. "This is my immortality," I thought. As long as there is a Library of Congress, my name will remain forever. And every time I publish a new book or article, I feel that I am adding another link to my reputation and my name. And anyone can search for my name on the Internet and find my work. That will take care of my legacy.

Yet I am also curious to know what will happen to "me" after I am gone. I don't expect to come back. My grandchildren will remember me, but I doubt that my great-grandchildren, if I have any, will know anything about me or care to find out. Most likely, the energy I represent will return to the source of energy of the universe and become one with it.

In the meantime, I firmly believe that we should make up for the brevity of life by heightening its intensity and learning how to live richly, creatively, and nobly. As the Jerusalem Talmud puts it, "A person is obliged to give account before the judgment seat of God for every legitimate pleasure that he denied himself in this world" (Kiddushin 4).

And to this I say amen.

---

1   All biblical quotations are taken from JPS Hebrew-English Tanakh (Philadelphia, PA: The Jewish Publication Society, 1999).

2   James B. Pritchard, ed., *Ancient Near Eastern Texts Relating to the Old Testament*, 3rd ed. (Princeton, NJ: Princeton University, 1969), 96 (henceforth ANET).

3   Rifat Sonsino, "Did Eve Eat an Apple?" in *Did Moses Really Have Horns?* (New York: Union for Reform Judaism, 2009), 38–46.

4   Catechism of the Catholic Church (Ottawa, ON: Canadian Conference of Catholic Bishops, 1992), 404.

5   Harold S. Kushner, *How Good Do We Have to Be?* (Boston: Little, Brown and Co., 1996), 21.

6   Claus Westerman, *Genesis* (Grand Rapids, MI: W.B. Eerdmans, 1987), 28.

7   *ANET*, 106–108.

8   Sefer haHinnuch, *The Book of [Mitzvah] Education*, vol. 1 (Jerusalem: Feldheim, 1992), 69.

9   George F. Moore, *Judaism*, vol. 2 (Cambridge, MA: Harvard University, 1962), 389.

10   Louis Jacobs, *A Jewish Theology* (New York: Behrman, 1973), 306.

11   Flavius Josephus, *Antiquities*, trans. W. Whiston (Grand Rapids, Michigan: Krengel, 1963), xviii, 1:3, 4.

12   Richard Levy, "Upon Arising: An Affirmation of Techiyat Hametim," *Journal of Reform Judaism*, CCAR (Fall 1982): 12–20.

13   Neil Gillman, *The Death of Death* (Woodstock, VT: Jewish Lights, 1997), 259.

14   For these different views, see, among others, Rifat Sonsino and Daniel B. Syme, *What Happens After I Die?* (New York: Union for Reform Judaism), 1990.

15   Ibid., 136.

Rabbi Rifat Sonsino, PhD

Rabbi Rifat Sonsino, PhD, is the rabbi emeritus of Temple Beth Shalom in Needham, Massachusetts. He taught various courses in the Theology Department of Boston College from 1999 to 2015. He is now on the faculty of the Framingham State University Department of Psychology and Philosophy, teaching ethics.

Born in Turkey, he received his law degree from the University of Istanbul (Faculty of Law, 1959), his rabbinic ordination from the Hebrew Union College–Jewish Institute of Religion (Cincinnati, 1966), and his PhD from the University of Pennsylvania (Philadelphia, 1975) in the field of Bible and ancient Near Eastern studies. In 1991 the Hebrew Union College–Jewish Institute of Religion bestowed upon him a DD.

Before coming to Needham, Rabbi Sonsino served congregations in Buenos Aires, Philadelphia, and Chicago.

Rabbi Sonsino has authored numerous books and articles and has chaired various committees both regionally and nationally. He was also the editor of the *CCAR Journal* (1997–2001).

Rabbi Rifat and Ines Sonsino have two children, Daniel Sonsino and Deborah Seri, and four grandchildren: Ariella and Dalia Sonsino, and Avi and Talya Seri.

Contact Information:
e-mail: rifatsonsino@gmail.com

DEATH TEACHES US HOW TO LIVE

A Christian's Perspective on Mortality

B. Glenn Wilkerson, DMin

Introduction

I N 1986, DR. Duke Samson shared with me his paper "Mortality and the Neurosurgeon" and invited my response as a clergyperson. While I agreed to his request, I had to spend more than forty years in the practice of ministry before I felt I could offer a relevant, possibly helpful response.

Dr. Samson mentioned that probably no other medical specialists, other than oncologists and hematologists, encounter incidences of death and the dying process with the frequency of neurosurgeons. Similarly, other than morticians, I doubt that any other professionals interact with those who are dealing with death as often as the typical clergyperson. The human mortality rate is 100 percent, and the vast majority of those who are at the point of dying or who are engaged in the process of mourning seek some form of spiritual counsel or emotional support from clergy. I presume that the practitioners of all the major world faiths look to their spiritual mentors and guides to help them make peace with personal mortality issues and, in the process, to frame the reality of death within the context of living a meaningful life.

The majority of young clergy graduate from seminary equipped with a starter set of theological formulas regarding the function of death as a passageway to eternal living. They soon discover, however, that there is no substitute for personal, existential experience in understanding the continuum of life within which death plays such a pivotal role. As for me, while a believer in Paul's powerful assertion that nothing in all creation, *including death,* can separate us from the love of God revealed through

Jesus Christ (Romans 8:38–39), moving to an acceptance of my own mortality has proven to be a difficult struggle—and yet, one that I must undertake if I am to assist others on that journey.

My struggles reached full flower sometime in my late thirties. Several times I awakened in the wee hours of the morning, feeling myself standing at the edge of a black, bottomless abyss. I would peer into that abyss and be confronted by an elemental fear of my own death. The ensuing feelings of terror were so intense that, on one occasion, crying and trembling, I awakened my wife Karen and asked her to hold me.

For her, a life-threatening automobile accident in her teens led to what Elisabeth Kübler-Ross described as an out-of-body experience, provoking such feelings of comfort and hope that she has no subsequent fear of death. After one of my bouts with my night terrors, Karen asked me, "What caused you to be so restless last night?"

I told her, "I'm wrestling with my mortality again."

She didn't understand; so I explained,

"It's the question of our lives ricocheting off the wall of existence … and then hurtling out into the abyss. Is there meaning in that brief encounter with the wall?"

She answered, "I think the meaning is found *in* life—in the encounter. Without life, the universe itself is without meaning. The tragedy lies with those who don't fully participate in the possibilities for living and loving during the encounter."

"In the living and loving lies the possibility for meaning?"

"Yes. So why do you feel anxious about that moment on the wall?"

"Because of its brevity. We're wisps of wind."

"My concept of the universe of existence is that there is more. But even if this is all there is, it's still good," concluded Karen.

That exchange summarizes the difference between a person who has come to terms with her mortality and a person who has not. The importance of that acceptance lies in the fact that those who are at peace with their own mortality are empowered to live courageous lives. They are the ones who dance at the edge of the abyss, savoring each moment for its potential for joy.

In the service of those who seek relief from their death-and-dying concerns, clergy and physicians would seem to be joined at the hip. They share a mutual responsibility to effect a compassionate, empathetic response that transcends both religious formulas and rote biomedical practice. In the past, however, issues of turf and denial have frequently precluded such a melding of efforts.

For the clergyperson, denial usually centers on an afterlife emphasis that ignores the emotional trauma and feelings of loss associated with death and dying. To speak blithely of the "hereafter" without dealing with those feelings is a blatant form of denial.

Dying is the most ubiquitous, and arguably one of the most important, aspects of living. Therefore, it is important that those of us in the healing professions pay close attention to theologian Martin Marty's contention that the key to a good death is "to die meaningfully."

I believe that a meaningful death is a product of meaningful living. In this regard, contemporary culture is of little help. Our omnipresent, primordial fear of death manifests itself in a societal worship of wealth, beauty, youth, sexual prowess, and power—all of which are subconscious means of distancing ourselves from the realization that one day we will get sick, will not get well, and will die. So, we busy our lives worshipping the ultimate con: "If I acquire enough stuff, generate enough wealth, and remain sexually attractive and virile, then surely I will never die."

A terminal prognosis negates these cultural myths. Social status and material possessions are of little interest to a person who is dying. Not once during the course of multitudinous deathbed vigils have I heard a person reminisce over his or her stock holdings, club memberships, or business deals. The conversation always turns to cherished memories regarding time spent—and love shared—with family and close friends.

I have discovered that the sheer volume of funerals and graveside services can lead a tired clergyperson to become temporarily desensitized to the personal aspects of the dying process. Also, if I truly open my ears and heart to the deep, profound expressions of fear, hope, and love being shared by a dying person, I run the risk of being reminded of my own mortality. The temptation, then, is to distance myself from dying parishioners and grieving families through means of formulaic responses and canned theology.

As a young clergyperson, rushing to the bedside of those who were about to die or to the home of a family dealing with raw grief, I would rehearse as I drove, trying to remember the theological assurances I would share as a means of imparting comfort and hope.

I have since learned that when people are hearing the quick steps of death's boots in the hallway, theological explanations are of little avail. At that point, they already believe what they believe. What gives solace are assurances that they are loved by family, friends, and God, and that their lives have meant something to others. My own illusions regarding the imparting of spiritual support through theological exhortation were exposed by the crib death of my six-month-old son, Shane. While hundreds of people offered their condolences, the only words of comfort that resonated within my soul were "I'm sorry" and "I love you." And what counted most was the company of people who, by the very fact of their presence, signified that the life of our child mattered to them.

It is important for clergy to remember that theology is important in preparing people for death. However, at the point of death, the only real condolences are empathy and unconditional love.

The Components of a Good Death

How does one go about dying well? When a group of physicians from Duke University Medical School participated in a study entitled "In Search of a Good Death," two of the themes identified by the researchers were "pain and symptom management" and "preparation for death."[1]

The positive outcomes of proper pain and symptom management have been vastly improved by technological advances in hydration, nutrition, and respiratory maintenance that are now available to dying patients. While palliative medicine makes it possible for the vast majority of the terminally ill to die in an environment relatively free from physical pain, questions remain, such as When? and How much?

A nurse who was interviewed during the course of the aforementioned study said of one of her patients, "His disease was very widespread. One of the interns or residents said, 'We don't want you on morphine. You're going to get addicted.' I replied, 'You must be joking. This guy is having pain, and he's not going to make it out of the hospital.' He stayed on the medical protocol; and he died in four days, in pain."

As Dr. Samson indicated, a more typical response from most attending physicians is to administer appropriate pain-relieving drugs and then to remove themselves as much as possible from contact with the dying patient and his or her family. As poignantly pointed out in Dr. Samson's chapter, a primary culprit is the mistaken notion that death indicates failure on the part of the doctor.

An important role of a caring therapist (including clergy) is to release physicians from the terrible burden of this occupational hazard. Irrespective of the considerable skills of professionally trained practitioners, death ultimately is impervious to the abilities of even the most competent physicians. As Charles Meyer has noted, if a patient's condition is "incompatible with life," it is the height of arrogance to assign failure when death, a natural process, has followed its normal course.

As for the minister or priest, clergy have little room to cast stones at others in regard to an honest interaction with a dying parishioner. When we are confronted by the unavoidable reality of another person's impending death, the cork pops out of the bottle and the genie of our own personal mortality emerges. And all too often, we try to placate that genie by offering comforting platitudes—not only to the dying person but to ourselves as well.

Clergy are as susceptible to the fear of death as anyone else. A colleague of mine, who is as deeply spiritual as anyone I know, once told me, "I believe that heaven is home, but I ain't homesick yet." And it is telling that while religious jihadists preach and teach the joys of life beyond this existence and encourage the faith-induced suicides of others, they themselves almost never carry backpacks of death into a marketplace. Thus, we clergy frequently find ourselves all too eager to respect (even embrace) the admonitions of the dying patient's family: "Let's all maintain a stiff upper lip in front of George. We want him to keep fighting the cancer." So we join the bedside chorus of "You're looking good today, George. I believe you're getting better."

Physicians and clergy are, more frequently than not, mutually complicit in this tactic of distancing, ostensibly "for the sake of the patient" and the desire to enable him or her to cling to hope and "fight the good fight." In reality, the professionals may simply be kicking the can down the road as a means of avoiding any serious consideration of their own mortalities. These denials are a reflection of our realization that if others die, then someday so shall we.

The words of Kübler-Ross and Ernest Becker (author of *The Denial of Death*)[2] ring as true today as in the times in which they were written. As indicated in their books, we will have difficulty in effectively ministering to those who are dying until we first come to terms with the reality of our own mortality. Only then can medical practitioners and clergy be emotionally and spiritually empowered to play a significant role through their continued, caring presence in the lives of those who are dying.

It is the responsibility of attending physicians to offer a terminal patient the pain and symptom management that will allow, as much as possible, the caring presence of others to be a source of mutual joy, and that will enable all participants to experience the ensuing transition in an atmosphere of comfort and peace. Then those who have chosen to journey with the patient can take their courage in their hands and—casting aside personal fears regarding their own mortalities—open themselves to candid, caring discussions of the patient's current condition and prognosis as well as the feelings that emanate from that diagnosis. Through that process, they help prepare the patient for a "good death."

The Role of the Clergyperson

Science basically deals with the *how* of existence while religion essentially deals with the *why*. Of the two disciplines, religion should lead the way in providing insight into living a life that affords a meaningful death. To this end, clergy must summon the courage to accept their own mortality and open up opportunities for others to deal with their own.

As indicated earlier, the difficulty resides in the fact that death and concerns regarding what lies beyond have constituted humankind's greatest fear since our earliest moments of self-consciousness. It should come as no surprise that in the Western world, the words "death" and "dying" are almost never heard in personal conversations. We are uncomfortable with anything that serves to remind us of our own mortality.

In the face of this cultural denial of one of life's most crucial ventures, I believe that the clergy's role is threefold:

- to be an interpreter of death,

- to provide a "ministry of presence," and,
- to facilitate people's journey as they work through the grieving process.

A Spiritual Interpretation of Death

I believe that we are spiritual beings. While it plays a part, sheer intellect is neither the perpetrator nor the definer of self-awareness. Chemical synapses in the human brain interact in ways beyond our present comprehension, and something called spirit emerges, whereby a sentient being becomes cognizant of self in a manner that transcends the types of awareness found in other high primates. Mammals with high intelligence, such as chimps and dolphins, appear to have no conception of life's extension beyond this mortal existence, while that concept has been a source of spiritual comfort to humankind since our earliest origins. Drawings depicting supreme beings exercising powers over life and death decorate the walls of our ancestral caves. Some of the earliest cave art, found in the Chauvet Cave in southern France, dates to 30,000–32,000 BC. Many anthropologists believe there is a ritual or shamanist aspect to the paintings and that our ancestors created them to communicate their religious beliefs and ideas.

On November 25, Billy Graham reportedly opened his 1994 London Crusade with these words: "Today marks the twentieth anniversary of the death of my good friend, U Thant, who served as Secretary General of the United Nations. I was present at his bedside, and I'm happy to report that, at the time of his death, U Thant was at peace with himself, with his family, and with his savior. U Thant's savior was Buddha. Now, let me tell you about my savior, Jesus Christ!"

Graham then proceeded to deliver a powerful message proclaiming the unconditional love of God revealed through the Christ-event and the triumph of that love over physical death. Like Billy Graham, all I can offer is witness to the spiritual truths that enrich *my* soul as a Christian, and I do so while according full respect for the faith perspectives provided by other world religions.

There are a variety of ways to describe what takes place at the moment of death. All parties can agree that there is a cessation of the physical processes by which we measure a person's corporeal existence. Most clergy would additionally argue for a spiritual interpretation of death that offers hope of a continuation of the cognitive/spiritual self that lies at the heart of human self-awareness.

My interpretation of death resides in the belief that the Holy Spirit of God consists of pure, unconditional love (manifested in human form through Jesus Christ). At the core of our beings, we are spiritual "knockoffs" of the Spirit of God—and spirit communes with Spirit in ways that transcend our conscious awareness.

One summer, when our son, Kevin, was eight years old, he went to our subdivision courts to play tennis with some of his buddies. An hour or so later, Karen suddenly felt an overwhelming urge to drop everything she was doing and rush to the tennis courts to see Kevin. The feeling was so overwhelming that she told our daughter, Kelly, to keep an eye on her sister Shay in her crib. Then, not wanting to waste time getting the car out of the garage, she ran the two blocks to the tennis courts.

At first glance, her behavior bordered on the bizarre. We had lost our six-month-old Shane to crib death four years earlier. There was no possibility, under normal circumstances, that Karen would leave a six-year-old alone to watch our one-year-old daughter. But the feeling that she needed to see Kevin was so intense that she didn't think she had time to gather up the two little ones to take with her.

When she arrived at the subdivision courts, she found that Kevin and his friends had stopped playing tennis and had started climbing on the monkey bars alongside the courts. The way Kevin's friends explained it, a couple of minutes or so before Karen's arrival, Kevin had climbed to the top, slipped, fallen ten feet, and landed on his head. So when she ran up, she saw him lying unconscious on the ground. At the moment he lost consciousness, something apparently passed between his spirit and the spirit of his mother, signaling to her that he was in trouble.

There is something of the spirit that transcends time and space. And Kevin's spirit reaching out to Karen's, in a manner infused with such power that she became consciously aware of the connection, is not an isolated incident. Many people have told me of similar incidents when they felt the strong urge to pick up the telephone and inquire about someone close to them, only to discover, when the call was answered, that something traumatic had just taken place on the other end.

These incidences of the human spirit mysteriously connecting with others emboldens my belief in a spiritual resurrection. I believe that when my mortal, earthly life comes to a close, the unique, self-conscious part of me called spirit (or soul) will continue in relationship with the Holy Spirit of God throughout eternity. I don't know what heaven is going to be like, but I believe it to be a spiritual reality. My faith informs me that when our spirits pass through that stage of living called death, God is going to be waiting on the other side because things of the spirit have the ability to transcend the space-time continuum.

The concept of a spiritual continuance of life beyond physical death is, of course, a matter of faith. One of my mentors was an older minister by the name of Dr. Richard Crews. One summer I roomed with Dick while both of us were serving as counselors at a Christian youth conference. A highlight of that particular outing was staying up until three or four o'clock in the morning sharing thoughts with Dick. A particular conversation has lingered with me over the years. Dick and I were discussing the subject of eternal life, and I asked him if he believed in heaven.

He replied, "Yes, ninety-five percent of the time, I do."

I said, "How about the other five percent?"

Dick said, "I hope it!"

This seems to me to be what faith is all about—believing and hoping and centering one's life on such hopes and beliefs. That faith comforts me as I prepare for my own death.

All the major world faiths, and tribal religions as well, deal in some fashion with the concept of life beyond physical death. I once heard church consultant Lyle Schaller remark that the primary function of Christianity is to provide a "Christian interpretation of death." While conversations regarding an afterlife are most certainly a part of the discussion, they by no means constitute all—or perhaps even the most important part—of that interpretation. To be truly helpful, religion and spirituality must focus on what it means to live this life well, and living well is greatly facilitated by achieving a sense of peace regarding our mortality.

The Ministry of Presence

In his book *The Wounded Healer*, Henri Nouwen says that the best we can offer people who are facing major surgery is to tell them we will be there after the procedure. It is comforting and provides hope when we let people know they are not going to have to face life's critical moments alone.[3] It is a great gift to say to a loved one, "When you come out from under the anesthetic, I will to be waiting for you. We'll see this thing through together. I'm going to be there for you."

In similar fashion, clergy can play an invaluable role as a listening, caring, continuing presence in the lives of those actively engaged in the process of dying. A patient who becomes aware of the terminal nature of his disease typically will begin to mourn his own death and will process through the same stages of grief that his loved ones will embark upon following his actual death. By offering a caring, nonjudgmental ear, which is a primary element in a "ministry of presence," clergy can help enable a dying person, and those around him or her, to embrace the dying process with a sense of dignity, grace, and hope.

Often, those who would like to be a source of comfort to the dying say that they don't know how to begin. Through a simple, private declaration— such as "I'm here for you to talk about anything you want to talk about," or "It's a little scary right now, isn't it?"—a practitioner of care can signal that he or she is open to sharing the patient's journey. Clergy can model this sort of caring presence for family, friends, and medical staff who are having difficulty in opening themselves to the patient's feelings. Once all barriers to honesty have been dropped, everyone involved can, in the words of Nouwen, "open up the possibility of a new, more radical communion, a new intimacy, a new belonging to each other"[4] that death offers to those who love and care for one another.

Whenever that possibility is realized, an amazing thing happens: the dying process can become a source of previously inconceivable enrichment for all who have the courage to share the journey. It's one of the great paradoxes of a ministry of presence—those who come to give comfort to the dying person often find themselves being immensely comforted.

The importance of providing a caring presence to those who grieve cannot be overstated. When a nineteen-year-old member of my church named John Reano died, I jumped in my car to drive over to the home of John's parents, Charlotte and Louis Kuehn. Bill and Pat Meek beat me there. Bill was an elder at the church, and the Kuehn family had just been assigned to Bill's shepherding group. Bill had not even had the opportunity to meet the Kuehns; but, when he got word of their son's death, he and his wife Pat immediately went to the Kuehns' home. When I arrived, the Meeks were sitting in the living room across from the Kuehns, silently grieving with the family. I don't remember them saying a word until we said our good-byes. And when I left, the Meeks left with me.

Ten years later, Charlotte Kuehn and I were talking about John's death, and she brought up the fact that Bill and Pat Meek coming over that evening was one of the nicest things and most powerful pieces of ministry that she had ever experienced. Bill and Pat had said hardly anything, and they didn't have to. Their simply "being there" said it all. It was a wonderful example of the effectiveness of a ministry of presence.

Facilitating the Grief-Work Process

Elizabeth Kübler-Ross has provided us a valuable tool for understanding the stages of the grieving experience. Her "grief-work process" (so-called because grieving *is* hard work) explains not only the feelings experienced by those who are mourning the death of a loved one but also the emotional journey of terminally ill persons who are mourning the reality of their own impending deaths. The Swiss-born psychiatrist's list of the stages of grief includes shock/denial, bargaining, anger, depression/isolation, and acceptance.[5] They are not stages in the literal sense of a step-by-step progression. They are simply a list of emotions commonly experienced (sometimes more than one at a time) by persons immersed in the grieving process.

Begging the indulgence of those who are familiar with Kübler-Ross's work, I will briefly recap her stages for those who are not. I will do so by referencing my grief-work process regarding the death of my infant son, Shane.

- **Shock/Denial** (*"I can't believe this has happened. It's surreal."*)
  Six months after Shane's death, I would awaken in the middle of the night, exclaiming, "I just had a horrible nightmare that Shane is dead!" This would be immediately followed by the realization that the nightmare was reality.

- **Bargaining** (*"If only …"*)
  Karen and I would lament, "Shane often cried during the night. *If only* we had taken him to the doctor and gotten a diagnosis of infant sleep apnea, Shane might still be alive."

- **Anger** (*"Why me? I am so angry at God and at the world about the injustice of my loved one's death!)*
  Months after Shane died, I was driving to my church; and, for no apparent reason, I suddenly began screaming and violently cursing God. Surprised by the violence of my angry outburst, I finally pulled my car over and reflected on my behavior. Then I remembered the stages of grief, and I turned around and drove back home. I said to my wife, "Now I understand why fifty percent of couples who lose a child get a divorce within two years. I am still furious over the death of Shane, and because you're the safest person with whom I can share my anger, I've directed a lot of it at you. Please forgive me."

- **Depression/Isolation** (*"I'd like to just crawl into a hole and sleep for the remainder of the year."*)
  Sometimes the seemingly interminable sadness resulting from the death of Shane rested so heavily upon my soul that I wanted no contact with the larger world. I just wanted to close my eyes and make it go away.

- **Acceptance** (*"I don't like what happened, but life is good, and I'm ready to get on with the living of it."*)
  The first year following Shane's death was the worst for me as I struggled with the task of hard grieving. I went

through the stages, regressed and relapsed into some of them, and finally arrived at a point where I began once again to experience joy in my family and my work.

As a result of my involvement with a wonderful support group for grieving parents called Compassionate Friends, I would add a sixth stage to Kübler-Ross' grief-work process: guilt.

Prior to experiencing feelings of acceptance, a dying person will often express feelings of guilt over things done or not done or words said or not said. Offering responses such as "You did the best you knew to do at the time" or "Everyone makes mistakes; God forgives you—forgive yourself" might be helpful. But the most beneficial role clergy and others can play is simply to be good listeners and to affirm the guilty feelings as being a normal part of the grieving process. In fact, the role of the clergyperson in facilitating movement through all the stages of the grief-work process is to listen compassionately, without judgment, and then to reflect back the feelings being expressed (e.g., "You're really angry right now, aren't you? It's a normal reaction to what you're going through.") so that the patient feels he is really being heard and understood.

Kübler-Ross's research indicates that patients frequently are subconsciously aware of their impending deaths even before the health care professionals arrive at that diagnosis. I attended a Houston conference where Elisabeth contended that, excepting a catastrophic accident, the human psyche often (and mysteriously) senses that its biological clock "is running down" and, without consciously being aware of the process, begins taking care of any "unfinished business" with families, friends, and loved ones.[6] My own experience of this phenomenon took place when my father, who was a co-owner of a West Texas oilfield supply company, became suddenly and inexplicably obsessed with selling his interest in the company so that when he died, my mother would not become an innocent pawn in an operation in which she had no experience or understanding. I vividly remember him saying to her, "Jessie Lee, I want to get my share of the company sold so that you won't have to worry about selling your interests when I'm gone." Then, for four weeks, he worked feverishly to get the papers and agreements in order. He completed the sale on a Friday afternoon and died on the golf course the following morning, the victim of a massive and unexpected heart attack.

Sometimes a person intuits his or her own impending death; other times it's a matter of picking up the clues from the behavior of an unwittingly transparent family and nursing staff. The patient begins to sense the fear behind the smiles. Unfortunately, it is the rare patient who has anyone with whom he or she can share those intuitions. The typical scenario is for doctors, nurses, family, and clergy to enter into a subconscious conspiracy to keep themselves and the patient in a state of denial. Even when the terminal diagnosis is out of the bag, the conversation of family, friends, and medical staff typically alternates between outright denial ("Your nurse says you're doing better today") and bargaining (discussing alternative treatments, etc.).

When a patient senses that those around him or her are in a state of denial, he will not burden them with either his feelings or his whereabouts on the grief-work continuum. The net result is that many patients die alone, bereft of the company of anyone genuinely willing to share their deaths with them.

At that same Houston conference, where she addressed 4,500 clergy, doctors, nurses, psychologists, and other health care providers, Kübler-Ross talked about the phenomenon whereby the dying, although not consciously aware of their condition, often will begin saying their good-byes and expressing their love and appreciation toward family and friends. She spoke of the tragic loneliness of those who are prevented from sharing their feelings because of the self-serving denial of those around them. Her words produced a hush—you could have heard a pin drop in that vast auditorium—as each listener pondered his or her own culpability.

Two weeks later, Karen and I traveled to Ohio for a large gathering of her family. Her eighty-year-old grandfather and I were assigned the task of cooking hamburgers over the outdoor grill. He was a wonderful man: strong and robust—an absolute picture of physical health. I had watched him carry a 120-pound birdbath across the backyard earlier in the day. As he turned the hamburgers, he said, "You know, we may never pass this way again. I want you to know how much I love you."

My first impulse was to launch into denial and say something like, "Granddad Bennett, we're going to be cooking burgers together for years."

Then, remembering Kübler-Ross's admonitions regarding denial, I paused a moment and said, "I want you to know how much you mean to me and that I love you, too."

The old man and I stood quietly over the coals for the next few minutes, softly weeping together.

During the meal that followed, I saw him look around the table and say three different times, "We may never pass this way again. Isn't being together wonderful?" His words were greeted by a chorus of denials, "Oh, Granddad, we'll be doing this forever!" and "We need to start planning for next year's reunion." At each occasion, he simply smiled and said nothing more. I told my wife on the flight back home, "I think your grandfather might have been trying to tell the family good-bye."

Sure enough, he was diagnosed with pancreatic cancer three weeks later, and within six months, he was dead. Somehow he intuitively knew, and I will be forever grateful to Kübler-Ross that he and I were able to share our farewells.

The readiness of a doctor or clergyperson to enter into the emotional world of a dying person and to listen to his hopes, fears, and concerns is a beautiful gift—one of immeasurable value in helping the patient prepare for death and to achieve a sense of acceptance and completion.

Discovering Redemptive Possibilities

In most sectors of this temporal world, death is viewed as the final defeat. Hopes, dreams, and aspirations are laid to rest with their owners. Yet, truth be told, death often gives rise to new possibilities. In his brilliant tome *The Will of God*, Leslie Weatherhead observes that there are redemptive possibilities to be found within even the worst of personal tragedies.[7]

I know a young woman who was literally jilted by her fiancé the day before the wedding. She was brokenhearted and felt that she could never trust men again. However, once her grieving was done and she began to move on with her life, she encountered another gentleman who was much more suited for her. Now years later, happily married with two children, she claims her former calamity as one of her greatest blessings.

Two of my friends each lost an adult child in automobile accidents. Their deep, almost inconsolable grieving ratcheted up and down through the various stages of the grief-work process for years. The two friends now co-lead a Compassionate Friends group and serve as immense sources of hope and encouragement to others whose children have died. They offer a degree of empathy and compassion that can be accessed only by those who have suffered a similar loss. In response to their own personal tragedies, they sought and found a meaningful, redemptive possibility.

Other parents who have lost children confide that the loss has made them much more sensitive to the fragility of life and, as a result, more appreciative and loving in their roles as spouses, parents, and friends.

Finding meaning and purpose in the wake of tragedy does not come easy and often is years in the making—especially in the case of death. And because it requires intentional revisiting of the tragic event, it is a brave course that honors those who have died. However, for those sojourners who have the courage to persevere and to seek, the subsequent discovery of redemptive possibilities is one of the latent benefits of death.

Becoming Aware of the Preciousness of Life

When death is proximate, the preciousness of relationships is seen with greater clarity, frequently bringing together families whose members have been estranged from one another for years. As the final curtain begins to drop, the poignancy of the moment shatters any illusion (for a time, at least) that petty things matter. People lower their emotional safeguards and open themselves to love, which is the most important component of a good death. Death can lend immense quality and dimension to life.

Death has a way of cutting through the social pretense and enabling people to discern that which is truly important. Shorn of petty grievances and meaningless power struggles, people can begin to relate to one another on a level that would be beyond their reach without the intervention of impending death.

The demise of Shane put me in touch with that which is truly of value and importance, more so than anything else I have ever experienced. Death can teach us so much. We cannot really live until we first come to recognize the reality of death. Those who have come to terms with their own mortality become more vibrant and alive and appreciative of the gift of *this* life.

The words of a Thai meditation master underscore the role death can play in precipitating vibrant, grateful living. He was asked the question:

> In this world where everything changes, where nothing remains the same, where loss and grief are inherent in our very coming into existence, how can there be any happiness? How can we find security when we see that we can't count on anything being the way we want it to be?

The master teacher, with a compassionate look, held up a drinking glass that had been given to him earlier in the morning and said,

> You see this goblet? For me, this glass is already broken. I enjoy it. I drink out of it. It holds my water admirably, sometimes even reflecting the sun in beautiful patterns. If I should tap it, it has a lovely ring to it. But when I put this glass on a shelf and the wind knocks it over or my elbow brushes it off the table and it falls to the ground and shatters, I say, "Of course." When I understand that this glass is already broken, every moment with it is precious. Every moment is just as it is and nothing need be otherwise.[8]

When we recognize that, just like that glass, our bodies are in the process of being broken, then life become precious; and we open to it as it is, in the moment it is occurring. When we understand that all our loved ones—our children, our mates, our friends—are in the process of being broken, how precious they become!

When openly acknowledged, the immediacy of death can become the catalyst for the celebration of life. We awaken to a newfound sense of appreciation. Our priorities change. New values emerge. The mad quest for treasure and power falls away, and for at least a time, we embrace the true joy that can be found only through relationships of love and care.

Conclusion

In a moment of complete candor, a clergyman friend of mine said to me, "I was a human being a long time before I became a minister. What most of my parishioners don't realize is that I am open to the same fears, superficialities, and temptations as are they. My anxiousness concerning personal mortality is the same as well." As for me, the soft music of Andrew Marvell's words in his poem "To His Coy Mistress" rings louder, and with intensified pace, with the passing of each year.

At my back I always hear

Time's winged chariot hurrying near.[9]

While I am a frequent companion on the terminal journeys of others, I still deal with the natural questions and trepidations that accompany my personal encounter with the ultimate unknown. In spite of my faith and theological training, death and the dying process continue to awe and mystify me.

Strangely, as my own death becomes more imminent, I find myself feeling increasingly at peace with it. I believe I should live this life with all the fervor I can muster and simply trust God for whatever comes next. In the meanwhile, the giving and receiving of empathy, compassion, and unconditional love are revealed as the ultimate values through which meaning and purpose are achieved. As a clarifier of that truth, death provides great blessing.

1   Karen E. Steinhauser, et al., "In Search of a Good Death: Observations of Patients, Families, and Providers," Annals of Internal Medicine 132 (May 16, 2000), 827.

2   Henri Nouwen, *The Wounded Healer* (Doubleday, 1979).

3   Ernest Becker, *Denial of Death* (Free Press, 1973).

4   Henri Nouwen, *Life of the Beloved* (New York: The Crossroad Publishing Company, 1992).

5   Elisabeth Kübler-Ross, *On Death and Dying* (Simon and Schuster, 1969).

6   Elisabeth Kübler-Ross, speaking at a Houston conference for professional caregivers, Houston Astrodome Arena, March 6, 1975.

7   Leslie Weatherhead, *The Will of God* (Abingdon Press, 1999).

8   Stephen Levine, *Who Dies?* (New York: Anchor Books, 1982), 98f.

9   Andrew Marvell, "To His Coy Mistress," *The Oxford Book of English Verse, 1250–1900* (Oxford University Press, Arthur Quiller Couch, ed. 1919), 357.

B. Glenn Wilkerson, DMin

B. Glenn Wilkerson was born in San Diego, California. Raised in Odessa, Texas, he graduated from Odessa High School and majored in prelaw at the University of Texas. He received postgraduate degrees at Brite Divinity School at Texas Christian University (MDiv and DMin) and Union Theological Seminary/Columbia University in New York City (STM).

Dr. Wilkerson is an ordained minister in the Christian church (Disciples of Christ) and served as senior minister of a Northwest Houston congregation for thirty-five years.

He is president and founder of the ARKGroup, a nonprofit organization whose mission is to help adults learn ways of disciplining behavior while still enabling children to feel respected and valued. As an architect and developer of nurturing relationship models, he is nationally recognized for his work in improving the social and emotional climate within families and schools. His research in cooperation with the late Dr. Ron Lorimar at the University of Texas School of Public Health established a new paradigm regarding the primary role of caring adult–child relationships—characterized by unconditional love—in creating positive self-concepts in children.

Glenn is the author of *Trekking: Searching for Love and Self-Esteem*, *If Jesus Had a Child*, and twelve manuals for the nationally acclaimed ARK (Adults Relating to Kids) Program, which incorporates best practices in parenting and teaching. His research-based and evidence-proven materials are widely shared in schools, churches, prisons, juvenile justice venues, and community service organizations.

He is a world traveler and has spent time in over fifty countries, absorbing the beauty of foreign vistas and cultures. As a participant in various athletic endeavors over the years, he has played a lot of softball and earned a black belt in taekwondo. Believing that exercise is one of the keys to aging gracefully, he is a semiserious powerlifter and participates in state and national meets as a means of "flogging myself into making the required, regular trips to the gym." His most cherished times are those celebrated with family and close friends.

Contact Information:
e-mail: glennwilkerson@sbcglobal.net

SUMMARY

B. Glenn Wilkerson, DMin

During time spent in India, I was struck by two seemingly irreconcilable insights. The first had to do with the degree of poverty experienced by the vast majority of the population. It was scathing—in some areas almost unbelievable. The sanitary conditions in the countryside and in vast areas of the major cities were beyond the pale, with trash scattered everywhere and grown men urinating and defecating on the streets. The second observation was that, in spite of their impoverishment, the people on the whole appeared to be happy and at peace with their lot in life. While I realize that my appraisal of other people's "happiness" is subjective at best, all fifteen of my fellow travelers expressed the same sentiment every day: "I don't understand how people can be so poor and yet appear to be so blissful and content!"

The dichotomy was astonishing. How could a people so impoverished experience any sense of tranquility or joy? My first thought was that they simply were not aware of the higher standards of living enjoyed by other cultures across the world, but that is not the case. Everyone—even the lowliest street beggar—had a cell phone.

A possible answer came to me during a visit to Varanasi, where people bring deceased loved ones to the cremation sites located there. Situated on the banks of the Ganges, the fires burn twenty-four hours a day as family and friends sit on the embankment, silently praying, mourning, and observing as their loved ones are consumed by the fire. Bodies are cremated in Western culture, but are done so in a manner whereby we are not intimately involved. In India, people actually watch as their loved ones disappear in the flames, releasing their spirits to the universe and to God.

Staring in wonder from a boat floating just offshore, I watched as the flames softly illuminated the night, divulging a mystical intertwining of humanity and wood and water. The entire scene—cast in rich shades of reds and browns and oranges and yellows, spiked by a flash of royal blue from a light in the background—was surreal and beautiful. Far from being ghoulish or macabre, the scene was an unforgettable vista of a people making their peace with one of the great transitions in life. For me it was a profound spiritual experience. I wept, as did others in my company. We were witnessing a people accepting death as an ongoing aspect of the human journey rather than something from which to seek escape.

Subsequent reflection upon that experience produced this thought: Does an open acceptance of the reality of death somehow release the living to live more joyfully in the present? If so, that helps explain the dichotomy of a people who, while materially impoverished, appear imbued with the ability to be content and happy.

I would not want to live in India's poverty, but I think there is something to be learned from its people. With its emphasis on youth, beauty, wealth, and power, our Western culture is fixated on the denial of personal mortality. The intent of this book is to provide an open, honest sharing of thoughts and feelings regarding death and dying. My hope is that it will help readers come to the realization that our fear of death and accompanying feelings of denial are common to everyone; and that, when we are enabled to push through that denial, we are prone to live more expansively.

To that end, *Reflections on Mortality* comprises a diverse cadre of nineteen authors offering their perspectives on dying and death. Included are practitioners of the Christian Protestant, Catholic, Jewish, Hindu, Muslim, and Buddhist religions; a humanist/atheist; the director of Pediatric Oncology Social Work at St. Jude's Hospital; two psychologists; medical doctors from the specialties of neurosurgery, oncology, and cardiology; a funeral director; two hospice directors; a helicopter pilot who fought in Iraq; a philosophy professor; cancer survivors; and a mother who lost her adult daughter to suicide.

Four themes emerged from the musings of these authors:
1. Fear of death is a common human condition.
2. Denial of death is the common response to that fear.
3. Recognition and acceptance of our mortality can sharpen our appreciation and subsequent enjoyment of life.
4. Living full, joyful lives centers around meaningful, caring relationships.

A common thread among those who shared their observations and feelings regarding death and dying is that the denial of our mortality can translate into a denial of the preciousness of life. We slog through our everyday activities without being intentionally thankful for the gifts of laughter, love, and good health. Instead of savoring each day for the exquisite joys and opportunities that it provides, we become numb to those possibilities. We have this terrible tendency to waste life—a propensity for nonappreciative living reflected in Thornton Wilder's classic stage play *Our Town*.

In the play, Emily dies and then is granted her request to return to the land of the living to relive one day of her life. She chooses her twelfth birthday. She is transported as a child back to that birthday scene and stands in the midst of the festivities, observing all the participants, while they remain totally unaware of her spiritual presence. She sees her twelve-year-old self being inundated with gifts but is dismayed by her inability to get anyone to pay attention to her. Her mother is so busy getting breakfast ready and pointing out the various birthday presents that she scarcely even acknowledges her daughter's existence.

Finally Emily cries out on behalf of her alter self, "Oh, Mama, just look at me one minute as though you really saw me." But the mother is so involved with her mundane kitchen chores that she remains oblivious to the child's desperate attempts to secure her attention. Emily finally gives up and comes to the front of the stage and addresses the audience.

> I can't go on. Oh! Oh! It goes so fast. We don't have time to look at one another.

> I didn't realize. So all that was going on and we never noticed. Take me back—up the hill—to my grave. But first: Wait! One more look. Good-by, Good-by world. Good-by Grover's Corners … Mama and Papa. Good-by to clocks ticking … and Mama's sunflowers. And food and coffee. And new-ironed dresses and hot baths … and sleeping and waking up. Oh, earth, you're too wonderful for anybody to realize you.

Then, through her tears, little Emily asks, "Do any human beings ever realize life while they live it?—every, every minute!"[1] The answer to her question is "Probably not, dear Emily … unless we are able to summon up the emotional courage to fight through our denial and come to terms with the finiteness of our existence."

Recognition of our mortality can make us aware of the fragility of human existence and induces a sense of pleasure in the simple joy of being alive. The consequences of that awareness and sense of pleasure are vividly depicted in Nikos Kazantzakis's marvelous book *Zorba the Greek*. Very earthy, very human, and possessed of a tremendous spirituality, Zorba, with all of his being, says yes to life. He is consumed with a tremendous vitality—a burning desire to experience all that life has to offer. One incident in Kazantzakis's book offers a classic summary of Zorba's philosophy of life. He tells about going into a little village and seeing a ninety-year-old grandfather planting an almond tree. He asks the old man, "What, granddad! Planting an almond tree?" The elderly man says, "My son, I carry on as if I should never die." Zorba replies, "And I carry on as if I was going to die any minute."[2]

I am *not* saying that we cannot live wonderful lives without coming to terms with our mortality. I *am* saying that when we recognize that life is incredibly finite and fragile, it sharpens our appreciation of the exquisite nature of our existence and propels us to live even more fully and wonderfully. As Kübler-Ross suggests, "It's only when we truly know and understand that we have a limited time on earth—and that we have no way of knowing when our time is up—that we will begin to live each day to the fullest, as if it was the only one we had."[3]

The authors within these pages conclude that the key to vibrant living is not to live as fast as we can but rather to live as meaningfully as we can. What does that entail? It requires those of us in our Western culture to relinquish our insane desire to acquire wealth, fame, and power as a means of denying our mortality. It means slowing down, rearranging our priorities, and paying more attention to the ultimate source of human meaning: relationships. All the possessions and accolades in the world will not produce the joy experienced through laughing with friends, working and playing with our families, or joining others in helping those in need. As for me and my personal search for meaning, it has been the receiving and giving of unconditional love that, in the words of Loren Eiseley, "sounds down across the years and tingles among the cups on my quiet breakfast table."[4]

While I choose to believe in (and hope for) a continuation of my personal identity after I die, I embrace Bob Brooks's sentiments, which take issue with the belief "… that the main reason for leading a kind, charitable, compassionate life on earth is for the reward that follows—namely, being accepted into heaven." He says, "I believe we should lead such a life not as a guarantee of entry into a heavenly afterlife but rather because leading such a life is what contributes meaning and purpose to our existence, whether an afterlife exists or not."[5]

Various authors say it differently. Some talk about showing care through the exercise of their professions; others approach the topic more personally. All, however, would seem to agree that kindness, charity, and compassion are primary contributors to a sense of purpose and meaning.

I have been with many terminally ill persons who, upon reflecting back upon their lives, alternately smile and cry as they talk about the meaningful experiences that have enriched their existence. They share the stories—the cherished memories of funny, sad, poignant times shared with friends and loved ones—and they dwell on how much those relationships meant to them. They may also touch on events or achievements, but even then, those memories usually settle around the people with whom those events were shared or the persons whose lives those successes benefitted.

The deaths of people with great relational memories typically are peaceful and serene. On the other hand, the last days of persons who are largely bereft of those memories are typified by bitterness and regret. Meaningful dying requires meaningful living.

Several authors commented on how recognition of their mortality brought a welcome sense of urgency to the importance of meaningful, relational living. Shall we join them on that journey while there is still time?

---

1   Goodreads, Elisabeth Kübler-Ross > Quotes, accessed October 22, 2015, https://goodreads.com/author/quotes/1506.Elisabeth_Kubler_Ross.
2   Thornton Wilder, *Our Town* (New York: Harper and Row), 99–100.

3   Nikos Kazantzakis, *Zorba the Greek* (New York: Simon and Schuster, 1952), 123.

4   Loren Eiseley, *The Incredible Journey* (New York: Vintage Books, 1959), 192.

5   Robert Brooks, *Reflections on Mortality* (Bloomington, Indiana: iUniverse, 2016), 16.

INDEX